TALES
FROM THE
LOGBOOKS:
An Airline Memoir

LARRY HOLTZAPPLE

Printed in the United States of America

Second Printing, 2025

ISBN 979-8-89390-039-2

Library of Congress Control Number: 2024926192

Holtzapple Illustration and Photo credits
Picture of Linda Blair and Larry is a Mike Nicholson photo.

Picture of five picketing flight attendants is a Dorie Watts photo.

Picture of four of flight attendants in masks and gloves is an Antonio Diaz photo.

All drawings/illustrations are courtesy of Stephen Moore.

Ordering Information: Special discounts are available on quantity purchases by bookstores, corporations, associations, and others. For details, contact the publisher at sales@braughlerbooks.com or at 937-58-BOOKS.

For questions or comments about this book, please write to info@braughlerbooks.com.

**Braughler
Books**
braughlerbooks.com

This book is dedicated to Karen...my wife, best friend, and travel buddy. I love our life together!

Contents

Introduction

By the middle of the year 2020, like many Americans, I was isolated due to numerous Covid-19 restrictions. In addition, my wife was recovering from two very serious strokes and my son and I had become her full-time caregivers. Although the idea for writing this book goes back at least five years before that, the actual compilation and organization of the material didn't begin until I started looking for something to occupy my time, while staying with her at the hospital after her second stroke.

Despite those Covid-19 restraints, our hospital had tweaked its visitation policy and had finally allowed one family member to stay with any gravely ill patient. Since I was already off work from my airline job with a Covid-related leave of absence, I chose to spend almost 20 hours a day with my wife at that hospital. Eventually, the stories of my flying adventures began to be used to distract her from her condition and to entertain the severely overworked staff as well. After a number of doctors and nurses told me: "You should write a book about this stuff"...I decided to write a book about this stuff!

At some point that summer, I started to earnestly search through my airline files where I began to uncover the logbooks that I had kept for each year of flying. You see, when I first started working as a flight attendant for USAir in 1983, we were required to keep a written record of each day's flights. That data included flight numbers, airports, crew members' names, and any incidents onboard our aircraft. The information was then noted in our small, maroon-colored company notebooks, called a logbook. That little book was also the best way to verify that you were in fact paid for all of your flight time, and was very helpful with filing any paperwork regarding passenger behavior or safety concerns. In short, it was my airline diary.

Even after USAir eventually created their computer system in the early 1990s, I stubbornly continued to maintain my logbooks. As a former educator and trained historian, I was used to keeping records of the things going on around me. Plus, my logbook was usually stashed in my uniform breast pocket, so it was easy to access while in flight or when a computer was not available.

As I began to gradually amass my 38 years' worth of logbooks, it was a real treat to look back and recall so many amazing experiences. It also dawned on me that I was just so incredibly fortunate to meet, and often chat with, so very many interesting personalities; many of which were noted in that day's records.

While going through those logbooks, I also realized that I only had a very small space on each page on which I could make additional "notes." Therefore, a lot of my stories are based largely on a very condensed notation, usually scribbled before going to bed or while in flight the next day. For example, my Alice Cooper story comes mostly from my memory of that encounter, spurred by that day's note which read…"Sat behind A. Cooper at Expo's game. Very cool guy!" Consequently, some of my stories are based more on years of retelling them and less on actual accumulated data.

However, as a former teacher, I have always wanted to be as factual as possible, and in this case my dates and locations are exact. I also have numerous autographs, photos, and lists of crew members who were with me at the time these stories happened. As with any good storyteller, the details are sometimes secondary to the actual story. I have also changed some of the names of the people involved in my stories for security purposes and to protect the innocent, and/or the easily embarrassed. I hope you enjoy my trip down memory lane!

Chapter One

Job Interview and Flight Attendant Training

It was Autumn of 1982 and I was a hot mess. While on the surface it may have appeared that the 27-year-old version of me was doing well, it was not the case. At that point, I had in fact achieved a number of successes such as graduating from a terrific high school and going on to wrestle in college. There were diplomas on the wall heralding both a Bachelor and Master's Degrees in History. I had already been a Social Studies teacher and wrestling coach for a total of three years and between teaching gigs, I had succeeded in reaching my ultimate goal of going to law school at the University of Dayton. I had even purchased what was going to be my first "starter" house. But as they say, "things aren't always what they seem to be."

As I recall, there were a number of issues that I was trying to cope with at that time. My teaching position at Lebanon High School had been eliminated due to a "reduction in force" in the Spring of 1982. My first year of law school had drained most of my savings and made me realize that maybe I wasn't cut out to be a lawyer. The sweet young lady that I had dated in college and eventually proposed to, had decided that she liked someone else, and had returned the engagement ring. Worst of all, the cost of my new house was taxing my remaining limited finances.

Looking back now, I suppose I was somewhat fortunate. Most people have faced, or will face, a stressful time like mine at some point in their lives. I at least had good health, the love of my family, and great support from some wonderful friends. In fact, it was one of those friends who literally changed my life.

That friend was Wendee Wilson. She and I met when she started dating my best friend Steve Moore while they both attended Columbia College in Missouri. She was sweet and funny and could out-drink most guys. I liked her immediately. Although those two only dated for a few years, I somehow managed to stay in contact with her after their breakup.

Wendee's family was from the Pittsburgh area and most of them worked in the airline business. I got to meet a lot of them in the summer of 1976 when I accompanied Steve on a road trip. They were loud and fun and even had a keg of beer in their house, which made quite an impression on a naive Ohio farm boy. Her mother, Barb, had an office job with USAir's supervisory staff and her step-father worked in their Load Control department at the old Pittsburgh airport. After college, Wendee had followed in their footsteps and became a flight attendant for USAir. Through her, I began to hear lots of wonderful stories about the places she got to see and the interesting people she had on her flights.

In the Spring of 1982, I even got a chance to meet up with her and her flight crew during their layover in Cincinnati. Over drinks and dinner, I was entertained with amazing stories of famous passengers and unbelievable life experiences. Before heading home that night, I shared with Wendee the rumors of possibly losing my teaching position. My memory was of her saying that if that happened, I should come work for the airlines. I do remember thinking, "Yeah sure, I've never even been on an airplane!" I told her I appreciated the thought, but I was sure the teaching situation would work out.

It didn't. Less than a month later I was formally notified that the Lebanon School District would be laying off 18 teachers and that I would be one of them. I would however be paid through the summer, with the last check arriving on August 1st.

Thus began the process of looking for work. Although my first choice would have been a teaching position, I was willing to consider just about any job offer. I figured that a healthy male with two college degrees and credible references would not have much of a problem finding employment. I was wrong.

As the summer wore on, my stack of rejection letters grew. When I couldn't land another teaching or coaching position, I ended up taking whatever odd jobs I could secure, including surveyor's assistant, substitute teacher, and even going back to the farm and bailing hay for my father.

Sometime around mid-July of 1982 I received a call from Wendee saying that she and a girlfriend were coming to visit Kings Island amusement park which was located 15 minutes from my house. She also wondered if I could meet up with them while they were in the neighborhood. Seeing that I did in fact have quite a bit of time on my hands, I agreed. That weekend was the first time I recall Wendee really pushing the notion that I should give the airline business serious consideration.

About a month later, Wendee mailed me a job application form. It was for a Flight Attendant position with USAir, which I found a little amusing, because again at that point in my life I had never flown. However, I was desperate for work, so I filled out the application and mailed it in, thinking that there was no way that an ex-teacher/farm boy from Ohio would even be considered!

Well, never say never. Several months later I received a call from someone at USAir who informed me that I had an interview scheduled for December 16th at 10 am. There would be a plane ticket mailed to me for a round-trip flight from Cincinnati to Pittsburgh and back.

My memory of December 16th, 1982 is still pretty clear, even to this day. I dressed in my best sport coat and tie, borrowed my roommate's fancy leather briefcase, and left very early for the drive to the Greater Cincinnati airport. Since there were no real security screenings in 1982, I checked in at the ticket counter for my seat assignment and then walked to the gate. I also carefully watched every flight crew in hopes of picking up any helpful information, should it come up during the interview.

The flight to Pittsburgh was a little over one hour, and it was the most amazing hour in my life. I had a window seat and the memory of that first taxi and takeoff still warms my heart. As most folks do during their inaugural flight, I carefully watched the flight crew's boarding rituals and dutifully noted where all the door and window exits were located. I also closely observed what the flight attendants did, and when they did it, in case it needed to be discussed during my interview. In short, it was a very interesting first flight!

However, my interview that morning was less than inspiring, and lasted no more than 10 minutes. One of the flight attendant supervisors gave me a very cursory review, mostly verifying my work history and references, and really only asked me one question...

"So, why do you want to be a flight attendant?"

If I would have had a chance to peer into the future at that point and reflect on what allowed me to be an effective and successful flight attendant, I would have stated that my twisted sense of humor will deflect most criticism and help defuse tense situations. My inherent people skills will allow me to anticipate my passengers' wants and needs and create positive travel experiences. More than anything else, my outgoing, yet subtle, personality will not only make my fellow crew members comfortable, but also earn me the chance to have some wonderful life experiences with some amazing people.

However, I couldn't have known any of that at the time. Although my answer seemed to me to be honest and sincere, but in hindsight was probably the most un-original response they heard that day...

"Because I love people and I love to travel!"

That supervisor just blankly stared at me...and sighed.

I do remember thinking as I gathered up my things, that at least I had gotten a free airplane ride out of the deal. However, just before I left the office, a secretary stopped me and asked if I would be able to attend a second interview later on. My first thought was that it would be a month or so down the road and that I might be able to score my second, career round trip off this company.

"Sure!" I said, "When would that be?"

"How about this afternoon," she replied, "before you head home?"

Based on my less than impressive first interview, I could only assume this was a normal and usual progression of events, so I agreed. I was told to meet with Mr. Fred Kocher, a vice-president of something or other, at 1 p.m. on the upper floor of the airport building. The interview would also include a Mr. Rice, who I believe was then in charge of USAir's airline security.

That meeting was really the beginning of a new life for me. As uneventful as the first interview had been, this second interview could not have gone any better. Fortunately for me, Mr. Kocher had a daughter who was a teacher, and Mr. Rice's son had worked at King's Island and was a Cincinnati Reds fan. Every topic discussed had us all in agreement and every story I told had them both nodding and laughing. In short, our two-hour meeting was outstanding!

As I was preparing to leave, Mr. Kocher asked if I would be willing at some point, to take a physical exam. Again, imagining that this would be done at some future date, and include another free airplane ride, I said that would be fine.

"What about right now?" he asked, "We could squeeze it in before your flight home tonight."

I agreed and then walked down the hall for the 20-minute exam. Afterwards, I eventually made my way to the gate for my flight home. I also recall telling one of the flight attendants on that return flight that I had been interviewing all day, and that perhaps one day I might become a co-worker. I remember her telling me it was the best job she ever had and wishing me good luck.

As soon as I returned home that night, Wendee called and inquired as to how the day went. Still really not convinced that USAir would actually hire someone like me, I replied with,

" You know...the usual. I had two interviews and took a physical."

Wendee squealed with excitement and explained that what I had experienced was not the norm, and that they would only have done that with someone they were seriously considering hiring. She also relayed that her airline loved teachers and were actually starting to hire more males for what had been the traditionally female-dominated flight attendant position. She also thought I would probably hear from them some time after the first of the year.

It was on February 8th, 1983, that I did indeed receive a certified letter from USAir stating that I had been accepted into their training program which would start on February 21st in Sewickley, Pennsylvania. It was to be a five-week program and should I graduate, I would be hired as a flight attendant. There was also a package of information which included a list of all the cities that USAir served, the official names of all the airports, and each three-letter airport code. All that had to be committed to memory, as there would be a "pass or go home" test on that first day. The elation of finally getting a great job opportunity was exciting, but now the pressure was on!

The next two weeks were a whirlwind. I had to prepare my roommate on the care and maintenance of the house and I had to organize my upcoming bill payments. There was specific clothing (required to be worn on our practice flights) that had to be procured. Although we would be staying at a local hotel for the length of the training period, I still needed information on the Pittsburgh area. And of course, there was all that new airline material that had to be memorized. In what seemed to be no time at all, I was saying goodbye to the folks and heading off to Pittsburgh in my crammed-to-the-ceiling Ford Pinto.

That five-hour drive went well, until highway construction on I-70 led to an unanticipated delay and created an unexpected crisis. We were to have been checked in at the Sewickley Holiday Inn at 5 p.m. and seated at our introductory dinner at 7 p.m. Because of the traffic delay, I pulled into the hotel parking lot at 6:45 p.m. and raced to the sign-in desk, still in my somewhat rumpled blue jeans and plaid flannel shirt combo. With no time to spare, I made the first of what would be many, many critical airline-related decisions and entered the dining hall without changing into my "make a great first impression" suit. To my chagrin, all the rest of my soon-to-be classmates were dressed in their finest outfits. The farm boy from Ohio was looking like...a farm boy from Ohio!

The dinner went well, however. When it was my turn to stand up and introduce myself, I managed to deflect attention from my low-keyed garb with a simple heart-felt apology, and a promise to work so hard that no one would remember what I was wearing at dinner.

We were assigned a roommate later in the evening and mine was a local guy named Bryan Hunt, whose sister was already a flight attendant with USAir. We hit it off immediately and spent the rest of the night testing each other's knowledge of the assigned airport information in preparation of the first day's test.

That first day was indeed stressful. Our three instructors were a short, burly guy named Hank Rogier, a former flight attendant supervisor named Jeannie Grano, and the newly hired Colleen Gamelier. They quickly let us know that for the next month, we would be tested daily on anything and everything that was related to our flight training. That included not only service procedures, but catering, flight scheduling, the 24-hour/military clock, grooming, emergency procedures and responses, airline security, and the theory of flight. Oh, and by the way, we all passed the first day's tests. (I only missed the three-letter code for Detroit's Metropolitan Airport (DTW) which I never, ever forgot for the rest of my career!)

Our first training flight, or "observation flight" was a few days later. Half the class went from Pittsburgh to Memphis and back, the rest went on a Nashville turn. It was our first real chance to watch a veteran crew perform their duties, and by the end of the day, I knew that I would probably enjoy this occupation.

In the following weeks we took four additional training flights and generally things went pretty well. On each trip we were allowed to try different flight attendant duties. I discovered that making the flight announcements and greeting passengers came easily to me. Other duties like working the drink cart would take more time.

The veteran crews were generally pretty nice to the trainees, with the exception of a few good-natured pranks. One story included a crew asking one of our female classmates to take a plastic bag and collect some air for the "official air sample." (She agreed, and then enthusiastically swooped through the cabin waving her bag above the customer's heads, while attempting to get the best possible sample!)

There were also numerous rules that we were expected to follow during our training time. Among them was the mandate that we should never, ever leave the airport during our brief between-flight layovers. In addition, it was also crucially important that we always follow whatever commands our captain gave us. However, on my fourth practice flight I was confronted with a real dilemma.

We had flown from Pittsburgh to Denver on an older Boeing 727-100 and were facing a three-hour layover before heading back to Pittsburgh. Our cockpit crew included two real colorful characters in captain James Doke and first officer Harry Sickafuse. (They were actually the first in a long line of interesting pilot personalities that I would have the pleasure of working with over my career.) Both of them radiated that subtle confidence that most pilots display, but they also gave us a sense that anything could happen with them around.

Upon emerging from the cockpit after our Denver arrival, captain Jim called the crew together and stated that he had a car parked in the commuter lot and that we were all going out for lunch at a place called the Monterrey House. When one crew member seemed concerned about the foot of fresh snow on the ground, he countered that he had just put new snow tires on his station wagon commuter car and that we would indeed be safe. I then spoke up and said that because of my training status, I probably needed to stay behind.

"Nonsense," he said, "You are coming with us...and that's an order!"

"Oh man, you are going to get me fired before I even get started," I pleaded.

"Son," he countered as he put his arm around my shoulders, "Let me worry about that."

I then reluctantly followed the crew out to the parking lot, and after being informed that my very junior status demanded it, I was stuffed into the tiny, rear fold-up seat of a vintage 1960s era station wagon. We then proceeded to career wildly over the snow-covered streets of Denver, while I was bounced around that back storage area like some sort of lottery ping-pong ball. I also vividly recall lots of maniacal laughter from the front seats and at least one or more 360° spin-outs on some icy parking lots. Despite my trepidation, I tried to keep a positive outlook on the situation and not worry about the outcome. (Just in case you were wondering, the Mexican food was indeed terrific...and captain Jim picked up the tab for all of us!)

The return trip to Pittsburgh also went well. However, when called upon during the next day's class to summarize my experience, I elected to avoid mentioning my off-airport adventure and tried to stick to the more mundane aspects of my flight. It didn't quite work out that way.

"Are you sure there wasn't anything else you want to tell us?" our instructor Hank gruffly inquired.

"Ahh...I don't think so." I stammered, knowing that I was possibly going to be sent home shortly.

"Well, according to this report, I see that the captain enthusiastically praised your work." replied Hank as he shuffled through a rather thick stack of papers. "In fact, he says you are about the best trainee he has ever seen, and that we would be foolish not to graduate you at the top of the class."

Upon hearing that, my jaw dropped and I somehow managed to offer up a stammering reply by stating,

"Well...they really were a nice crew!"

I also recall that our other instructor Jeannie chimed in and said that if we would just give this job a chance, we would all be pleasantly surprised how much we would enjoy this occupation. Those words turned out to be so very accurate!

The rest of our training was a bit of a blur. I know there was lots of anticipation about the future, and probably quite a few tension-relieving games of Euchre. (Pronounced "yoo-ker"...it is a card game where you only play with half a deck...something that may have fit my mental state some days.) Despite the stress, we all managed to survive that final week. On the next-to-last day, we had the opportunity to bid for our "home" crew base from a choice of either Pittsburgh, Washington D.C., or Boston.

Based on our class seniority, I was awarded Pittsburgh, while most of my younger friends and colleagues were assigned to Boston. (I would in fact, end up working the Pittsburgh crew base for the next 21 years.) We were also informed that we would have five "settling days" after graduation, in order to get prepared for finding housing and moving into our new base. My Euchre buddy Scott Parks was the last guy to get Pittsburgh, so we decided to be roommates.

Graduation day was March 22, 1983. From the original group of twenty-two, 18 of us managed to survive the rigors of training and were given our wings at a short ceremony at our hotel. To my surprise, I was voted the "Outstanding Trainee" by my classmates. I was also elected as the speaker for our class, which required me to give a brief talk about every classmate, as well as each of our instructors. My speech lasted about 15 minutes and must have been acceptable because everyone laughed at all the right moments. It was indeed a wonderful ending to a very tough five weeks. (In looking back, I would argue that it was every bit as demanding and stressful as my first year of law school.) Thank God we had a great group of trainees who supported each other. Many of them are still very close friends to this day!

While Scott went home to Texas, I went out and found what would become our home for the next three years; the house at 1501 Lynfield Avenue. The only catch was that it would not be available for a few days, so I had to get special permission from USAir to continue to stay at the Sewickley Holiday Inn after graduation. That was okay with them, as long as I went on immediate flying availability. I agreed and did not have to wait long to be called out for my first "real" trip.

Chapter Two

The First Week

In late March 1983, the world around me was a very different place. At that time in the airline business very little airport security was needed, as the only credible threat to an airliner was a highly unlikely hijacking. Although we had been schooled in what to watch for and how to react to possible bomb threats and/or other weapons, realistically there was little to worry about. Our gates were either monitored by our ground agents or coded to restrict unauthorized entry to the plane or the tarmac area. Our airline badges were only casually looked at and no one ever worried about what crew members may be carrying in their luggage.

I also recall that the general atmosphere at work was one of casual concern about the "real world." Once passengers boarded our aircraft, they could expect to be treated well by the crew. The captain was in charge of everything and the flight attendants were going to be their best friends for the duration of the flight. Also, the 1970s image of sexually charged crews (portrayed in the book "Coffee, Tea, or Me") was not really accurate in 1983...with a few notable exceptions that I unfortunately overheard through the walls of our hotel rooms.

Our passengers were generally businessmen and a few vacationing families, and almost everyone dressed up in their "church clothes" when flying. First Class was still the epitome of luxury and tickets were expensive. "In-flight entertainment" was determined by the kind of reading material you brought along with you. Our flights were rarely completely full, except during the holidays. That was the reality of my world at that time, and I was about to jump in with both feet.

March 26th, 1983 - I was awakened by a phone call to my room at about 5 a.m. The voice on the other end identified himself as "Bill from daily crew scheduling," and informed me that they needed me to work a one-day trip to Fort Lauderdale and back. My flight left at 8:30 a.m. so I needed to be checked in at the flight crew desk at the Pittsburgh Airport by 7:30 a.m. I thanked him and assured him that I would indeed be there. As I hung up the phone, I remember thinking of what I used to tell my athletes when I was coaching:

"It's game time and this is what you have been preparing for!"

After a quick shower and a shave, I double-checked my travel bag and headed out the door for my first real trip. I also made sure to give myself plenty of time to find a place to park my car in the employee lot. (We had been warned that the crew bus that dropped us off at the front of the airport was sporadic, so I didn't want that to be a problem.) As I boarded that bus, I remember thinking along the lines of how I felt during the first day of a new school year and whether or not the students would like me.

At that time, our crew room was located on a lower level of the airport. Our check-in involved actually going to the scheduling desk and signing a big book that showed that day's flight schedule and who was on each crew. As I copied the names of my crew members into my brand-new maroon logbook, I did notice that one of my training classmates was also going out later that afternoon on a two-day trip.

On that particular day, I was going to be on a Boeing 737-200, which fortunately was one of the planes that I had worked during training. My first crew included Julie Tierney who was the "A" or "Senior" flight attendant, a hilarious guy named Sal Arnone as the "B," and the "C" was a sweet young lady named Mary Lou Engle. I would be the "D" flight attendant and would be working the rear portion of the plane during our flights.

In short, everything went very well. I remembered which exits to point to during the safety demonstrations and I am pretty sure that I got all the drink orders correct. Also, the crew was really nice to me. In fact, it turned out that Sal was on the Pittsburgh base "welcoming committee" and gave me some great information about the flight attendant union as well as some tips on dealing with our crew schedulers. It turned out to be a really good "first day!"

March 27th-30th, 1983 - The next morning, I got a call from scheduling informing me that I was being assigned my first four-day trip. It too went fairly well, and included my first hotel stay (Orlando, Florida), my first "celebrity" (Harlem Globetrotters point guard Curly Neal), and my first attempt at trying to explain to some passengers why we were delayed. (Rain storm over Philadelphia)

April 1st-2nd, 1983 - The following two-day trip included a Toledo, Ohio layover at a most unusual hotel that featured shag carpet and a waterbed, right out of the 1960s! It was also my first trip on the old BAC-111 aircraft. (Those planes were very noisy and did not even have overhead luggage bins.) After a great dinner with the entire crew at a Mexican restaurant called "Loma Linda's" and a few too many margaritas, I also experienced my first hangover.

I suppose I should pause here, just to clarify a little bit of airline policy. In early 1983, airline crews were mostly on the "honor system" with regards to off-duty behavior. Throughout my career, there were established guidelines for flight crews regarding drinking alcohol and/ or taking any drugs or medications when not flying. (Actual drug testing and random drug and alcohol screenings would not appear until the early 1990s. Airport security lines and luggage checks probably appeared shortly before that.) Depending on the union contract in force at the time, the time limit for stopping drinking was 8-12 hours before reporting to work. As with any group of people, most of the crews respected those guidelines and only on very rare occasions did anyone have to be pulled aside and "reminded" what the rules were. Rumors of company-based spies who monitored the hotel lobby bars also helped curtail crew misbehavior.

Much of my early flight career during that period of time was memorable, mostly because of my relative youth and my "single" status. Let's face facts; most of the other flight attendants had outstanding personalities, so there was an absolute joy of being around fun and exciting new friends. We were also staying at some amazing locations with easy access to some great bars and restaurants. Perhaps those factors and the relative lack of immediate supervision did occasionally lead me to push those drinking boundaries. However, I am proud to say that I never broke those guidelines...but, I may have dented them a bit.

With that being said, throughout this book I will mention situations when some imbibing was going on during our layovers. Early on in my career, it was just an accepted tradition to meet up with your crew after checking into your hotel. I definitely remember a number of captains reminding us of the "mandatory debriefing" downstairs at the hotel bar and that they were buying the first round of drinks. Some captains would even pick up the tab for the entire evening! Because of those traditions, I never really questioned the "party culture" that came with my job. However, (and I cannot emphasize this enough) you were always, always expected to be ready to work the next day.

Chapter Three

1983-1984....The First Years

From this point on, I will be highlighting a number of notable moments from my logbooks and expounding on a number of memorable stories where possible. Generally, any flight attendant specifically named is (or was) a good friend and will probably be mentioned again later in the book. Please bear with me, especially during my first few years of flying.

May 9th, 1983 - I had the pleasure of meeting our CEO, Mr. Ed Colodny on our last leg from Washington, D.C. to Pittsburgh. He introduced himself to every crew member and seemed like a very nice man. They say he is really intelligent and has a phenomenal memory.

May 14th, 1983 - My first trip to Los Angeles. My fellow crewmember Dan Paich and I met a "valley girl" named Julie who drove us around L.A. that night in a very iconic red Mustang convertible. Other highlights from the evening included a fun bar that featured turtle races and a very cool hotspot called The Red Onion.

May 29th, 1983 - A fun trip with training classmates Jim Easton and Scott Parks to Tucson, Arizona. During a repositioning (or "ferry") flight, where there are no passengers on board, our captain was nice enough to invite me to sit in the cockpit jump seat for our takeoff and landing in Phoenix. What an amazing experience to witness everything that transpires during those phases of flight!

June 1st, 1983 - Scott Parks and I welcomed two new housemates to our place at 1501 Lynfield today. Training classmate Sherri Swanson and her friend Sally Pike had recently transferred into the Pittsburgh base and decided to move into the downstairs apartment of our big two-story house. They are both sweet and funny and will eventually end up being great, life-long friends!

June 2nd, 1983 - An Air Canada plane experienced a fire while in flight today and was forced to make an emergency landing in Cincinnati. Fortunately, the crew was able to evacuate a number of passengers once they landed, however there were multiple fatalities from the smoke and fire. According to our training instructors, a fire was the absolute worst thing that could happen during a flight. It also made me realize how vigilant and prepared you needed to be during your flights. A flight attendant's first and most important duty is to manage any emergency that may arise!

June 4th, 1983 - My first trip with my friends Rick Meyer and Mike Flores. On the Detroit-Buffalo flight we had a number of notable passengers onboard, including House Rep. Shirley Chisholm, New York Mets owner M. Donald Grant, and rocker Ted Nugent. (Being a music fan, I felt like the "Nooge" was definitely the most fun to interact with!)

June 22nd, 1983 - My first in-flight emergency. I had to administer oxygen to a lady who felt "light-headed" during our flight to LaGuardia. Fortunately, I remembered all that I was supposed to do, and I felt better when she started feeling better.

July 14th, 1983 - Today we flew a round trip from Pittsburgh to Cincinnati and back to Pittsburgh. Just before touching down in Cincinnati, we flew over the burned-out remains of the Air Canada plane that caught fire a month earlier. It was a very sobering sight to see.

August 27th, 1983 - My first trip with fellow flight attendant Billy Walton. Today we encountered football players Sonny Jurgenson and Sam Huff, and sports announcer Irv Cross on our Washington-Buffalo flight. All of them were very personable! We also celebrated another crew member's birthday at the Playboy Club in Buffalo that night.

September 22nd, 1983 - Today completes my six-month probationary period that all flight attendants must go through. So far, so good!

September 24th, 1983 - My first "no wake-up call" emergency occured this morning when our hotel failed to awaken any of our crew. It was a good thing that we were fairly organized and pre-packed, as all of us got dressed and ready in about 10 minutes. After a frantic cab ride to the airport, we managed to take off...on time! (I do however remember feeling a little "gamey" with not having had time to shower.)

November 11th, 1983 - We had two rock bands on today's flight from LaGuardia-Pittsburgh. The "Irish Rovers" were a pretty subdued group, but the "Stray Cats" were very nice. Although it is a rather common tradition now, I do remember thinking then, how strange it was that the Stray Cats were sporting so very many tattoos.

November 16th -17th, 1983 - This was a great two-day trip with training classmate Cyndi Veronesi and the very sweet Deb Cunningham. Our three personalities meshed immediately, and we ended up really enjoying the entire trip!

December 12th -15th, 1983 - One of my favorite trips so far with wonderful co-workers Mary Filipponi and Rich Dempsey. Just like last month, our crew bonded on all levels and we laughed hard every day. However, during one of our deplanings, I was trying to mix it up a little and not repeat the same phrases while saying goodbye to our passengers. In the process I accidently told one person, "Good...bye-bye"! (Mary just about wet herself laughing when she heard that!)

December 19th-20th, 1983 - A very interesting trip with my new friend Tom Kilheeney. On one flight we had two deaf girls who ended up on the wrong airplane. My logbook notes indicate that we tried to tell the gate agent that our passenger count was over by two. (That was how we verified with the agents about how many people were on board.) The agent basically disregarded our count and of course the two girls were unable to hear our announcement about what city we were going to. When they were surprised to end up in Boston instead of New York, we were questioned about it, but exonerated after they heard our side of the story. (That was also one of the many reasons we were told to keep a logbook; to protect ourselves from potentially incriminating situations.)

December 24th-26th, 1983 - This was my first trip flying during Christmas, but at least I had the great pleasure to fly with two of my favorite flight attendants, housemate Sally Pike and previously mentioned classmate Cyndi Veronesi! On Christmas day, the captain okayed giving out free drinks to the passengers on the Pittsburgh-Orlando flight.

December 28th, 1983 - Today, we got stuck on a DC-9 airplane for about four hours during an ice storm in Harrisburg, Pennsylvania. At the time, the Harrisburg airport was just a small cinder-block building that had only six gates...and apparently very little de-icing fluid. The passengers were fairly patient with us, mostly because they could see how bad the weather was outside.

December 29th, 1983 - Philadelphia Phillies All-Star third baseman (and Dayton, Ohio native) Mike Schmidt was on our flight from Philadelphia to Dayton today. He was a very nice man and even signed a few autographs for some of our young passengers.

December 31st, 1983-January 1st, 1984 - This was the first time I recall being upset with USAir's crew schedulers. Originally, I was awarded a trip with a long overnight in Louisville, Kentucky. That was going to allow me to spend New Year's Eve with some college fraternity brothers and would make working another holiday a little more bearable. However, as I was checking in for my trip, I was informed that I was being reassigned to a trip that would overnight in Grand Rapids, Michigan, instead. Upon boarding the aircraft, I discovered that our first officer and other flight attendant had also been reassigned at the last minute as well.

So, with that collective chip on our shoulders, we took off for what we all assumed was going to be a terrible trip. However, as it turned out, our misery bonded us and we had a rather enjoyable evening. We were treated to some free drinks at the hotel, and eventually enjoyed a memorable countdown to midnight. It also reminded me to always keep an open mind about whatever city I was in and to enjoy whatever opportunities that were there!

Jan. 24-25th, 1984 - My first trip with fun flight attendants Becky Russell and Mark Wagner. We ended up touring the "Old Town" section of San Diego and the next day we got to "deadhead" (that is, we got to fly like regular passengers do) on Republic Airlines up to Los Angeles. There we picked up our airplane and flew back to Pittsburgh.

Feb. 4th-5th, 1984 - A great trip with flight attendant Lynette M. who was a former cheerleader at U.C.L.A. Although she was just a few months senior to me, she already had some very interesting passenger stories to share.

Feb 10th, 1984 - The first of many strange coincidences where, despite the mathematical odds against it, I encountered a number of people from either my hometown, or from the schools that I attended. Today I had married high school classmates Greg and Sharon Davis on my flight from Cincinnati to Washington, D.C.

March 22nd, 1984 - My one-year anniversary...and a small pay raise! Yay!

April 21st-22nd, 1984 - A fun trip to Baltimore with my friend Judi Vanderweilen. Since everything was closed on Easter morning, we enjoyed a semi-religious experience at the only open facility we could find...McDonald's! (Instead of using bread and wine, our communion consisted of iced tea and hash browns.)

May 11th-13th, 1984 - This was a very memorable trip with housemate Sherri Swanson and fellow Cincinnatian Dan Schild, which also included two Cincinnati overnights. However, on the morning of our second day, our Florida turn cancelled, and we were given the day off. After Dan decided to go home to see his family, Sherri and I rented a car and drove 20 miles north to spend the day at the previously mentioned Kings Island amusement park. It was a glorious day, highlighted by both of us winning baseball caps at a pitching booth. We also observed a gentleman garishly clothed in a bright-purple jersey and bizarre shorts, who we nicknamed "Natty Dresser." Many, many years later, we still use that term and break up laughing when we are faced with anyone with let's say...questionable wardrobe choices!

May 16th-17th, 1984 - My first trip with flight attendant Ron P. He was an interesting guy who always wore a rosebud boutonniere on his uniform lapel. He was also a former teacher from the state of Oklahoma. Although we would eventually work quite a few trips together, it was only much later that I discovered that he was at one time married to Playboy's 25th Anniversary Playmate, Candy Loving.

May 24th-26th 1984 - A wonderfully memorable trip with fellow flight attendants Spence Tenhagen and Tony Shimkonis. In fact, we still laugh at the memory of this adventure some 40 years later! This trip involved a Friday night stay at the Indianapolis Airport Radisson hotel where their little four-piece house band was pleasantly surprised to have our enthusiastic support on a normally slow night. As the night progressed, they played every song request we came up with, and also allowed Tony and Spence to get up and sing with them. We danced with everyone in the room and we even bought the band a round of drinks, which was later reciprocated when the band sent us a round of drinks! (I think we even helped them load out their equipment after the evening was over!)

If that wasn't enough, the next day we had an easy day, and ended up with a long overnight at the Buffalo Airways Hotel. Now, I should pause here to briefly describe the unique facility that was the Airways Hotel. In the 1980s, we stayed at a lot of interesting places throughout our system, but the most interesting was this hotel located in the front yard of the Buffalo International Airport. The rooms were slightly smaller than a college dormitory and had paper-thin walls and wafer-thin sheets on the bed. However, those detractions were more than off-set by them serving the best Buffalo chicken wings ever created and also having the best hotel bar in the system. (You were always sure to see at least 10-12 of your airline friends there.) Additionally, there were two great nightclubs right across the street: the 747 Club featuring an airplane themed interior, and the very cool Playboy Club located next door. Suffice it to say that most USAir flight crews actually rejoiced at seeing a Buffalo overnight on their weekly trip schedule.

As I recall, we got checked into the Airways around dinner time. Spence and Tony had a friend from Buffalo who was going to meet up with us later, so we started the evening with a large order of wings and a pitcher of Genesee beer. We then hung out with a couple of other crews until their friend (named Butler) showed up. After crossing the street, we spent the next few hours at the Playboy Club. At some point after that, things got a little fuzzy.

Somewhere around 1 a.m., I decided that I had had enough and was going to head back to the hotel. However, Butler had made some calls and said he knew where there was a great house party, and that we were all invited. I again politely declined and started heading toward the door; only to be informed that I wasn't allowed to retire yet because I just HAD to accompany them to the party! I then got as far as the front entrance, before actually getting chased by my friends into the parking lot. While Butler circled the area in his car to prevent my escape, I vaguely remember the next ten minutes being a life-sized version of the game "Whack-A-Mole"; where I tried to hide between cars and periodically lift my head up to see where they were. Meanwhile, Spence and Tony were doing the same thing while searching for me!

At some point I was physically tackled and thrown into Butler's car and then driven to some frat house in downtown Buffalo. The party must have been really good because the next memory I have is of us sitting on the steps of the Buffalo Federal Court House watching the sun rise at 5 a.m.! (How and why we were there remains a mystery to this day!) Somehow, we managed to catch a cab ride back to the hotel and then grab a quick nap before reporting for our last day of flying.

If that wasn't enough, after that trip was over, the three of us then met up again the next night at a local restaurant/bar called the "Ground Round." (That establishment had become the favorite gathering place for our group of very junior, Pittsburgh-based, weekend-working, flight attendants.) Tony, Spence, and I then regaled our friends with the tales of our latest adventures. What a fun trip!

June 19th, 1984 - There were a number of WWF professional wrestlers on our Pittsburgh to Newark flight today, including the Iron Sheik, Sergeant Slaughter, and Mr. B. Brian Blair; a member of the "Killer Bees" tag team. After the drink service, Brian asked me why I looked familiar to him. I then reminded him that he and his friend Paul "Mr. Wonderful" Orndorff, had recently been to our house. Apparently, they had been introduced to my housemates Sherri and Sally at a Coraopolis bar called the Juggernaut, where Sally's sister and her roommate worked as bartenders.

If I remember correctly, Sherri and Sally had come home and told me that they had met a couple of professional wrestlers, and that they were going out with them the next night. As a very protective older brother with two pretty younger sisters, I immediately inquired as to where they were going and when they would be returning home that night. When Sherri tried to bust my chops about sounding like her dad,

I half-jokingly added that before they left, I also wanted to meet their dates and talk to them. She just giggled and we left it at that.

The next night I was upstairs in my kitchen doing the dishes, when I heard a car pull up, and then some muffled low voices as the girls met their dates at the door. I then heard the door to my upstairs apartment open, followed by some serious creaking noises coming up the stairs. Suddenly two giant shadows covered the kitchen wall, and I looked up from the sink to see these two behemoths standing in my doorway. It was Paul Orndorff who spoke up in his deepest, most-chilling voice and growled,

"The girls said we had to come up and meet you first."

I swallowed hard (and maybe even dampened my shorts a little) but stuck out my hand, introduced myself, and offered the guys a seat. We casually chatted for a few minutes before one of them noticed some framed pictures on my wall of the varsity wrestling teams that I had coached. When asked, I told them that not only had I coached, but had wrestled in both high school and college. Come to find out that both Paul and Brian had also wrestled in high school, and in fact Paul had been a state champion! It turned out that I also knew one of Brian's high school coaches as well. Before long, we were laughing like old friends and I was even invited to come and hang out with them the next time they were in town! Although I never took them up on the invitation, I always appreciated the offer. (Paul Orndorff passed away in 2021, so I am especially sad now, that I missed out on that opportunity.)

September 11th, 1984 - On our Pittsburgh to Ft. Lauderdale flight, our passengers included former Secretary of State, General Alexander Haig, and former president/CEO of Allegheny Airlines, Leslie O. Barnes. Mr. Barnes was personable and very interesting to converse with.

September 21st, 1984 - A nice flight today from Newark to Indianapolis on the DC-9. Onboard was newswoman Jane Pauley and her young twins, as well as talk show host Dick Cavett. As I recall, the twins had just learned to walk, so they had a great time climbing all over the folding table and rear-facing seats that were located in the first two rows of the DC-9 aircraft. That distraction also allowed Ms. Pauley and Mr. Cavett a chance to chat a little bit. (In my humble opinion, not only was she a great "hands-on" type of mom, but Jane Pauley was also one of the most naturally beautiful women I have ever seen.)

September 24th-26th, 1984 - My first trip with my good friend Ed Flowers. We ended up having a nice chat with professional boxer Ray "Boom Boom" Mancini on our Los Angeles-Pittsburgh flight. ("Boom Boom" seemed to enjoy the fact that Ed and I were both "Ohio guys"; mostly because he was also a fellow Buckeye from the Akron area.) I also saw my friend and local businessman Ralph Saltsgaver in the Pittsburgh airport. (Over the years, I would end up seeing Ralph four or five times on my flights!)

October 30th, 1984 - My housemates and I got invited to a great Halloween party onboard an old, paddlewheel riverboat that was scheduled to cruise up and down the Ohio River. For my costume, I dug out an old tuxedo jacket from the back of my closet, then put a paper bag over my head and went as the "Unknown Comic" from the 70s era television program "The Gong Show." There were also a number of fellow flight attendants at the party, and that made for a great evening.

The real kicker came after our ship was docked at the end of the cruise. That's when one of my housemates drunkenly decided that she wanted to take home one of the several carved pumpkins that were displayed on the dock. As we attempted to dissuade her, she lifted one of the bigger pumpkins and tried to throw her coat over it. It was then, from out of the silent evening air, (and from somewhere above us) that a deep, booming voice firmly requested us to..."PUT THE PUMPKIN... BACK!" We ran off the dock laughing like hyenas!

November 7th, 1984 - We took a large group of F.F.A. (Future Farmers of America) dairy farmers from Pittsburgh to Chicago. Having been raised on a dairy farm, I found that we had a lot to chat about. It was also the only time that I can recall having a public discussion about udder size that no one seemed offended by.

November 21st-22nd, 1984 - We had newswoman Diane Sawyer on our LaGuardia-Louisville flight. (Like Jane Pauley a few months back, she too was so naturally beautiful.) I also got a chance to visit with my high school classmate Kenny Adkins while overnighting in Los Angeles. The next day I also ran into fellow training classmate

Janet Hensley, who had elected to quit USAir and return to flying with her previous employer, United Airlines.

December 16th-17th, 1984 - This was a great two-day trip with my housemates Sherri and Sally. We all brought cameras and took lots of pictures, both inside and outside the airplane. It also ended up being the only time that the three of us had the opportunity to work together. (That was probably for the best, because we ended up using the phrase "Put the pumpkin back" much too often!)

December 23rd-26th, 1984 - A four-day Christmas trip on the 737-200 with one of my favorite flight attendants, Shawn Forrest. The highlight of that excursion was having a passenger in a full Santa Claus outfit (including his own long, white beard!) on our Pittsburgh to West Palm Beach flight. He brought gifts for the young passengers and special gift bags for all the crew. We even let him get on the P.A. and wish everyone a Merry Christmas. This was also my last trip for 1984, which allowed me to go home and celebrate New Year's with my buddies Mike Butts and Bryan Hutcheson and their wives.

Chapter Four

1985-1986....The Buffalo Blizzard and the Girl of My Dreams

January 2nd-4th, 1985 - This was a nice trip with my new friend, Janis Jackson. Our first overnight was in Newark, New Jersey, with a stay at the just-opened Newark Marriott Hotel. In fact, our crew members were the very first guests to stay there, which unfortunately wasn't as glamorous as it sounded. Although the rooms were sparkling clean, the restaurant was not yet functional, and there was very little available to eat. Janis and I avoided starvation by following the newly hired chef into the kitchen area and then asking him if we could raid his barely stocked freezer. The chef must have felt sorry for us because he kindly offered us a couple of beers and enough stuff to make a few sandwiches.

January 11th, 1985 - During a repeat of the previous week's trip, we again got to stay at the same new Marriott hotel. However, this time things were more functional and the restaurant was open. I also got a chance to visit with my youngest sister, Cindy, who in the last few months had decided to try the airline business. She was now a flight attendant with People Express and was based in Newark. What had once been my family of teachers, was rapidly turning into an airline clan.

January 21st-24th, 1985 - This was a great four-day trip with an outstanding crew of Carol Gorenflo, Stu Burke, and Sue Campbell Burns. On the third day we worked the first flight that had landed in Buffalo in five days. That was because a major blizzard (known locally as the "Six-pack Storm") had battered the Buffalo area for several days.

Consequently, all air traffic to that area had been cancelled or diverted. On our flight from Buffalo to Pittsburgh, we ended up taking about 80 of our crew members who had been marooned at the Airways Hotel, back to our home base of Pittsburgh. Oh, the stories they told!

As I had mentioned earlier, the Buffalo Airways Hotel had always reminded me more of a frat house than a proper hotel/motel. Evidently, during the five days our crews were stranded there, that's exactly what it turned into. Here are some of the more incredible stories that I heard about on our flight back to Pittsburgh.

At the beginning of the storm, about a dozen USAir flights in Buffalo were cancelled. Apparently, the Airways Hotel had enough room for the crews, but not for any of the passengers. As the storm worsened, everyone knew they were probably going to be there for awhile, so they headed to the bar to hang out and watch the weather reports. By the second day, the storm had intensified, and the snow drifts were starting to reach the second-floor windows. No one was getting in or out; not even the hotel staff. It was up to the crews to entertain themselves.

I did not mention it earlier, but the Airways Hotel also featured a rather unique perk at that time. They had installed an in-house video system that allowed them to play movies on certain channels of the televisions in each room. In 1985, that was pretty advanced technology, but the problem was that during that week, they only had three movies available to play. We were told that by the end of the five-day stay, everyone knew every line to the movies "Caddyshack," "Animal House," and "Stripes."

By the evening of day #2, almost everyone there had elected to leave the doors to their rooms open, mostly because they all knew each other. Someone had also set up tables in the hotel lobby, where crews were having jigsaw puzzle tournaments and trivia contests. Of course, the bar stayed open and the restaurant staff continued to pump out those delicious Buffalo chicken wings!

By day #3, the storm was still raging. Since most of the hotel workers were unable to get into work, and the crews were beginning to show signs of "cabin fever," many crewmembers opted to begin helping out by either working in the kitchen or the laundry facility. Also, according to eyewitness accounts, tragedy struck on day #3, when the restaurant (gasp!) ran out of beer!

Another endearing thing that you should know about the Airways Hotel, was the fact that USAir crews could call their restaurant before leaving on a flight, and they would then deliver your orders of wings when you arrived in Buffalo...right to the door of the plane! (Of course, this was before most of the current security checks were in place.) The young man who delivered most of those orders, also doubled as the van driver who picked up the crews when they overnighted in Buffalo.

Now, upon hearing the tragic news that the beer was gone, the hotel guests started brainstorming about how to secure more alcohol while in the middle of a raging blizzard. The roads were closed, the wind was howling, and it was getting dark. After several phone calls, the hotel manager discovered a place that sold kegs of beer, but then lamented that there was no way to get there.

It was then that the young van driver revealed that he, in fact, had his snowmobile on a trailer out in the parking lot, but unfortunately did not bring any warm clothing. Upon hearing that, the crews immediately volunteered winter coats, hats, gloves, and scarves. Once he was bundled up, he started up his snowmobile and disappeared in the swirling black snowstorm. An hour later, he returned...with a keg strapped to the back of his seat! According to the story, the crews then celebrated by carrying him around the lobby on their shoulders like a football hero!

By day #4, there were reports that the storm was weakening. However, all the roads and the airport were still closed, and the snowdrifts were now past the second-floor windows. Since the crews were apparently getting bored with wearing their same clothes every day, someone suggested pulling the sheets off the beds and having an "Animal House" style toga party. According to the smirking and giggling flight attendants who were telling us the story, that party was "insane!" (One even suggested that nine months from then, it wouldn't be surprising if there were some babies born with the middle name of "Airways.")

Day #5 started with the news that the weather was improving and that the snowplows had finally cleared both the airport runways and the main roads to and from the airport. USAir crew schedulers had contacted a few of the captains and informed them that most of them would be put on our flight that day and would be coming home at last. As I recall, once our flight finally landed in Pittsburgh, the stranded crews let out a great shout and gave us a huge round of applause! After hearing all those amazing stories, I spent the rest of my airline career hoping for my great five-day "stranding." (Alas, it never happened.)

February 3rd-21st, 1985 - This was my first real, extended airline vacation. During that time off, training classmates Sherri, Cyndi, and I decided to use our passes to fly to Los Angeles in order to try out for some game shows. Although we didn't get selected for "Tic-Tac-Dough" or "Jokers Wild," I did have some success with the game show "Sale of the Century." As I recall, one of the ladies who was interviewing candidates, revealed that she was related to sports broadcaster, Al Michaels. Therefore, during my brief introduction, I mentioned that I was from the Cincinnati area, and that I remembered listening to some Cincinnati Reds games that happened to feature a rookie broadcaster named...Al Michaels! I don't know if that helped, but I did end up being placed in the "contestants pool." Sadly, I never did get the call to actually tape a show.

Following our few days in L.A., the girls flew back to Pittsburgh. Meanwhile, I decided to use our interline travel privileges and hopped on an American Airlines flight to Hawaii, and spent some time with a friend of mine who was living in Honolulu. At this point, I was really starting to appreciate our airline travel perks!

April 4th, 1985 - While working our flight from LaGuardia to Pittsburgh, we had a small, engine fire on our taxi out to the runway. No one panicked, mostly because the captain came on the P.A. and calmly explained the situation to the passengers. Despite a three-hour delay to fix the problem, most of the folks were just glad that nothing tragic happened and that they were safe to continue their travels.

April 24th-25th, 1985 - A nice two-day trip with my friend Lynette M. again. During a long layover, we came up with a number of airline "sniglets." (This term came from an HBO comedy series which created made-up words for objects that hadn't yet been defined.) Some notable terms included "Man-a-fest" (The list of passenger names and seat assignments that female flight attendants could look at, to see who the cute, male passengers were.) and "Adult-lets" (Those human beings who claimed to be two-year olds, riding for free on their mother's laps, but smoked cigarettes and ordered Scotch!).

May 12th, 1985 - We took racing drivers Dan Gurney, Rick Mears, and Mario Andretti from Washington D.C. to Indianapolis in preparation for the upcoming Indy 500 race. They were all very nice gentlemen.

May 25th-26th, 1985 - A good trip on the 727-200 aircraft. Our first officer was a stunning blonde named Vera, who used to be the private pilot for attorney F. Lee Bailey. She had some very interesting stories to tell about lawyers and their clients.

June 25th, 1985 - In another very bizarre coincidence, I actually had my mom and dad on my flight from Washington D.C. to Cincinnati. As I recall, I had originally given them parental travel passes to go to Hartford through Philadelphia for a dairy farmer's convention. (Evidently, there had been some sort of delay and they had been rerouted to Washington D.C.) After my crew had boarded the plane and while we were storing our bags, one of our "through passengers" started laughing and in a very familiar voice stated, "I recognize that flight attendant!" It was my mom! I introduced them to my crew and my father ended up having a great conversation with our captain, who was also a Navy veteran. What a wonderful twist of fate!

July 24th-26th, 1985 - An interesting three-day trip with friends, Kim Solomon and Frank Matarazzo. On the first day we had astronomer Carl Sagen on our Pittsburgh to Ithaca flight. (He was surprisingly chatty, but I don't think he ever used his famous phrase, "billions and billions of stars.") On our layover in Erie, Pennsylvania, we went go-cart racing after dinner and Kim won every race! On the last day, we had an older gentleman on our Kansas City-Pittsburgh flight who unfortunately got a little disoriented and accidentally crapped his pants in the rear lavatory. Being a farmer, I was somewhat used to the smell, so I volunteered to assist in cleaning him up. It was just something that needed to be done for this particular passenger. (However, the next time someone mentioned how "glamorous" our jobs must be, I just snickered.)

September 1st, 1985 - This was a very eventful day for me. First, we began wearing new, navy-blue uniforms, effective today. Second, after two years, I finally had enough seniority to get off our reserve system and was awarded a regular "block" schedule. For non-airline people, this means that you know ahead of time where and when you will be flying. That also allowed me to start having a more "regular" lifestyle and not have to be on call to fly at a moment's notice. Because my September block allowed me to have the first two weeks off, I went home to hang out.

During this time off, a lot of things happened. I managed to squeeze in a little vacation time with my sister Cindy out in California. My good friends John and Kathi McComb had their first child, and local boy Pete Rose broke the baseball record for most hits in a career. But on September 1st, my life changed forever.

That day, I had gone golfing with my best friend, Steve Moore, and afterwards we had come back to his house for a beer. Upon looking out his window, I saw my old high school classmate Karen Epp across the street on the front porch of the house she was renting. As I recall, Karen had gotten married and divorced right out of high school and was a single mom with a young son. Over the years we had run into each other occasionally and had always enjoyed getting caught up with each other's lives.I remember telling Steve that I would be back in a few minutes, and I proceeded to cross the street to just say hello to Karen. The rest, as they say, is history.

We talked, we laughed, we hugged, and before we knew it, two hours had flown by, and it was dark by the time I got back to Steve's house. When he asked what had happened, I told him I wasn't sure... but I had a date for the next day! Long story short, things went great, and we dated for the next two years before finally getting married in 1987. Yep, September 1st was a really great day!

October 15th-17th, 1985 - A fun trip with friends, Joe Croft and Jeff Abbott. On our overnight in Toronto, we were offered tickets to Game #6 of the American League championships. If the Toronto Blue Jays won that night, they would be going to the World Series for the first time, and all of Canada would be celebrating! However, the Jays were then playing in an outdoor stadium and none of us had enough warm clothing to survive the chilly Canadian evening. We then borrowed the hotel "crew car," and went shopping for warm coats. (Yes, some of our hotels back then did indeed provide a car for the airline crews to use. It was a wonderful perk that would soon disappear.) However, the Jays ended up losing that night, but it was a really good game. We also had some great conversations with the people sitting in front of us, who turned out to be the parents of pitcher Bud Black. (After his successful pitching career was over, Bud Black then went on to have a long and distinguished run as a Major League manager for several teams.)

October 31st, 1985 - My housemates and I attended a great Halloween party hosted by our pilot friends, John Taylor and Hartley LeRoy. Seven of us went as the cast of the classic television show "Gilligan's Island," and we burst into the party while collectively singing the theme song from the show. It was hilarious! (We also won the prize for best group costume.) Additionally, it was my housemate Sherri's birthday, so Sally and I presented her with a special cake to help her celebrate.

December 28th-29th, 1985 - I surprised my girlfriend, Karen, and her son Brian, with airline "buddy passes" to Washington, D.C. for Christmas. Neither had ever been on a plane before, but they both handled it very well. We got to see the White House Christmas tree display and the panda exhibit at the Washington Zoo. It was the first of what would be many, many great trips for the three of us.

January 25th-26th, 1986 - My first trip with my fellow Cincinnatian, "Flyin' Brian" Lindsey. We had a New Orleans overnight and ended up going down to Bourbon Street to take in all the festivities of Super Bowl XX. It was so much fun.

January 28th, 1986 - The Challenger Shuttle air disaster. Although I was not working that day, I was watching it live on the television at my parent's house when it occurred. I later found out that a friend of mine was working on a flight to Florida at the time and actually saw it happen out of the airplane window. Her captain later had to make an announcement to the passengers explaining what had occurred and the crew had to quietly try to console a number of people. It was a very sad day.

February 17th, 1986 - We had another group of WWF professional wrestlers on our Pittsburgh to Albany flight, including Rowdy Roddy Piper, Brutus Beefcake, and my old acquaintance, Paul "Mr. Wonderful" Orndorff. Paul remembered me and was even nice enough to sign an autograph for Karen's son, Brian.

February 21st, 1986 - Today, USAir had a DC-9 slide off the runway in Erie, Pennsylvania, during some bad weather. The crew then had to evacuate the aircraft and there was every indication that they did it very well. It was another reminder that with this job, anything could happen at any time. (Get used to that phrase, as I will end up using it several times throughout this book!)

February 21st-25th 1986 - During this week of vacation, I made plans to move back home and start "commuting" to Pittsburgh for my trips. In the airline world, that meant that I would be living outside my crew base but traveling on our passes before (and after) each trip. Although it would be more time-consuming, it would allow me to move back into my house and continue to date Karen.

March 19th, 1986 - On our Raleigh-Pittsburgh flight, we encountered a female passenger who was ready to graduate from USAir's innovative "Fearful Flyers" program. That program was designed to assist folks who were terrified to fly, by offering them scientific answers for the things they disliked about flying, such as noises, vibrations, and so on. Our lady passenger was taking her first flight and was also going to be filmed by a Pittsburgh television crew during that flight. In short, she did very well. They even had balloons and a graduation certificate for her as she got off our plane.

March 22nd, 1986 - My three-year anniversary with USAir. According to our flight attendant contract, that achievement also came with a huge pay increase, which nearly doubled my salary. In anticipation of that pay raise, I had earlier gone out and purchased a 1982 Datsun 280-ZX sports car with T-tops! It ended up being the best car I ever owned.

May 7th, 1986 - On this trip, I got a chance to meet up with my good friend and former housemate, Mike Butts, while he was in Philadelphia for a lawyer conference. We had a nice dinner and afterwards we discovered a trivia bar near our hotels. We then entered their trivia contest and absolutely crushed all our competition. Mike was just so smart, which also made him so much fun to hang out with.

May 23rd, 1986 - Near the end of our flight from San Francisco to Pittsburgh, a passenger suffered a possible heart attack. True to our training, we all jumped in to help out. Fortunately, there was a doctor on board who assisted us. Once the passenger was taken off by paramedics in Pittsburgh, we had a lot of medical reports and paperwork to fill out regarding this incident. I never did hear what happened to him afterwards.

June 20th-29th, 1986 - This week I got to enjoy some wonderful vacation time with Karen, when we used our passes to fly out to Wyoming, Colorado, and Washington. We also returned to Pittsburgh in time to attend the wedding of my two flight attendant friends, Greg Parrill and Cyndi Veronesi. (The wedding was a blast!) Afterwards, I officially moved out of our house near the Pittsburgh airport, which was had been such a great place to live while starting my airline career.

July 10th, 1986 - Today I became violently sick with food poisoning, probably from our company-provided crew meals. As I recall, we had run a little late getting into Orlando, and apparently the caterers had just left our meals sitting in the hot jetway. Since we had no time to eat between flights, I remember wolfing down a roast beef sandwich that tasted a little "funky." Sure enough, two hours later I started sweating and feeling a little "green." Fortunately, my crew covered for me while I puked my guts out in the rear lavatory. Although I survived, I couldn't even look at another crew meal for the next few years.

August 14th, 1986 - During our overnight in Norfolk, Virginia, the entire crew decided to meet downstairs at the hotel bar. There, we ended up talking with two nice young guys, who eventually revealed that they were the drivers of the Oscar Meyer "Weiner-mobile." (For those who don't know, that vehicle is a 20-foot-long car that resembles a giant hot dog.) They eventually took a liking to our two hot, female flight attendants and in sincerely trying to explain their occupations, unconsciously and innocently offered up some of the funniest lines I have ever heard. Among them were...

" Wanna come out to the parking lot and see my weiner?" As well as...

"Would you like to sit on my weiner and get your picture taken?"

I know the captain and I both spit up our beers when we overheard that conversation!

September 27th, 1986 - I got a chance to walk over and check out the supersonic Concorde SST jet that was parked next to us in New York. It was smaller than I had imagined, but still very impressive. There were only two seats on either side of the center aisle and maybe only 15 rows. A digital display board on the forward wall showed their passengers how fast the plane was going. Their crew also explained that when the Concorde hit the speed of sound (Mach 1) the flight attendants would then pass out champagne to toast their accomplishment.

October 22nd, 1986 - Today we had a one-day training seminar on airline security. It went well and in fact when the instructors found out that I was a former teacher, they offered me a position in the training department. I told them thanks, but I was having too much fun flying.

November 18th-21st, 1986 - A nice four-day trip with my friend, Carolyn Martin. While on our Los Angeles overnight, Carolyn made some calls and ended up getting us front-row/VIP seats for a taping of the "Late Night with Joan Rivers" talk show on the new FOX network. As I recall, we even had our own private bathroom during the show. Guests included actor Martin Sheen, musician Ricky Scaggs and etiquette specialist Miss Manners.

November 25th, 1986 - In another strange coincidence, I had ESPN sportscaster Dan Patrick on our Washington D.C.-Cincinnati flight. He seemed to remember me, maybe because we grew up in the same area, and were close to the same age. Also, our mothers knew each other, our sisters worked at the local YMCA together, and we both went to Eastern Kentucky University at about the same time. (He played JV basketball and I was on the wrestling team.) Our meeting also caused me to remember this interesting little story.

Unfortunately for both of us, in the Spring of 1976, EKU had begun incorporating the recently passed "Title IX" legislation which provided better funding for women's sports teams. Eventually, EKU decided to cut several men's sports programs in order to create the new women's Cross-Country squad. Sadly, that meant ending the financial support for the wrestling and JV basketball teams.

On the day that our teams were informed of their fates, I remember seeing Dan afterwards in the locker room area and we talked about what we were going to do next. Since I was already a junior, I said that I was just going to come back the next year and finish my degree. Because Dan was only a sophomore, I remember him saying that he was going to look into transferring to another college and maybe try out for their basketball team as a "walk-on." In an interesting twist of fate, he did transfer to the University of Dayton, and in the year that he had to "sit out," he ended up calling UD basketball games for a local radio station. Eventually, he decided that he liked that better than playing...and has ended up being one of the most recognizable announcers in sports! (Thanks Title IX!)

December 7th, 1986 - By this date, we had started hearing rumors that USAir might be trying to buy or merge with California-based PSA Airlines. That seemed to make sense because a number of other airlines had attempted to do the same thing this year.

December 10th, 1986 - Today we heard reports that USAir would indeed be purchasing PSA Airlines for something like 400 million dollars. That was also the beginning of what would become an era of rapid airline consolidation.

December 17th, 1986 - My logbook notes for this day showed the initials "A.G." in a corner of the page. Since I don't remember ever having an "Attorney General" on any of my flights, I can only assume this was the time that I had the professional wrestler "Andre the Giant" onboard.

As I recall, we were on a smaller DC-9 airplane at the time. When the gate agent came down to inform us that our famous guest would be seated across all three seats of the last row, I think I sort of chuckled. That was because Andre was something like 7 feet tall and around 400 pounds. I guess I couldn't imagine how someone that large could even squeeze down the center aisle, let alone ride comfortably in those smaller seats.

However, when he did board the aircraft, he was pleasant enough to the crew, even though he appeared to be in some pain at the time. After he was seated, I do remember that we had to then connect four seat belt extensions end-to-end, in order to be able to secure him in his seat. Because of the limited legroom, he also had to sit sideways with his legs out in the aisle.

The other vivid memory I have of that encounter, came during the drink service once we were airborne. Aside from his wrestling fame, apparently Andre was also well-known for his ability to ingest large amounts of alcohol and not be affected by it. In fact, once we reached his row, he ordered eight small bottles of our white wine. After we set them on his tray table he then did the most amazing trick. After turning his huge hand palm up, he evenly placed all eight bottles between his fingers, and then cracked them open at the same time with his other hand! Afterwards, he then dumped them all into his own personal big plastic cup, and downed the wine in about three huge swallows. After thanking us, he leaned his head back against the rear bulkhead wall to try to catch a little nap. Later on, I recalled thinking how incredibly difficult it must have been for him to do any traveling at all, especially during his long wrestling career.

December 22nd, 1986 - We had a very bumpy flight into West Palm Beach today. In fact, there were numerous news reports afterwards about other flights in that same area that suffered some serious injuries to both passengers and flight crew. Officially it was listed as a phenomenon known as C.A.T. or "Clear Air Turbulence," and many pilots reported no indications of any problem areas on their radar screens at that time. Incidents like this are why flight crews continue to ask their passengers to keep their seat belts fastened while in flight.

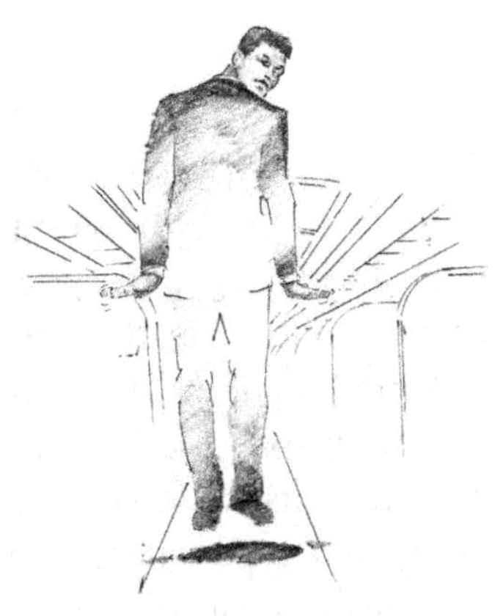

Chapter Five

1987....Mergers, Marriage, and Muhammad Ali.

January 14th, 1987 - Today we had about a dozen Clairol "hair models" on our West Palm Beach-Pittsburgh flight. Most of them did have beautiful hair, but several of them wore hats...which I found ironically amusing.

January 20th-23rd, 1987 - This was an interesting four-day trip with friends Sue Underhill and Jeff Davis. On the third day, we got stuck in Washington, D.C. due to a huge snowstorm which dumped 12 inches of snow on the airport area. Our company then decided to put about a dozen stranded crews on a bus, in order to drive us to our supposedly available hotel. However, after two hours of inching through the snow drifts, we found out that our rooms had been given to other stranded folks. After that, it was back on the bus for another long drive to another hotel. This time, the drive was more subdued, especially after we crossed the 14th Street bridge where the Air Florida flight had crashed five years earlier in very similar weather conditions.

February 14th, 1987 - While home for Valentine's Day, I proposed to Karen, after first getting permission from her son, Brian. Thankfully, they both said yes!

February 24th - March 10th, 1987 - During this two-week period, USAir made a bid for Charlotte-based Piedmont Airlines, only to be surprised a few days later by a bid from TWA to buy USAir. After officially turning down TWA, USAir finally secured the purchase of Piedmont several days later. "Merger Mania" continues!

March 30th, 1987 - On this trip, we had a very long overnight in Hartford, Connecticut. However, the company chose to bus us about 30 minutes north and put us up at a nice Marriott in downtown Springfield, Massachusetts. While out walking the next day, I discovered the terrific National Basketball Hall of Fame. In fact, at the end of the tour, there was an open-air display of 50 different basketball goals where you could shoot basketballs at each of the different backboards. It even featured a bowling-alley-type ball return for the basketballs. I didn't leave until I made at least one goal at every basket.

The following morning was even more entertaining, because one of the pilots made the hotel van driver divert to a rather unusual place for coffee. That coffee shop turned out to be a "topless" doughnut stand which featured waitresses without blouses...and really great doughnuts as well. (Needless to say, between the caffeine, the sugar-filled pastries, and the tatas, I was certainly wide awake for that morning flight!)

June 23rd-24th, 1987 - This trip had a great overnight in Burlington, Vermont, where I got a chance to walk the University of Vermont campus. At the campus dairy store, I discovered the most delicious ice cream I have ever tasted. When I returned to our hotel, the actors who played the unique characters of "Larry, Darryl, and Darryl" on the "Bob Newhart Show," were just checking in at the front desk.

July 20th, 1987 - We had USAir CEO, Ed Colodny, on our Pittsburgh to Washington, D.C. flight. I had only met him once about four years earlier, but true to the legend regarding his phenomenal memory, he did indeed remember my name! What a terrific man!

August 20th, 1987- We had a number of very angry passengers on our Columbus-Newark flight. At that time, the rules regarding the size of the smoking sections on each flight were determined by the number of non-smokers on board. On rare occasions, last-minute seat purchases by non-smokers could shrink or completely eliminate the smoking section. Apparently, that is what happened on our flight and several smokers were irate about it. We really had to keep an eye on a few people who wanted to "light up" anyway.

September 30th, 1987- Unfortunately, after this trip was over, I could not get a commuter flight home and I ended up with the absolutely worst room available at the old Pittsburgh Airport Hotel. (No heat, no window shades, and it was next to the runway, where I heard planes taking off all night long!) Ahh...the joys of commuting.

October 6th, 1987- While on a layover at our Cleveland hotel, we encountered several of the Cleveland Browns "replacement players" who were staying there also. As I recall, the NFL Players Union was out on strike at the time and these guys were being used by the owners to play in games anyway. One of them even helped load our crew bags onto the hotel van.

October 8th-26th, 1987 - I was off for most of the month to get married and then honeymoon in Hawaii for two weeks. The wedding went great, Karen looked beautiful, and the reception may have been the best party I have ever attended! I still feel to this day that I am the luckiest guy in the world!

November 13th, 1987 - Day three of a four-day trip. This great crew included friends Dave Brown and Kelly Crudep. Today we worked a flight that went from Pittsburgh to Phoenix to San Diego. Unfortunately, our 737-200 plane was one of the aircraft that had been "reconfigured" into a fleet of all-coach Boeings. Those planes had no First-Class section and were supposed to allow for more regular seats, and therefore more profit. (All it actually did was upset the frequent flyers, and ended up being scrubbed after a couple of years.)

Just before we started the boarding process, the gate agent came down and informed us that the famous boxer Muhammed Ali was going to be on our flight and would be going all the way through to San Diego. Sadly, he had recently been diagnosed with Parkinson's disease which had slowed him down quite a bit. Apparently, as part of his therapy, he was heading to Mexico for some medical treatment. Although he was traveling by himself, we were told that he was going to be met in San Diego by some of his associates.

Now keep in mind, when Mr. Ali was in his prime, he was probably around 6'4" and 250 pounds and was one of the finest athletes of his generation. He was also intelligent, well-spoken, and very charismatic. Unfortunately, the Parkinson's had slowed him down quite a bit and also kept him from being able to speak much above a whisper. Despite that, he was still a very impressive personality. In fact, I have repeatedly said that meeting Mr. Ali was the one time that I witnessed what true "star quality" was all about.

Again, because there was no First Class, the agent had seated him about halfway back in the main cabin. When he finally boarded, he quietly whispered "hello" to Kelly and I and then slowly made his way toward his seat. From my position at the front of the cabin, I could just see over his shoulder, and I witnessed nearly everyone's jaw drop as they recognized their famous fellow passenger.

To his credit, I have always thought that Muhammad Ali was one of the most gracious and patient celebrities that I ever encountered. Sadly for him, almost immediately after being seated, he was bombarded with requests from the other passengers for snapshots and autographs. Because of his Parkinson's, he was slower and more deliberate in his movements and consequently it took him a little longer to sign an autograph or pose for a picture. During that three-hour flight, I never saw him refuse any request from his fans. I did however feel sorry that he never really got a chance to rest or relax.

Once we landed in Phoenix, about half of our passengers deplaned, with the rest choosing to stay onboard. During that 30-minute layover, I saw that Mr. Ali (who had elected to stay onboard) was still being inundated with the attention of his fellow passengers. It made me feel sorry for him and that's when I decided to try to come to his rescue, and give the guy a little break.

I then asked the gate agent if she could close off the attached jetway for a little while, and she agreed. After that, I went up to Mr. Ali and very discreetly informed him that if he would like a little time to himself, he could use our jetway area where no one would bother him. I distinctly recall him looking to his left and right, then nodding his head and silently mouthing the words "Thank you" to me. (It was so sweet and sincere that it made me chuckle quietly to myself!)

After excusing himself, he came up to the front of the plane where he spent the next ten minutes walking and stretching out on the jetway. Meanwhile, our crew stood watch in the front galley to assure him some privacy. After a short time, I think he got a little bored, because he wandered over to the front-entry door and started up a conversation with the three of us.

For most of my adult life, I have been able to read and retain all sorts of information. That ability came in very handy when I was a teacher, but it has also allowed me to be able to engage in some very interesting conversations with our passengers. (I don't know why some of that stuff sticks in my brain, but it does!)

Anyway, once we started chatting with Mr. Ali, I suddenly recalled an article that I had seen about his interest in magic tricks. Once I asked him about it, I swear that his eyes sparkled, he grinned at us, and slowly and deliberately asked, "Would you like to see one?" Not sure of what I had done, I looked at the other flight attendants and cautiously replied, "Okay?" He then told us to watch his heels.

At this point, we looked at each other as if to say, "What is going on here?" However, he then turned his back to us, put his heels together, and began moving his hands in small bird-like motions. It was then that I witnessed perhaps the coolest thing I have ever seen. Muhammad Ali, the world's greatest boxer, proceeded to levitate off the ground about 5-6 inches, for about five seconds, before slowly settling back onto the jetway floor!

The other flight attendants and I gasped in amazement at what we had just witnessed. (To this day, I am not sure that my eyes didn't actually bug out of my head like some sort of cartoon special effect!) As he turned around, you could tell that he was delighted to have mystified our crew. I think that I then stammered out some semi-intelligent question like,

"Um, I don't suppose you are going to tell us how you did that?"

He just grinned and replied, "Sorry; I'm not allowed to tell."

Now, I am a very rational thinker and I knew there had to have been some logical explanation for what I had just seen, but I had no idea what it could have been. The jetway canopy was pushed back, so there was nothing above him that he could have used to pull himself up. I also clearly saw the bright, Arizona sunlight under both feet. It then slowly dawned on me that this may have been why his boxing opponents couldn't seem to hit him much. Just like his famous hype, he really did "Float like a butterfly!"

After a few more minutes of trying to pry an answer from him, we escorted him back to his seat and then started boarding for our flight to San Diego. Although that flight was much shorter, perhaps an hour or so, the new passengers also delighted in interacting with Mr. Ali as well. Again, he was so very polite and patient with everyone he came in contact with.

After landing and taxiing up to our gate, Kelly and I truly enjoyed watching our passengers get off the plane; all chattering about our famous guest and clutching their many autographed items. However, Mr. Ali chose to wait around until everyone else had deplaned, before getting up to leave. It was then that he surprised us with a little gift. To our amazement, (and because we were probably the only people on the plane who had NOT asked him to sign something) he presented us with three autographs! I remember telling him that he did not have to do that, but he told us that he really appreciated our kindness and wanted us to each have one.

He also wanted to shake hands with each of us. To this day, I still recall him having maybe the biggest paw I have ever seen on a human being. (I felt like a six-year-old shaking hands with a full-grown adult!) I also couldn't imagine getting hit in the face with that huge hand; let alone putting a boxing glove on it and making it even bigger!

Finally, as he was getting ready to leave, my friend Kelly asked if she could give him a kiss on the cheek. He playfully agreed and when she gave him a little peck, he made us all laugh when he grinned and pretended that his knees buckled! What a wonderful human being.

Although this is absolutely one of my favorite celebrity encounters, this story actually has a second part, which is almost as incredible as the first part. You see, some five years later, I was working a trip that overnighted at the beautiful Marriott Marquis hotel in downtown Atlanta. At some point I had shared with my crew the story about meeting Mr. Ali. After describing his amazing levitation trick, they all razzed me about what I had claimed to have seen. Some offered that he had used mirrors and others surmised that he somehow hoisted himself up using the jetway canopy. Basically, none of them believed me.

Now as airline crews often did, we had decided to meet up for dinner that night on one of the upper levels of the hotel. After we had all assembled, we began discussing our dining options. It was then that the captain leaned over, looked past my shoulder, and pointed out a store behind us called "The Magic Shoppe." Since he had been one of my biggest non-believers, I was not surprised when he came up with the idea for us to go into that store and have me share my story about

Muhammad Ali levitating. (I think he hoped that they could give us an idea of how he did it.)

We then strolled into the store and introduced ourselves as an airline crew. After relating to the gentleman behind the counter that we needed an explanation, I began to tell my amazing tale; being sure to carefully explain what I had seen and heard. To our surprise, at the end of my story, the shop owner was grinning from ear to ear. He said that not only could he confirm that Mr. Ali could in fact do that trick, but incredibly, they were the store that had sold him that particular trick! (Now what are the odds of that??) He then said that he wanted to show us something.

From behind the counter, he pulled out a large, dusty ledger and proceeded to flip through the pages. Meanwhile, he explained that when a magician buys a trick, he must swear that he will never reveal how he does that trick, and then signs a waiver to that effect. After a few seconds, he stopped and pointed to a particular entry. Sure enough, it was Muhammad Ali's signature, and it was dated six months before I had encountered him on my flight.

Now that my crew had independent confirmation of what I had seen, they grudgingly apologized, but still wanted an explanation of how that trick could have been done. Again, the shop owner chuckled and said that since he too was a magician, he could not reveal any details either. I then tried very hard to resist the urge to stick out my tongue and tell my disbelievers..."Nah-nah! Nah-nah!"

December 3rd, 1987 - The Washington Bullets NBA team just happened to be in the waiting area of our gate at the Washington National airport when we deplaned. Although they were all rather tall, one of their players was 7'6" Manute Bol who literally towered over everyone.

December 14th-15th, 1987 - During this trip, we had to deal with some really bad weather in the South. There were lots of storms and high winds which caused numerous flight cancellations. In fact, we just avoided a series of tornadoes that hit Memphis, Tennessee, right after we had taken off from there!

We also had a very interesting captain, who throughout the trip, offered us all a chance to participate in his version of "nose-wheel roulette." Apparently, he would go down to the tarmac and use white chalk to divide the front tire of each airplane into equal portions and then number each section. Each crew member could then throw a couple of dollars into the pot and pick a number. After each arrival, the captain would tell us which number was touching the ground and award the winner the pot. I got lucky and won three of the seven flights on the first day.

December 22nd-24th, 1987 - This was another rather interesting trip. On the first night, we overnighted in Albany, New York. As we were walking down that airport hallway, we passed a newly installed art display that consisted of some long, curved wooden staves that had been fashioned into a large ball. On each stave, was a collection of antique iron door knockers. As a former educator, I remember being somewhat impressed by the historical value of those iron rings. However, I did not really think before uttering out loud...

"Wow, look at those knockers!"

(Fortunately, my somewhat statuesque, female co-worker standing next to me just snickered and dead-panned... "Hey, thanks for noticing.") I was mortified.

On the second day of this trip, I ran into my old housemate Sherri in the Pittsburgh Airport. She then informed me that her crew had just encountered the famous PBS kid show host Mr. Fred Rogers, on their flight. According to Sherri, he was just as kind and personable as he seemed to be on his television show. He had even brought home-made chocolate chip cookies for each crew member. (To quote Mr. Rogers, that must have made for a... "wonderful day in the neighborhood!")

Chapter Six

1988-1989....Protecting the Cockpit and a Cabin Prep

January 26th, 1988 - I commuted in early today so I could do our annual weight check and yearly evaluation. When I first started flying, there were very strict physical requirements that would determine whether or not a flight attendant could actually work. If a person gained too much weight, they could be put on a type of probation until that problem was rectified. Our union eventually fought to change it to a more balanced "height/weight ratio" scale. Regardless, at every yearly recurrent training you still had to be able to squeeze through a standard airplane window exit.

February 2nd-4th, 1988 - My first trip with my friend Lynn Mendiola. On the second day, we had a long overnight in Islip, New York, where we drove the crew car to a nice restaurant out on Long Island. On the last day, we had former Pittsburgh Pirates first baseman Willie "Pops" Stargell on our flight to Atlanta. He was such a nice gentleman.

February 12th, 1988 - A very weird weather day. We started off in a snowstorm in Toronto and finished the day in sunny 80-degree weather at the San Antonio Riverwalk. Extreme changes like that sometimes make my sinuses want to explode.

February 13th, 1988 - We had the great privilege to meet and chat with basketball star "Dr. J" Julius Erving on our Philadelphia-Pittsburgh flight. He was also nice enough to sign an autograph for my son Brian who loves basketball.

April 14th, 1988 - What a fun flight from Cleveland to Washington, D.C.! We had several women's choral groups on board who spent most of the flight challenging each other to short singing performances. (I believe they were known as "Sweet Adelines") They were all wonderfully talented and it made for a very entertaining flight!

June 17th, 1988 - Sadly, we experienced huge, air-traffic delays in and out of the LaGuardia Airport. At one point, we were delayed for over three hours and were something like number 47 for take-off. Our passengers were all going to miss their connections and were not very happy with USAir, despite the fact that they could see out the windows that all the other airlines were running late as well.

July 5th, 1988 - Today, I enjoyed a very nice conversation with long-time Motown singer Gladys Knight on our Pittsburgh-Toronto flight. She was very sweet to everyone around her.

July 6th, 1988 - Just before we started boarding our flight in Pittsburgh, we had an angry federal mediator come down the jetway and try to barge into the cockpit. Not knowing what was going on, and since I was stationed at the cockpit door for boarding, it was one of the few times I had to physically manhandle someone. (For all I knew, this idiot was trying to take over the airplane!) I then used a favorite wrestling move, known as an overhook, that tied up both of his arms while pushing him back towards the jetway. The captain then came out of the cockpit and told me to let him go. It seems he and the mediator had some sort of a union-related argument earlier in the day, and the guy was still mad. Our captain then told the gate agent to take him off our flight. (He also said I did a great job protecting the cockpit and paid for my dinner that night.)

August 2nd, 1988 - An incredibly long, hot day on the DC-9. We worked a total of seven flights today and our crew was on duty for over 17 hours! I was exhausted.

August 16th, 1988 - Today I officially adopted Brian as my son. For a wedding gift, my law school friends had agreed to handle all the paperwork and fees for this procedure, and it may have been one of the best gifts ever given to us. The judge made a point of saying how happy he was to help form a new family. It was an amazing day. (I later sent out some "It's a Boy" birth announcement cards to a few friends and family members. On the lines where it said, "height and weight," I put Brian as 5'7" and 125 pounds with size 11 feet!)

October 12th, 1988 - Our crew got to deadhead on United Airlines from Ontario, California to San Francisco, and then work from San Francisco to Reno. While in Reno, I learned how to play blackjack with my friend and crew member Debbie Bodner.

November 9th, 1988 - During a long layover in Philadelphia, I went downstairs to the employee cafeteria and had a delicious lunch from Marie's Sandwich Shop. Marie was the owner and always took great joy in chatting up the crews. She almost always called you "Honey" or "Baby Doll" while she was making your meal and, in return, the more you complimented her, the larger your sandwich became! (By the way, there were a number of times that I went to Marie's, not necessarily because I was hungry, but just because I enjoyed the verbal stroking.)

November 22nd, 1988 - While at the gate in Philadelphia, our plane was accidently hit by a United catering truck. That truck hit the end of the wing and collapsed the left-wing light. Although it wasn't a lot of damage, it was enough to cancel the flight and probably cost that caterer his job.

December 16th, 1988 - We had a number of NFL athletes on our flight from Pittsburgh to Denver tonight including players Larry Csonka and Conrad Dobler, as well as ABC Sports president Roone Arledge. Mr. Csonka was very nice, but Mr. Dobler was a real pain regarding a relatively simple double-seat assignment.

December 21st, 1988- The tragic crash of Pan Am flight 103 over Lockerbie, Scotland, happened while we were in-flight from Las Vegas to Pittsburgh. The captain called our senior flight attendant up to the cockpit during the flight and shared the few details that he had at the time. It was only later on that we learned it was a terroristic act which devastated us all. I also found out later that a young couple from my hometown perished on that flight.

January 12th, 1989 - Unfortunately, an elderly lady died on our flight to West Palm Beach today. When her sister asked me to look at her, the lady looked like she was sleeping, but already had a grayish skin color. When I couldn't find a pulse, I immediately pulled her out of her seat and started CPR on her. At that point, my crew made an announcement, and a doctor came up to assist me by doing the chest compressions while I continued doing the rescue breathing.

Our captain then made an announcement that he was diverting the flight to Orlando and he landed with us still in the aisle performing CPR. The paramedics were on board in no time, but it was pretty clear to all that she was already gone. I felt so bad that I even apologized to her sister that I couldn't have done more for her. However, the real kicker came during the hour or so that we were on the ground, when some well-dressed businessman came up to me and callously asked "So... exactly when ARE we going to get to West Palm?" (That passenger has no idea how vividly I imagined putting him in some sort of wrestling "sleeper hold.")

January 13th, 1989 - In another strange coincidence, our high school English teacher, Mrs. Francis Drake, and her husband were on my flight to Dayton, Ohio. They were returning from a short vacation and she couldn't have been happier for me to see that I had found a job that I was truly enjoying. (As I write this paragraph, I can only hope that my composition, syntax, and punctuation are correct. That alone would have made her proud!)

April 8th, 1989 - After almost two years, the company announced that the USAir/PSA merger will be completed as of today. It's a little sad to see such a fun airline just disappear.

April 22nd, 1989 - We had the Indiana Pacers NBA team on our flight from Indianapolis to Milwaukee today. Some of the taller players looked very uncomfortable trying to sit in some of our slightly smaller coach seats.

May 2nd, 1989 - After USAir's failed attempt at going to all-coach seating, they decided to re-establish First Class on most of their planes. Today we had to attend a one-day seminar on our "new" First-Class procedures. It was a fun day because I got to hang out with my old housemates Sherri, Sally and Scott. We even managed to squeeze in a few games of Euchre for old times' sake.

June 15th, 1989 - First-Class service started back up today. Unfortunately, there were lots of complaints from passengers and crew that things did not go smoothly.

July 6th, 1989 - This was my first time seeing our brand-new terminal at the Washington National Airport. I didn't like the color scheme or the layout, but it was still a vast improvement over the old terminal. My crew was underwhelmed as well.

July 18th-19th, 1989 - According to my logbook notes, this was "The 2-day from Hell!" We had angry passengers on our LaGuardia-Pittsburgh flight due to the agents going to an "open seating" arrangement. We also had a large number of double seat assignments on our Pittsburgh to San Francisco flight as well. On the second day, the San Francisco-Pittsburgh flight had very strong headwinds and we had to divert to St. Louis for additional fuel.

On top of that, once we got back to Pittsburgh, we found out that a United flight (flight 232) had a major mechanical problem and had to crash land in a cornfield outside Sioux City, Iowa. Later we learned that their pilots exhibited some tremendously heroic actions which limited the fatalities. I have always had the greatest respect for the piloting profession and this was another reminder of how much they have to perform under pressure.

August 4th, 1989 - Today was the last official day for Piedmont Airlines. Again, another sad day due to the demise of another wonderful airline.

September 20th, 1989 - USAir flight 5050 crashed during takeoff at LaGuardia Airport. There were several fatalities but the crew did well managing the situation after the accident. The plane ended up resting on one of the piers at the end of the runway and evidently several people did end up in the water. Again, due to the heroic actions of the crew, apparently it was not as tragic as it might have been.

October 16th-19th, 1989 - This was an interesting trip, mostly because we had just taken off from San Francisco about two hours before a major earthquake hit the Bay area. Once we arrived in Philadelphia, we spent most of the night glued to the television watching the tragic reports coming out of San Francisco. I heard later that one of our crews was stuck at the downtown crew hotel for five days afterward.

November 14th, 1989 - Tonight we stayed at the new Westin Bonaventure hotel in downtown Los Angeles. To our surprise, we were delayed checking into our rooms because there was a film company making a movie in the lobby. (I believe the name of the movie was "Solar Crisis.") Despite the delay, it was still very interesting to see all the things that go on behind the scenes of a movie set!

November 27th, 1989 - Because of all the holiday traffic and high passenger loads, I had to commute from Dayton to Pittsburgh through Cleveland in order to get to work today. For us "commuters," that kind of deviation is not really unusual during the holidays.

November 28th, 1989 - I was the "A" or "Senior" flight attendant on this trip and about 15 minutes from landing in Baltimore, I was called up to the cockpit. Our captain informed me that there was a problem with the nose gear and that we would be flying low over the control tower to see if they could tell if our nose gear was in fact down and locked. In the meantime, I should start preparing the cabin for a possible emergency landing.

Now every flight-crew member lives with the knowledge that you must always be ready to handle any emergency that may occur at any time. You train over and over for any and all possible scenarios, and then hope that you never have to actually use that knowledge. However, when something does happen, you are confident that you can do the right thing.

After the captain had given me the pertinent information, (we had about 15 minutes and that there was a possibility of the nose gear collapsing.) I called up the other flight attendants and briefed them on the situation. We only had about 40 passengers, so the cabin preparation was relatively easy to accomplish. I made all the announcements and surprisingly no one seemed that stressed. I was amazingly calm as well.

Long story short, the nose gear held up and we made a somewhat routine landing in Baltimore. It was only when I looked out my jump-seat window and saw all the fire trucks and emergency vehicles following us down the runway, that I allowed myself to wonder about what might have been. Fortunately, it was the only time in my 38-year career that I had to organize a "cabin prep," but it was always comforting to know that I could successfully do it again if I had to.

December 13th, 1989 - On this three-day trip, I was again flying with my friend Mary Filipponi. On our Reno-Los Angeles flight, we encountered a very chatty passenger who turned out to be the owner of the Mustang Ranch brothel. He took a liking to us and then eventually presented us with a number of interesting gifts. They included passes for a free "visit" and key chains that featured a number of simulated sex acts. (Just to be clear, I never used the free pass, but I do still have one of the key chains!)

December 18th, 1989 - Today I was an "extra" flight attendant on a Washington-based trip. (That meant that I would sort of float around the system and help out different crews on full flights.) While at the gate, several of the crew got off the plane in Pittsburgh to get something to eat. After a hectic boarding process, we pushed back on time, only to find that we were missing Shelly, one of our flight attendants. We then had to return to the gate to pick her up. That delay quite possibly cost her some sort of suspension, if not an outright termination.

Chapter Seven

1990-1991....Drug Testing, a Boy Band,
and Love in the Air

January, 1990 - During this month, I flew the same trip three weeks in a row. The highlight was a 24-hour layover at a beautiful Hyatt hotel right on Sarasota's main beach. Every week we either rode bikes on the beach or checked out the Ringling Brothers Circus Museum. We also enjoyed a number of meals at a great seafood restaurant right on the water. (I only felt a little guilty that while my family was freezing in Ohio, I was "chilling" on the beach in Florida.)

February 12th-15th, 1990 - A great trip with fellow flight attendants Monica Andyshak and Lisa Manfredi. On our overnight in Miami, we went out to celebrate Monica's final trip before she left the airline business. What really bothered me was that another airline crew at the table next to us was pounding down pitchers of Sangria. (I will only say that they were an international crew based in a foreign country.) When they finally left us and staggered back to their rooms, I remember hoping that they weren't going to go fly anytime soon.

February 25th, 1990 - Today was the last day that smoking would be allowed on any domestic flight in the U.S. For those of us who were non-smokers, it couldn't have come at a better time. I was getting tired of always smelling like smoke. Additionally, I had been having a little trouble breathing at work.

April 3rd, 1990 - During our flight from Tampa to Dayton, the cockpit windshield began to crack a little bit. Although we were able to safely land in Dayton, our captain later admitted to being a little nervous about the possibility of losing that piece of glass before we landed. In fact, we had slowed our air speed a little, just in case that happened.

April 12th, 1990 - We had the rock band "Slaughter" on our flight from Cleveland to Toronto today. They were all nice, but a little subdued. In a strange twist of fate, a few years later their lead singer Mark Slaughter would end up marrying my flight attendant friend Becky Russell who was mentioned earlier in Chapter 3.

May 22nd-23rd, 1990 - We went through two days of training in Pittsburgh to learn about the new Boeing 767 aircraft. It was bigger than most of our other planes, and I wasn't sure if I would like it enough to want to work on it. However, since it would be used to go to some international and Caribbean destinations that I had not yet seen, I wanted to keep my options open.

June 19th-20th, 1990 - This was my first trip on another new plane: the Fokker F-100. They were smaller (only 99 seats) and harder to work because there were only two flight attendants. On the second day we had NFL Hall of Famer Paul Hornung on our flight to Atlantic City. He apparently had enjoyed quite a few drinks before joining us but seemed like a very cool guy.

June 28th, 1990 - Tonight, we had another famous football player on our flight to Hartford, Connecticut: Chicago Bears running back Walter Payton. He was nice enough to take time to chat with each of our crew members during the flight.

July 6th, 1990 - On our flight from Dayton to Washington D.C., we had a sweet little unaccompanied minor named Amanda who was terrified to fly. After talking to her before we left, she asked me to sit with her during takeoff so she wouldn't be scared. After getting permission from the captain, I did and she was shaking but didn't cry. At the end of the flight, she wrote me the nicest little thank you note (in crayon) that I still have to this day.

July 12th, 1990 - The van driver who took us to and from our hotel in Raleigh-Durham was a very talented ventriloquist. During our ride, he absolutely amazed us by throwing his voice apparently from out of the glove box, from under his seat, and from the hotel mailbox.

August 2nd, 1990 - This was a really fun trip with flight attendants Barb Peters and Donna Chatari. The second day featured a long layover in Orange County, California. The three of us ended up riding the bus to Huntington Beach where we accidentally stumbled upon the O.P. National Surf Championships that were taking place that day. Watching the surfers and enjoying the warm sunshine was a wonderful way to spend an afternoon.

August 15th, 1990 - When we pulled up to our hotel in Greenville-Spartanburg, we were surprised to see hundreds of young fans surrounding the building. Apparently, the boy band "New Kids on the Block" was staying at the same hotel and were going to be leaving soon for a concert that evening. As we unloaded our luggage, you could feel everyone looking at us, in case we were "somebody with the band!" After we checked into our rooms, I changed clothes and decided to go downstairs for a bite to eat. I then took the elevator and when the doors opened on the main floor, I was greeted with five seconds of squeals and applause. That is, until I stepped out and the crowd in the lobby realized that I was NOT one of the "New Kids." (Then it was a collectively disappointed sigh of..."Aww"). Now I hate to admit it, but I actually enjoyed the attention so much, that I faked that I had forgotten my wallet and went back into the elevator. After a few minutes, I rode back down...and got the same crowd reaction again! (I chuckled about that for the next few days.)

August 22nd, 1990 - A fun night in New York City with the whole crew. We ended up at a very trendy dance club called the "Palladium" which had been featured several times on MTV. I even ended up "Vogue"-ing to the Madonna dance song of the same name.

September 25th, 1990 - While on another New York overnight, I took the United Nations tour and had the chance to hear Russian diplomat Eduard Shevardnadze speak to the U.N. Security Council. As a former teacher, I found it very educational to observe how the U.N. conducted their business and to also watch the interactions of their diplomats.

October 25th, 1990 - We had the Boston Celtics basketball team on our flight from Boston to Buffalo. Unfortunately for them, we were on an F-100 airplane which had slightly smaller seats and only one row of First Class. We were told that the four tallest guys would be sitting in First Class and the rest would have aisle seats in the back. Therefore, I got to take care of Larry Bird, Kevin McHale, Robert Parrish, and backup center Joe Kleine. I felt sorry for all of them because even with the First-Class seats, they still all had their knees up around their ears.

November 18th, 1990 - In another series of strange coincidences, on successive flights I had a U.D. Law School classmate (Veronica Winwood) and a college fraternity Little Sister (Terri Stuck Anderson) onboard. It was great to catch up with both of them.

December 7th, 1990 - This was an occurrence that showed the crazy fun days of our airline world were coming to an end...my first drug test! Our union had fought against it for a while, but for everyone's safety, they finally agreed. Supposedly, drug testing could only be done at the beginning or end of a trip, or for "good cause."

December 17th, 1990 - We had a really friendly group of Russian tourists on our flight to New York's JFK airport, who all wanted to try speaking English to us. By the end of the flight, we had all been given lapel pins and other Russian souvenirs by nearly every member of the group. Later in the day, on our Dayton-Evansville, Indiana flight, we encountered Yankee's star Don Mattingly and his wife. I even made him laugh when I tried to appear sincere when asking if he could recommend a good restaurant in Evansville. (Most people already knew of "Mattingly's"; a well-known eatery that was owned by Evansville's famous son, Don Mattingly!)

December 27th-28th, 1990 - There were really big snowstorms today in both Philadelphia and Cleveland. I also had one of my college wrestling teammates, Gene Smith and his wife, on our flight from Cleveland to Miami. I ended up meeting them for lunch the next day before we left for Philadelphia. I still can't believe how lucky I have been lately with running into people I know.

January 16th, 1991 - We found out during a deadhead flight to Kansas City that the United States had launched an attack on Iraq. I am not sure what this means for the airline business, but I don't think it will be a good thing. I only hope President Bush knows what he's doing.

January 25th-26th, 1991 - This was a trip with a Dayton, Ohio overnight; so rather than stay at the hotel, I drove home to see my son's varsity basketball game. (He scored 12 points, and they won the game.)

Later that night, we found out that our entire next day was cancelled due to more bad weather, so I got to stay home for an extra day. Yay!

February 1st, 1991 - USAir flight 1493 was involved in a crash today while trying to land at the Los Angeles International Airport. It seems that a small plane somehow ended up on the wrong runway and was crushed when our flight landed on top of it. The crew again managed to professionally evacuate the plane and properly care for our passengers despite a very chaotic situation. I later would work a trip with one of the flight attendants from that flight, and he said it was so weird how in 30 seconds that flight went from "normal" to "crazy."

February 11th, 1991 - My first trip with my friend and fellow E.K.U. alumnus, Nadine Freeman. USAir also announced today that because of reduced passenger traffic, they will probably be implementing cutbacks and layoffs in the near future.

March 13th, 1991 - We had actor Dennis Hopper on our flight from Albuquerque to Los Angeles today. Although he seemed a little confused at times, he was really a nice guy!

March 22nd, 1991 - We experienced an aborted takeoff (where our captain stopped the plane before we reached the end of the runway) on our Raleigh Durham-LaGuardia flight because of a problem with one of the baggage compartment doors. We ended up delayed for over four hours while they tried to fix it. Fortunately, most of our passengers were able to get on other flights to New York.

March 26th, 1991 - For the first (and only) time in my career, we had a young couple on our Pittsburgh-Houston flight that apparently joined the mythical "Mile High Club." As I recall, they both had aisle seats in the very last row, which were also right in front of the rear lavatories. I was working the rear galley on that flight, and once we had reached our cruising altitude, the captain then turned off the seat-belt sign. At that point, I got out of my jump seat and started getting the drink carts ready for our service. With my back turned to the cabin, it was then I heard one lav door open and close...then the second one. When I turned back around, both of the couple's seats were empty, so I assumed they each had decided to use the facilities. After turning to start up the coffee makers, I again heard both doors open and close. This time however, both their seats were still unoccupied, as was one of the lavatories. (Hmmm...)

I then put my ear to the door of the occupied restroom and could faintly hear them "getting busy." With a giant smirk on my face, I then discreetly called the captain to inform him of what was happening. He just laughed and said he would take care of it. The captain then made a cabin P.A. announcement that there was some turbulence ahead and that everyone should stay seated for the time being.

In what I would argue was the slickest and smoothest exit ever, the lady waited until I turned my back to hang up the interphone, then very quickly opened and closed the door and returned to her seat. A minute later, the young man exited the same lav in a more normal fashion, and even casually asked me if I knew what our current altitude was. Trying to stifle a grin, I replied that we were probably at about 25,000 feet. He then nodded and returned to his seat; quietly high-fiving his girl as he sat down. With the extremely limited space in those lavatories, I can only assume that they were both double-jointed, ex-Olympic gymnasts!

April 10th, 1991 - While on an overnight in Toronto, my crew and I decided to take in a Toronto Blue Jays baseball game at the new Sky Dome Park. Unlike the last time I saw the Jays play, I did not have to go buy a coat, because it was now a closed, indoor stadium with a retractable roof. What was really memorable was the fact that a Hard Rock Hotel actually abutted the outfield wall. In fact, a few select hotel rooms actually had windows that allowed people to see the game from their room through the outfield wall.

As I recall, it was a pretty low-scoring and somewhat boring game until around the 8th inning, when suddenly the crowd in a certain area of the stands started whistling and cheering wildly. Although we couldn't see it from our seats, apparently a young couple decided to get "romantic" in their room at the Hard Rock and didn't know (or didn't care) that some of the fans could see what was taking place. Once we figured out what was happening, I started laughing and then told my crew about the Mile High Clubbers on my recent flight to Houston. I could only then assume that either love was truly in the air...or it was possibly that same couple; busy trying to complete some sort of bizarre "things-to-do" list!

July 19th, 1991 - Today I got to meet my son, Brian, when he arrived in Pittsburgh for a week at the prestigious Five Star Basketball Camp. He ended up having a good week competing against future

NBA stars Jason Kidd and Alan Henderson. He also tied the camp record for consecutive free throws made, which earned him high praise from Indiana University's head coach Bobby Knight.

July 24th-26th, 1991 - This was a nice three-day trip with friends Susan Roth and Kathy Wegman. During our overnight in Champaign, Illinois, we stayed at the very interesting Jumer's Castle Hotel. It had kind of a Bavarian decor, with heavy canopy drapes over the beds and a stuffed, black bear in the lobby. For the only time in my career, we also got a chance to rent a canoe and paddle around the big lake behind the hotel.

July 31st, 1991 - In a good news/bad news scenario, we had a legless man in First Class that did not receive his specialized wheelchair when we arrived in New York City. (Apparently the baggage guys in Greensboro had failed to load it before we left.) The good news was the Herculean effort that our gate agent in LaGuardia made to find him suitable transportation until his own chair arrived on the next flight. The gentleman even wrote a nice letter to the company later, praising the efforts of our crew and the gate agent in trying to rectify the situation.

August 13th, 1991 - We had musician Glen Campbell on a flight from Nolfolk, Virginia, to LaGuardia today. He was such a nice man. He even remembered visiting my little hometown many years earlier. (Apparently, he was acquainted with the owners of Pasquale's, which had been my favorite local restaurant when I was young.)

August 17th, 1991 - My wife and I had recently decided to try for more children. Because of that, I had to call off sick from my trip today after my wife informed me (while I was busy packing my suitcase) that she was in her "prime time" this week. I then made up some excuse when I called crew scheduling to avoid telling them, "Hey, I won't be able to work this week because...I'm attempting to reproduce!"

September 17th, 1991 - There was a huge power outage in the New York City area that also knocked out power to the air traffic control center for much of the East coast. This caused a great many flight delays over the next few days.

October 21st-22nd, 1991 - During these two days, we had to attend a company-mandated seminar called P.P.F. or "Putting People First." It was a program designed to make us more sensitive to the needs of our customers, but was so hokey, it was actually hard to resist making fun of it. At the end of the seminar, I found out that I was equal parts of "personality categories" Panther, Owl, Peacock, and Dolphin. (I can't tell you how comforting that has been for me to know that throughout my airline career!)

November 14th, 1991 - Our company was now having us stay at a nice hotel in Orlando that was right across from Universal Studios. Since USAir was now the "official airlines" of Universal Studios, my crew went over to the park after we checked into the hotel and discovered that we could get in for free, just by showing our airline ID. We then had a great evening checking out all the rides and shows.

December 19th, 1991 - In what might have been my worst flight yet, two people in coach and four in First Class got sick on our flight from Sacramento to Pittsburgh. I recall one of my fellow crew members calling it the "Barf-O-Rama."

December 22nd, 1991 - In a case of "you just never know," the fire alarm went off in the middle of the night at our hotel in Kansas City. Because of smoke in the hallway, everyone had to evacuate their rooms. Although apparently there was no fire, it still took over two hours to clear the air before the firemen allowed us back into the rooms. That made for a very short night.

December 31st, 1991 - After she complained about stomach pain, I had to rush my wife to the emergency room this afternoon. It turned out that she had a tubal pregnancy and the doctors needed to operate immediately in hopes of saving the embryo. Sadly, things didn't work out, which unfortunately ended our hopes of having more children. But to me, the most important thing was that Karen was okay.

Chapter Eight

1992-1993....Hurricane Andrew
and the Presidential Suite

January 9th, 1992 - On our Fort Lauderdale-Pittsburgh flight we had Miami Dolphins quarterback Dan Marino and his family. They were all very polite and personable. In fact, one of his three boys drew a nice picture with his crayons and gave it to me.

January 16th, 1992 - Today we had the 1991 Women's World Cup Champion soccer team on from Seattle to Pittsburgh. That team included stars Michelle Akers, Mia Hamm, Julie Foudy, and Brandy Chastain. They were all very pleasant and they all seemed to enjoy each other's company.

March 9th-12th, 1992 - My first trip with my friend and training classmate David Marchetti. Dave was a great storyteller and had the same twisted sense of humor as me, so we always got along well. He also always entertained his passengers with his ability to make paper flowers out of our USAir napkins. His sweet wife Carol also worked as one of our gate agents in Pittsburgh.

March 17th, 1992 - I barely got home in time for our son's basketball awards banquet tonight. Brian had a terrific season and ended up being the league's top scorer and was voted Most Valuable Player as well. He also ended up with a partial scholarship to Baldwin-Wallace College, near Cleveland, Ohio. Despite my sometimes-crazy flying schedule, I never missed a game his senior year.

March 22nd, 1992 - While attempting to take off in a snowstorm, USAir flight 405 crashed today in LaGuardia. This accident involved one of our smaller Fokker F-28 planes and sadly, there were 27 casualties, including one of the flight attendants. From what we heard later, there had been some problems with the de-icing procedures, which contributed to the accident.

April 6th, 1992 - On our Pittsburgh-Boston flight, our guests included the UConn girls' basketball team. However, we found out after we landed that there had been a mix-up, and that they had all wanted to go to Hartford instead. Again, our crew made all the proper announcements for boarding and also several destination announcements during the flight. After the flight, I heard the coaches saying they had some friends in Boston who could bus the team back to Hartford that night.

April 29th, 1992 - At some point early in my career, I decided that I wanted to try to see a baseball game in every one of the Major League stadiums. Tonight, we ended up staying at a hotel in New York that was just down the street from the New York Met's Shea Stadium. When I saw there was a game that night against the Houston Astros, I headed over to see if I could get a ticket.

As I was walking up to the ticket window, a very sweet, elderly lady asked me if I knew anything about baseball. When I assured her that I did, she told me that I could have her extra ticket, as long as we talked baseball throughout the game. It turned out that she was one of the Mets' original season ticket holders and our seats were right behind the Met's dugout. She knew every usher by name and some of the players even waved at her. She was the most interesting baseball fan I ever sat next to...at least for the next couple of years. (hint, hint!)

May 2nd, 1992 - Today we had the wife of World War II General Douglas MacArthur on our flight from New York to Norfolk. Mrs. MacArthur was probably well into her 90's and very frail, but she took great pride in telling everyone around her that she was Mrs. Douglas MacArthur! (over and over...and over!)

After we got to our hotel in Norfolk, my old housemate Sherri and her husband Bruce came over and brought me back to their house for dinner. When I told them that I had recently started playing music again with some friends at home, Bruce got excited and wanted to show me his home studio. We then had a great musical jam with me on guitar and Bruce on drums. It was so much fun.

June 16th-18th, 1992 - This was a really nice three-day trip with overnights in Tampa and Philadelphia. While in Philly, a few of us walked down to the waterfront and got to see the three replicated ships of Christopher Columbus make their way into the harbor. (It was part of the 500-year anniversary of Columbus' discovery of America celebration.) Again, for an old history teacher, it was a very special and educational moment.

June 24th-27th, 1992 - A great four-day trip with a fun crew of Tom Kilheeney and Cathy Lazlo. We had some enjoyable nights in Tampa at the Yucatan Liquor Stand and in Bethlehem, Pennsylvania, at The Station Club.

July 10th, 1992 - While sitting around the Indianapolis Airport on a three-hour layover, we saw a number of notable personalities walk by, including NFL Hall of Fame running back Jim Brown and musician Stevie Wonder. In addition, I also witnessed one of my fellow flight attendants wave at Mr. Wonder as he was escorted by us. I then had to turn and ask her afterwards,

"Do you think he saw you wave?"

(Apparently, she knew who he was, but didn't know he was blind.)

July 15th, 1992 - I got some unsettling news this weekend when I learned that my dear friend, former housemate, and the Best Man at my wedding, Mike Butts, had been diagnosed with malignant melanoma. At this point he was just 37 years old and the father of three small children. Besides being maybe the smartest guy I knew, he was also my musical mentor and the guy who talked me into going to law school. As good friends often do, a group of us would spend the next few years supporting and rallying around him and his family during his cancer treatments.

July 21st, 1992 - We had the comedian Sinbad on our flight to Newark today. He was so very nice, and really intelligent. I also found out that he played a little college basketball back in the day.

August 6th, 1992 - During our Philadelphia overnight, our captain Dick Floyd and I went to the Phillies-Expo's game at Veterans Stadium. It was a pretty good game, highlighted by the fact that after all these years of watching baseball, I finally caught my first foul ball!

August 20th, 1992 - We finished up early today in LaGuardia, so I ended up having a really nice day sightseeing in New York City. Among other things, I got to watch the 60s era female vocal group "The Shirelles" perform a lunchtime concert on the World Trade Center Plaza area between the two towers. (While there, I definitely remember looking up at both towers and watching them gently sway back and forth.) I also toured the New York Stock Exchange and then rode the subway to Times Square and ate at the very cool Planet Hollywood restaurant. (I still love the fact that my job allowed me to have days like this!)

August 24th-27th, 1992 - A fun trip with friends Jim Dattilo and Laurie Johnson. Unfortunately, there were a lot of delays and trip changes because the monster hurricane Andrew was sitting off the Florida coast causing lots of flight disruptions. In fact, our entire third day was cancelled and we ended up with a very long overnight in Philadelphia. As flight attendants often do, we tried to make the best of the situation. That included acknowledging the storm by drinking a few "hurricanes" in a bar on South Street. (It seemed like a good idea at the time.)

August 28th, 1992 - I knocked another ballpark off my list tonight by attending a Padre's game at old Jack Murphy Stadium in San Diego. As a side note, one of the crew members who went to the game with me was our first officer named... Davey Crockett. (According to him, he is a distant cousin of the famous frontiersman.)

September 23rd, 1992 - Supposedly, our mechanics were going out on strike tonight at midnight. If that happened, it would strand our crew at the hotel in White Plains, New York, for a few days. As it turned out, they decided to delay the strike for one week, which did allow us to get home on time.

October 1st, 1992 - Today was the grand opening of the new, state-of-the-art Pittsburgh International Airport terminal. People were saying that it was now the nicest airport facility in the nation. It would also allow USAir to expand its flying operations and open even more new cities. The only downer today was that the mechanic's union announced that they would indeed be striking soon unless a new agreement could be reached. (Fortunately, a new contract did get signed soon afterwards.)

October 13th-16th, 1992 - A good trip with a fun crew. Upon arriving at our hotel in Toronto, we were offered champagne because the Toronto Blue Jays had just won their playoff game and were going to the World Series. Also, during our Washington D.C. stay, I took the guided tour of the Pentagon which I found very interesting. (Did you know that it had to be designed as a five-sided building because that was the only shape that would fit the limited space of the plot of land that it was built upon?)

November 21st, 1992 - This afternoon, we almost had a full-blown fistfight on our New Orleans-Pittsburgh flight. I had to yell at both passengers and then I moved their seats to opposite ends of the aircraft. Both of them apparently had too much to drink.

December 8th, 1992 - While in San Antonio, my fellow flight attendant Ben Ezell and I scalped a couple of tickets to the San Antonio Spurs/Utah Jazz basketball game. Strangely, the game was delayed in the 3rd quarter when a bat somehow got into the building and began dive-bombing the players and the fans. Eventually, a towel boy managed to safely catch the bat in his towel, which led to a huge standing ovation! After they released it unharmed outside, the courtside announcer got some laughs when he mimicked the famous Elvis Presley phrase..."The bat has left the building!"

January 12th, 1993 - A tough day because our flight to Minneapolis was first delayed by a mechanical problem, then by a fuel spill that had to be cleaned up, and finally a two-hour weather delay because of a snowstorm. The only good news was that I finally got a chance to check out the Mall of America while in Minneapolis. It was so big, it had its own amusement park right in the middle of the mall!

February 18th, 1993 - I worked an "extra" trip where I floated around the system helping out on full flights. It was okay because I got to work with crews from other bases, but it was bad because I was essentially on my own all week. One of my more interesting crew members was a lady named Debby Pastranna. It seemed that her son, Travis, was already a National Motocross Champion at nine years old. (He would in fact, go on to win a lot more races over the years and eventually become one of the best Motocross racers ever!)

March 22nd, 1993 - Today was my ten-year anniversary as a flight attendant. At this point, it seemed like it was going by pretty fast.

April 1st, 1993 - Effective today, USAir initiated a one-year pay cut that was the company's response to the continuing decline in passenger traffic. None of us like it, but with the continued fighting in the Middle East, a lot fewer people have been flying.

We also had a great crew on our MD-80 trip this week including friends Bunny Haase and Dan Schild. We did, however, encounter one small "situation" on our Philadelphia-Ft. Lauderdale flight. On that flight, we had a 12-year-old boy who vomited so much, that Dan nick-named him "the puke monster." In fact, there was so much regurgitation on his way up to the First-Class lavatory, that we had to ask for everyone's newspapers so we could use them to cover the soiled carpet! That at least allowed everyone to finally disembark...and I can't recall seeing a flight unload faster!

April 13th-16th, 1993 - Another great four-day trip with my crew of Joe Croft, Mark Wagner, and the really fun Jenni LaDue. On the second day we had Buffalo Bills quarterback Jim Kelly on our LaGuardia-Buffalo flight. During our conversation with him, I mentioned that my friend Mike Butts (who was a former high school quarterback as well) really admired his passing skills, but that Mike was no longer able to throw because of his cancer treatments. Upon hearing that, Mr. Kelly immediately wanted to send a personal note and an autograph to my friend to keep up his spirits. (I will never forget how kind he was to Mike!) The only thing cooler this week, was watching Jenni hustle some unsuspecting patrons at billiards at the hotel bar in Charlotte.

May 4th, 1993 - I had a really unusual thing happen in San Antonio tonight. Our crew had experienced a very long day and by the time we arrived at the very nice Marriott Hotel located right on the San Antonio Riverwalk, it was probably about midnight. Upon arriving at the check-in desk, the manager came up to us and said he needed to talk with us before we got our room keys. It seemed that there was a big convention in town, and they were short on rooms. He knew that every crew member got their own room, so he threw out the possibility of any two of us sharing a room for the night, in exchange for $50 cash each. When we politely declined, he bumped the offer to $75 each. Again, we declined and said that we sympathized with his situation, but we were all tired and just wanted to get to our rooms. Not wanting to take no for an answer, the manager then upped his offer to $100 each AND a free breakfast the next morning.

At this point, my buddy Rick Meyer and I looked at each other, shrugged our shoulders, and grudgingly agreed. The manager was delighted and immediately plopped down $100 cash each. He also surprised us with the announcement that because we were the first ones to take him up on his offer, he was going to put the two of us up in the Presidential Suite on the top floor! Upon hearing that, the captain and first officer also agreed to split a room, but since there were no more fancy rooms left, they got a regular room. (They told us later, that the manager did send them up a nice bottle of wine.)

Once Rick and I got our keys, we were then directed to the private elevator that only went to the top floor. Once we arrived at the penthouse and opened the oversized door to our hotel room, I am sure our eyes probably bugged out of our heads. The Presidential Suite ran the entire length of the hotel. It also featured floor-to-ceiling windows that offered a stunning view of the illuminated downtown area and the entire Riverwalk. There was also a wood-burning fireplace with a baby grand piano in front of it. The suite also featured three bathrooms, each with a different amenity like a sauna, a hot tub, or a steam shower. (With all that space available, they could have very easily accommodated our entire crew of five in that one room.)

The only dilemma we faced was where each of us would sleep. Our choices were either the master bedroom which featured an incredibly ornate king-sized bed with a canopy top, or the basic single roll-away bed that the hotel manager had sent up to us. After we agreed to a coin flip, I won the toss by calling "tails." Rick grudgingly accepted his loss, but sort of got even with me by telling me to remember all the rock stars and sleazy politicians who probably had sex on that fancy bed. (Because of that, I know I restlessly tossed and turned all night!)

The next morning, our fancy doorbell chimed and sure enough, our free breakfast was delivered on an elaborate cart with a number of entrees served under glass. Then, after a soak in the hot tub and a relaxing time in the sauna, I reluctantly packed up my suitcase and headed back to my normal "run-of-the-mill" existence as a merely mortal flight attendant. (I also vowed to take some piano lessons in the future, so that the next time this happened to me, I could properly take advantage of my in-room baby grand piano!)

May 20th, 1993 - While at our hotel in Detroit, I got to watch the final episode of "Cheers." It was a fun ending to a great television series. That show also featured actor Woody Harrelson, who just happened to grow up in my hometown and went to our high school with some good friends of mine. They said he was always a fun guy to be around!

July 27th-30th, 1993 - A nice four-day trip with training classmate Jeff Forbes. On the first day we had Duke University basketball coach Mike Kryzewski on our Washington D.C. flight. On the second day, we overnighted in New York City and had dinner at the Planet Hollywood restaurant. Our waitress was an actress who also read our palms during dinner. (She did say that I had been a teacher in a former life...which was sort of accurate.)

August 11th, 1993 - This was one of the few times that I wished I had a video camera on a flight. On our late-night flight from Indianapolis to Washington D.C., almost everyone had gone to sleep. Since we really didn't have much to do at the time, I grabbed a vacant window seat and spent a few minutes looking up at the Perseid meteor shower which happens annually in early August. (I think I counted something like 15 shooting stars in about three minutes.)

At just about that same time, we started flying over an area of weather which featured a lot of tall Cumulus clouds. Those clouds then started lighting up with the phenomenon called "summer lightning". Between the glowing clouds and the shooting stars, I think I must have uttered "Jeez" and "Wow" loud enough that the sleeping folks around me woke up. When they then peeked out the window, they also started "ooh-ing" and "aah-ing" as well. It was the only time that I recall witnessing both of those amazing sights simultaneously.

October 21st, 1993 - On all four flights today, we took a delay because the gate agents were allowing way too many bags and suitcases to come on board. On those full flights, the overhead space filled up rapidly and anything that didn't fit completely under the seats had to be gate-checked before we could close the doors and push the flight back. No one was happy about that, especially us!

November 3rd, 1993 - On our Cleveland-Pittsburgh flight, I had to deal with possibly the most "complicated" passenger that I ever encountered. In short, the gentleman was grieving the sudden loss of his father and therefore had been drinking before the flight. When I went to take stock of the situation, he started crying and then blurted out (in a very thick Cajun accent) that he was scared to fly and had not been on an airplane since he was shot down over Vietnam in 1970. When the reality of his situation sank in, I chose to quietly offer my sincere condolences, thank him for his service to our country, and gently remind him that it was a short flight and that he would be in Pittsburgh in no time. He gave me a little nod, closed his eyes and actually did reasonably well on our flight. Of all the drunk, grieving, Cajun, shell-shocked, fearful flyers that I have had on board, he was the best.

November 18th, 1993 - The American Airlines flight attendant union went out on strike today, which caused a few of them to be on our Baltimore-Chicago flight. In talking with them, they were very nice, but very confused about what they were striking for. Because of that conversation, I even made a note in my logbook that said, "Glad I don't work for them!" (Oops...never say never.)

December 1st, 1993 - A really good trip with friends Laurie Sismour and Kim Traister. When the hotel van in Indianapolis broke down, their manager sent a very fancy stretch limousine to pick us up and take us to the hotel. It was also the first time that this farm boy was ever in a limo! (I liked it.)

December 5th-8th, 1993 - My first trip with my dear friend Jody Compton, who was always so brassy and funny. I also found out later that her husband was a rock drummer and was currently touring with the Johnny Winter Band.

December 15th, 1993 - This story just emphasizes how much I admire my wife Karen. Tonight, after we got checked in at our hotel in West Palm Beach, I called home to see how things were going. It was then that she revealed that our furnace had gone out and couldn't be re-lit. I then reminded her of the list of repairmen that I had left for her, just for situations like this. However, she then countered that she did not need that list and had "taken care of it herself."

Now at this point, I must let you know that my wife has always been rather independent. Not only had she been a successful single parent for over ten years before we married, but she had also grown up around her family's hardware store in our hometown. Apparently, she had retained much of her mechanical knowledge because when she inspected the furnace, she realized that it just needed a new thermocouple. She then had gone to the hardware store, purchased the new parts, and repaired the furnace in less than an hour.

This story not only emphasizes how lucky I was to have married such a functional female, but it also reminded me that I always wanted to stay on her "good side." After all, I reasoned that if she could fix a furnace, she could also change the locks on the doors just as easily! (I am also glad to report that throughout my long airline career, I never had to get new house keys made!)

December 19th, 1993 - During our Sunday afternoon flight to Indianapolis, I found out that our hotel was just down the street from the RCA Dome, where the Colts would be playing the Philadelphia Eagles in the Sunday Night Football game that night. Once we got to the hotel, I quickly changed clothes, walked over to the stadium, and scalped a ticket for the game. I then was lucky enough to find that my seat was in the end zone behind the goalposts. Fortunately, the Colts won so everyone sitting around me was happy.

Chapter Nine

1994....Hello to Alice, Goodbye to Mike

February 9th, 1994 - Today we arrived in Baltimore just ahead of a major ice storm. Unfortunately, that airport soon discovered that it had very little de-icing fluid which led to multiple cancellations. We spent the next six hours huddled in the Baltimore operations room with many other crews, before learning that the rest of our trip was cancelled and we were free to go. I then tried for the next 18 hours to get a flight home, before eventually giving up and staying in Pittsburgh until my next trip.

March 15th, 1994 - By this date, there were lots of rumors going around about USAir being in financial trouble. We were also hearing that more pay cuts were possible as well.

April 5th-6th, 1994 - In another wonderful coincidence, I had my old friend and fellow Lebanon High School alumnus Joe Henderson on our Charlotte-Tampa flight. Joe started off as a sports reporter for our hometown newspaper "The Western Star" and after chatting with him, I discovered that he was now a sportswriter for the Tampa Tribune newspaper. (Many years later, he would also be kind enough to show me the sportswriters' seats and the official scorer's booth when I attended a Tampa Bay Rays baseball game.)

At the end of that same day, we had an overnight in Dayton, Ohio so I drove home to help my friend Mike Butts pick players for our annual fantasy baseball draft. Despite his weakening condition from the cancer, it was still fun to see his razor-sharp mind at work. He was also amazed at my accidentally running into Joe Henderson, especially since Joe had often written about him when Mike was our high school quarterback.

May 10th, 1994 - In a very weird confluence of events, my friend Mike Butts had to be operated on to remove some cancerous lymph nodes on the same day as a total eclipse of the sun. I don't know if that's a good sign or a bad omen.

May 19th, 1994 - While in Rochester, New York, I discovered the coolest music store called "The House of Guitars." It was in a regular house in a regular neighborhood and each room of the house contained groupings of musical items like drums, guitars, or keyboards. The garage featured giant piles of unsold concert T-shirts and other memorabilia. If that wasn't enough, when I got back to our hotel I found out that ZZ Top, one of my favorite bands, was also staying there. For a wannabe musician like me, it was quite the day.

June 15th, 1994 - You might as well get comfortable, because this is one of my best days and one of my favorite stories yet. (Again, there are so many details to this story that I may or may not, accurately recall. Please bear with me.) As you remember, I had been making a serious effort to see as many baseball games in as many different stadiums as possible. This story starts with us arriving in Montreal around noon, and after checking the local newspaper, I saw that the Montreal Expos were going to play an afternoon game that day with a 1:15 p.m. start. On the way to our hotel, I tried to talk my crew members into going to the game, but to no avail. Once at the hotel, I quickly changed my clothes and hopped on the local subway, which dropped me off directly underneath the ballpark.

It turned out that Olympic Stadium would not be one of my favorite ballparks, mostly because it was an old, domed stadium with poor lighting and a bad AstroTurf playing field. Evidently, the local fans thought so too because despite having a decent team, very few people went to the games. (The Expos tried for years to get a better place to play but in the end, the local government refused to build them something better. They eventually packed up and moved the team to Washington D.C.)

After I made my way upstairs to the ticket office, I saw that there was about ten minutes left before the first pitch. I then recall asking the ticket lady about the best seat available for that day's game. Because so few people attended Expos' games, my little query must have amused her because she laughed out loud! After she assured me there were plenty of seats available, she then asked where I wanted to sit. When I inquired about the seats behind home plate, she grinned and said that nobody was in section 206 and that I could have a whole row to myself. I thought that was wonderful, and with the Canadian exchange rate my ticket was only about fifteen dollars.

Sure enough, the ticket lady was correct. Nobody was in that area and there was maybe only about 300 people total in attendance. However, just when I thought that I was going to have an unobstructed view of the game, this rather long-haired guy with a beat-up old hat comes walking down to my wide-open section and sits (of all places) in the seat right in front of me! Because of the irony of the situation, I kind of chuckled and leaned over close to his ear and said somewhat sarcastically,

"Man, I didn't think they could find me a seat for this game."

When he realized I was just teasing him, he laughed and mockingly replied,

"I know, I didn't think they could squeeze me in either!"

With that exchange, the game started, and I settled in to watch.

Somewhere between the first and second inning, their very high-tech "Diamond-Vision" scoreboard lit up and showed a live shot of a long-haired guest in the crowd. Just about the time I thought that he looked familiar, the scoreboard flashed the following message,

"Montreal's Olympic Stadium welcomes...Alice Cooper to today's game!"

After seeing that, I remember softly uttering,

"Alice? Cool! I wonder where he is?"

Knowing that with such a small crowd I had a good chance of actually seeing him, I even stood up from my seat to start scanning the area to see if I could spot him.

Now I have heard it said that everyone experiences a really embarrassing moment (or two) during their lifetime. Well...mine is just about to arrive! Because, as the scoreboard camera started zooming in on Alice Cooper, here is this chucklehead in the row behind him standing up, looking around, and mouthing the words, "Alice? Cool...I wonder where he is?" (Uh, That chucklehead would be me!) I even looked up just in time to see my giant lips on the big screen slowly uttering "ALLLICE?...COOOOL!...I WONNNDER...WHEREEE... HE...IS?" It was indeed my most embarrassing moment ever.

Although this sounds really humiliating, in my defense I never really saw Alice Cooper's face as he walked to his seat. (His long hair was sort of hanging down over his face and he had his hat pulled down low.) In addition, because he was sitting directly in front of me when I was chatting with him, I was actually talking into the back of his ear and never really got a good look at his facial features. Despite my embarrassment, I do recall rationalizing that because there was such a small crowd there, very few people had actually witnessed my social boo-boo. I also was relieved that there apparently were no major sports news groups in attendance that day. I could only imagine how much fun a media group like ESPN would have had with my little "blunder" during that evening's broadcast!

Anyway, after the laughter of the other 299 people in the stadium died down, I finally leaned forward and realized that Mr. Cooper was in fact sitting right in front of me. I think I uttered something really intelligent like, "Oh, that's you!", then asked a more reasonable question, "So where is your entourage?" (He was with one other gentleman who I assumed was some sort of driver/bodyguard/personal assistant.) He then leaned back in his seat and related that whenever he was on tour, he enjoyed taking in whatever sporting event that may be happening in the city that he was performing in. Since he was doing a concert the next night in Montreal, he had decided to go to this game. He also said that he had asked all his musicians and roadies about going with him, but no one took him up on his offer. I then laughed and replied that I had also tried to talk my entire airline crew into going but was turned down as well.

At this point, (and being the extremely cool guy that he was) he then surprised me by asking if I wanted to come down and sit with him during the game. Upon hearing that, I think I might have swallowed my chewing gum, but tried to maintain my composure. I also made him chuckle when I pretended to "think it over" and finally said okay.

After stepping down to his row, I shook his hand, introduced myself, and to thank him, I offered to buy him a beer. He politely refused, and went on to explain that he hadn't had a drink in something like ten or eleven years. He then shared that he was at one time a pretty bad alcoholic and in fact had survived a period of time where he was drinking up to a case of beer a day! When I inquired as to how he was able to sober up, he said that his wife and his manager had basically kidnapped him and put him in an asylum for something like six months. Although that seemed extreme, he said that was what it took for him to get cleaned up. I told him that I respected that, congratulated him on his sobriety, and offered to buy him a bottle of water instead. He laughed and said that he would take me up on that offer!

The rest of the game was filled with a number of great conversations and amusing stories. I remember telling him that I played in a little garage band and that we did a couple of Alice Cooper songs. That interested him, and he then wondered why we had picked those songs. When I guessed that it was because we only knew a few chords and therefore had to choose the easy ones, he chuckled and encouraged me to keep practicing.

Later in the game, I recall asking which sports he liked the best and he surprised me when he picked golf. (I mean, crazy shock rocker Alice Cooper...and golf?) When I seemed puzzled by his answer, he went on to explain that after he got sober, he was looking for something positive to do with his free time. His wife had suggested to him that since there were so many golf courses in the Phoenix area where they lived, he should try golfing. He said that once he tried it, he liked it so much that he started playing 36 holes almost every day. When I asked about his golf handicap, he humbly admitted that he was a 3 or 4 but was hoping to improve on that in the near future. (For non-golfers, that is nearly professional level.) To this day he still participates in some Pro-Am events and has won quite a few!

Later on, I also remember him telling me a story about how his wife was sort of upset with him because their garage was packed full of gold records and other rock and roll memorabilia. He then told me,

"Can you believe it? She actually wants to park a car in our garage."

I remember shrugging my shoulders and sympathetically replying,

"Yeah, go figure."

He then said he wanted to share an idea with me. It seemed that he was considering opening up a restaurant. His rationale was that he could clear out all the stuff in his garage, hang it on the walls of his eatery, AND therefore make his wife happy at the same time. I recall telling him that I thought it sounded like a pretty good idea.

Although it is now closed, Alice Cooper's restaurant (known as "Cooperstown") did open up a few years later and was located just down the street from the Arizona Diamondbacks ballpark. Sure enough, when I finally got a chance to visit, I found that it was a combination of sports bar and rock-and-roll restaurant. The walls indeed were completely covered with the coolest photos, autographed guitars, and other rock memorabilia. (From the sheer volume of it, I could see why Mrs. Cooper wanted her garage cleared out!)

The other fun thing about the restaurant was the menu. On it were a number of meal choices that were named after local Phoenix-area celebrities. The one that I vividly recall was the sandwich named after Hall of Fame pitcher Randy Johnson, who had pitched for the D-backs the year they won the World Series. (Just fyi…Randy Johnson's nickname was the "Big Unit" mostly because of his height of 6'11".) That sandwich quickly became a restaurant favorite, and when ordered, came with a great table presentation including sirens and flashing lights!

In fact, I remember the first time that I got a Phoenix overnight and had a chance to go eat at this newly opened facility. After first walking around the restaurant and taking in all the great memorabilia, I finally settled into my seat. I also recall telling the waitress that I had once met her boss at a Montreal Expo's game. Soon after I ordered my dinner, I heard the gentleman behind me ask about the house specialties, and he eventually decided to try the Randy Johnson-inspired "Big Unit." She giggled and said he wouldn't be disappointed.

When they finally brought his order out, it was indeed quite the spectacle. The house lights started flashing, sirens started wailing, and every guest cheered and applauded. As the waitress approached the table behind me, I could see her struggling with a large, oversized tray. As she set it down, the guy behind me wrinkled his nose and disgustingly asked,

"What in the hell is that?"

She replied that it was what he ordered; it was the "Big Unit!"

I immediately started laughing when I finally saw what it was. The Big Unit was a two-foot-long sausage on a platter and may have been the most obscene looking thing that I ever saw delivered from a kitchen. In fact, during the time that the gentleman was deciding whether to eat it or send it back, three different women came over and took pictures of it with their cameras. (That guest eventually decided to try it and I heard him later say it was actually pretty tasty!)

Anyway, toward the end of the Expos game, I remember thanking Mr. Cooper for the great stories and wished him good luck with his show the next night. I also politely inquired if he would mind signing an autograph. (At that point, he just chuckled because a number of other fans had stopped by to get his signature throughout the game.) He was then nice enough to sign my 1994 All-Star ballot that they had handed out to all the fans at the game. I also recall wishing that I had brought a camera, but in 1994 I didn't yet own a cell phone and even so, none of those phones included cameras. Despite that minor regret, it really was an amazing day!

Also, once I got home from my trip, I immediately went over to visit my ailing friend Mike Butts and entertained him with the story of my celebrity encounter. I then presented Mike with the autograph, which just about made him cry. It was a wonderful moment, courtesy of the coolest guy ever; Alice Cooper!

June 30th, 1994 - This was the last day for our old duty rigs. Starting tomorrow, our minimum flight pay guarantee of four hours and 30 minutes per day, would shrink to just four hours. Basically, more work for less pay.

July 2nd, 1994 - On this date, USAir flight 1016 crashed just outside Charlotte while trying to land during a rainstorm. Apparently, a sudden downdraft pushed the plane down into some trees and a residential area. There were multiple fatalities, but again the crew performed heroically and were able to rescue some passengers out of the wreckage. The captain on that flight was a friend of mine who also commuted out of Dayton. Thankfully, he survived.

July 14th, 1994 - A great trip with my friend Janet Renda and my old training instructor Colleen, who had retired from the training department and was now a flight attendant. On our Orlando overnight, we ended up checking out the comedy club at our hotel. The comedians that night were hilarious, but I also remember thinking afterwards, that I had just as many funny "work stories" as they did.

August 23rd, 1994 - On our flight from Philadelphia to Buffalo, we carried 1.6 million dollars (all in ten-dollar bills) in our front cargo area. It was apparently a shipment from the Federal Reserve office to the central bank in Buffalo. There was lots of security before and after that flight, which included some federal agents coming on board and checking our flight attendant ID's. Supposedly, each of the 200 boxes contained about $8,000 each.

September 8th, 1994 - Another really unfortunate day because USAir flight 427 from Chicago to Pittsburgh crashed just outside Pittsburgh, killing all 132 people on board. At first, the accident seemed like a complete mystery. No obvious reasons for what happened were apparent. The subsequent investigation took over four years before they finally concluded that a rudder malfunction had caused the plane to nosedive into the ground. It was a very sad day indeed.

September 29th, 1994 - This was another very sad day for me. I found out after returning home from a trip that my friend Mike Butts had passed away that morning. He had battled his cancer for over two years and was only 39 years old at the time. The funeral was held a couple of days later and I was one of the pall bearers. His wake that night was one of the most endearing experiences I have ever encountered. Our circle of friends all promised to continue to do whatever it took to assist his wife and three small children with whatever they needed.

October 14th, 1994 - Today, we had actor James Doohan up in First Class from Pittsburgh to Norfolk, Virginia. He might best be remembered for playing the role of "Scotty" in the original "Star Trek" series. He was just the nicest man. (Fun fact: he actually had a Scottish accent...and also drank Scotch!)

October 18th-22nd, 1994 - A great trip on the MD-80 with friends Mark Wagner, Nancy Blake, and Kathy Grimm. While in Boston we checked out the historic Freedom Trail and Faneuil Hall, and then had a terrific dinner at an Italian restaurant in North Boston. We had so much fun that we all decided to fly the same trip the next week. However, the next week's trip wasn't as entertaining because Nancy forgot to check in for that trip and was replaced by crew scheduling.

November 14th-17th, 1994 - This four-day trip was notable because we had a total of three Larry's on board. Besides me, there was also captain Larry Taylor and flight attendant Larry Weckerly. The other two crew members took great joy in occasionally yelling out, "Hey, Larry!" just to watch us all turn around at the same time!

November 21st, 1994 - We had an extremely turbulent flight from Philadelphia to Manchester, New Hampshire today. Apparently, a slow-moving, 40,000-foot-high storm cloud was hovering right over Manchester, and we were forced to circle the outskirts of the storm until it was safe to land. It took over an hour to finally get there and when we did land, I was as green with motion sickness as I had ever been! I don't think I felt like eating for the next 24 hours.

December 13th-16th, 1994 - A fun trip with my crazy friend, captain Jack Ballard. Although he sometimes gave the impression that he might say or do just about anything, he was really a very nice man. He also pleasantly surprised me on the second night, when they started up a karaoke machine in the bar at our Philadelphia hotel. Jack then got up and sang "The Green, Green Grass of Home!" (It was the most heart-warming version of that song that I have ever heard.) When finished, he even got a standing ovation from the rest of the bar patrons!

December 19th-21st, 1994 - This three-day trip had 33 hours off in Dayton, Ohio, so fellow Dayton commuter Dorie Watts and I both decided to spend those two nights at our homes. It was nice to have a little extra time with the family and get paid for it!

Chapter Ten

1995....Buttsfest (With a Little Help From My Friends)

January 18th, 1995 - We landed in Roanoke, Virginia today on just one engine because of a bird strike. Although bird strikes are not a common occurrence, they do happen occasionally and pilots train for just such a thing. It was only after we landed and had the mechanics look at the engine that they discovered it was a very large bird, and the damage was enough to cancel the rest of our flights that day. Our captain said that we were at a pretty high altitude when it hit, so it may have been some sort of raptor that was riding the air currents over the mountains. Eventually, one of the mechanics came up and told us that the engine had almost completely pureed the bird. He then showed us what he found in the engine. It was the claw foot of a golden eagle, and it was the only thing left. (Note to self: Always stand clear of those big engines!)

April 4th, 1995 - On our flight from Pittsburgh to Raleigh-Durham we had "M*A*S*H" actor McLain Stevenson onboard. Later in the day, we had a number of Pittsburgh Pirates on the flight to Sarasota, Florida. Included in that group was pitcher Paul Wagner, infielder Jeff King, and their very personable manager Jim Leyland.

April 20th, 1995 - I had my first overnight stay in Asheville, North Carolina. The downtown had a very laid back, kind of Grateful Dead-ish vibe to it. There were also a number of great old-style record stores that I enjoyed visiting. Because my little garage band had been working on some newer songs lately, this gave me a chance to rummage through their record bins and pick up some of that music.

May 18th, 1995 - While on an overnight in Portland, Maine, I went out walking after lunch and happened upon a big tour bus idling outside one of the hotels. Just about the time I was getting ready to continue my walk, the bus doors opened and out walked musician Stephen Stills, who is probably best known for his band "Crosby, Stills, and Nash." (and sometimes Neil Young!) He said hello to everyone and seemed very friendly. The only thing I could think of asking him about was how his bandmate David Crosby was doing. (Mr. Crosby had just recently had a liver transplant and was still recovering at that time.) You could tell that Mr. Stills was moved by someone asking about his dear friend. He nodded and told me that so far, he seemed to be recovering nicely, and then thanked me for asking about him.

May 20th, 1995 - One of my favorite interests has always been music, especially what I would call "classic rock," which would include bands like the Beatles, Rolling Stones, and The Who. One of the best gifts my friend Mike Butts ever gave me was allowing me to be included in the re-formation of Mike's law school band, "The Bombastics."

That band had originally included friends Ken Krochmal on guitar, Bryan Hutcheson on bass, and Mike as the lead vocalist. Mike had always enjoyed performing and after he had moved back home, he eventually wanted to put the band back together. He then recruited our high school classmate John McComb to play the drums and our friend Bob Michaels and myself as the other guitarists. It would become one of the most entertaining things that our circle of friends enjoyed doing together.

During the early 90s, we would gather every few months to jam or just hang out. Once Mike was diagnosed with cancer, it also became something we could all do to lift his spirits. Although his voice changed some after his cancer treatments, we still loved watching him perform. After he passed, it was also something we could do to keep his memory alive.

On May 20, 1995, we had our first "real" gig playing at a backyard party. Although it didn't pay much, we did get to play a couple of sets. However, some neighbors complained about the noise and when the police showed up, they said we had to stop playing. Although that upset us, somebody then remembered that Mike had once said,

"It ain't rock and roll until the cops get called!"

Therefore, we left that party happy with the thought that Mike would have indeed been proud of us!

June 23rd, 1995 - My drummer, John McComb and I came up with the idea that since our circle of friends were about the same age, we should all celebrate turning the big "4-0" together. Therefore, we rented a party hall, invited all our friends and entertained them with our band. True to form, we again had the police show up both at practice and at the party, but this time we were allowed to continue. Again, we were happy to think that Mike was smiling down on us for apparently keeping up our new "tradition."

July 4th, 1995 - This was another situation where I truly wished that I had access to a video camera. We were working an evening flight from Pittsburgh to LaGuardia and were scheduled to land at about 10:15 p.m. With this being a holiday evening, we had very few passengers onboard, and most of them were sleeping. It was dark as we started our approach into the New York area, and we were coming in from the west over the water near Ellis Island and the Statue of Liberty. On that approach path, you usually fly up the East River, bank left, and then eventually land after following the Hudson River into the airport.

We were about ten minutes from landing when Captain Ron Faraday called me up to the cockpit. After entering, he told me to close the door...and take a look! The interior cockpit lights had been turned down and therefore I could clearly see the amazing spectacle that was laid out before us. Since it was a little past 10 p.m., about twenty or thirty fireworks displays were going off in every direction. From our vantage point, we could look down on fireworks going off over the Statue of Liberty, Ellis Island, the World Trade Center, the Empire State Building, and Times Square. Not only could we see them from above, but we also could see the reflections of the multi-colored sparklers off the water as well! (We were literally surrounded by fireworks!) I stayed up in the cockpit for as long as I could, before having to head back to my jumpseat for our landing. Again, it was just great timing and absolutely one of the most amazing spectacles I have ever witnessed.

July 10th, 1995 - At a "Bombastics" band practice, we were kicking around ideas of how to do something to help Mike's family since his death. Somehow, we came up with the concept of a fundraiser and gathering which we loosely termed "Butts-fest." It would be a huge party with all his friends and family in attendance. We would also feature a silent auction of items that we knew Mike would have approved of. We eventually settled on the date of September 30th, which would be close to the one-year anniversary of his passing. All proceeds would then go into a trust fund for the education of Mike's three small children.

July 13th, 1995 - Today, we had singer/actor Michael Damien on our flight from LaGuardia to Syracuse and he was nice enough to autograph a photo for each of the crew members. Afterwards, I decided to donate my signed photo to our "Buttsfest" fundraiser. It also got me thinking as to whether other flight attendants, who had encountered other celebrities, would be kind enough to donate some of their memorabilia to help us raise some money. I then sat down and fashioned a letter which described my life-long friendship with Mike, his battle with cancer, and what we were trying to do with our fundraiser. Over the next several days, I stuffed my airline friends' mailboxes with that flyer and hoped for the best.

August 2nd-3rd, 1995 - This was an interesting two-day trip with friends Dolly Larson and Christine Drall. On the first day, hurricane Erin was close to coming ashore in Florida, so our Orlando flights were delayed and some were cancelled. Our passengers, and especially their small children who were hoping to visit Disney World, were pretty upset about that.

On the second day, we had five college boys on a flight from Ft. Lauderdale to Pittsburgh who tried to pull a prank on the crew. While Christine and I were working the drink cart mid-cabin, one of those college guys put a note on the cart in front of Christine. I saw her open and then close the note, then silently mouth the words, "I'll be right back." While I continued serving drinks, she then went up front and talked to Dolly, who then went into the cockpit. Meanwhile the college boys were laughing and high-fiving each other.

Within a few minutes, Christine returned and informed me that we had to put the cart away "right now!" Once we got to the back, she explained that the note had stated "Give us all the drink money. We have a bomb." As required by company regulations, she then had to inform the captain about the note. She told him that she didn't think it was more than an idiotic prank, but the captain said he wasn't taking any chances and would inform the authorities. He also said to not let those five guys deplane when we landed.

Nothing was said to any of the passengers, and we had a normal landing in Pittsburgh. The captain then called me on the interphone and wanted me to tell the offenders to stay seated, because someone was going to come onboard to talk to them. When I got to their row, I'm pretty sure they knew something was up. In my sternest "teacher voice," I informed them that they were not to get up or try to leave the airplane. When one of them asked if this was about the note on the cart, I just shrugged and sarcastically replied, "Now what do you think?" I also reminded them that our airline took ANY bomb threat seriously and that they could not have picked a worse subject to joke about.

In short, all five of them were arrested and taken off in handcuffs. We heard later from our supervisors that they spent the night in jail and were banned from our flights for a certain amount of time. Although this was my only experience with a possible bomb threat, at no time did I ever really feel like we were in any danger. However, I did feel bad for those teenage boys who thought they were being funny, but really just messed up their short-term (and possibly long-term) futures with that stupid prank.

August 10th, 1995 - While on a Boston overnight with my buddy Billy Walton, we decided to take in that evening's Red Sox-Orioles game at Fenway Park. Keep in mind that at the time, Baltimore shortstop Cal Ripken was just a few games away from breaking the record for most consecutive games played. Therefore, that particular game was close to being sold out. We finally scalped a couple of tickets right before the game started, which ended up being pretty good seats on the first base side, about 20 rows up from the field.

One of the reasons that I wanted to see this game was because Cal Ripken had been willing to hang around after each game and sign autographs for his fans. Since his breaking Lou Gehrig's record was the biggest sports story of the year, I thought an autograph would be something that might raise a lot of money at our fundraiser in September. I just didn't anticipate the other amazing thing that happened to us.

About halfway through the game, I started looking around and finally asked Billy if he had ever seen the popular baseball movie "Field of Dreams." In one scene from that movie, Kevin Costner and James Earl Jones are watching a game at Boston's Fenway Park, and after seeing a dreamlike vision during the game, they get up and leave their seats. When Billy acknowledged that he had seen the movie, I wondered aloud if we weren't sitting in the same area where that scene was filmed.

That's when the guy sitting behind us poked me in the shoulder and with his best Boston accent said,

"I wondered if you two morons were going to realize where you were sitting!"

He then confirmed that I was, in fact, sitting where Kevin Costner sat and Bill was in James Earl Jones' seat. Although the game featured home runs by Jose Canseco AND Cal Ripken, our seat location just made the game even more special. The only disappointment was that the game ran late, and we were not able to hang around long enough afterward to secure Mr. Ripken's autograph.

September 5th-8th, 1995 - This was a really good trip with friends Mark Wagner and Laurie Sismour. While sitting around the Boston airport on a layover, tough guy actor Charles Bronson was seated right across from us, so I went over and introduced myself. I also explained about our upcoming fundraiser and afterwards he graciously agreed to sign an autograph. However, as we all got up to leave, he accidentally handed me his packet of tickets as well as the signature. A few minutes later, I realized what had occurred and had to chase him down to return his airline tickets. Although he was about 75 years old then, he still looked like he could have crushed my spleen if he had wanted to. However, he was nothing but gracious and polite to me, and I have always appreciated his kindness toward Mike's family.

September 14th, 1995 - While on an overnight at the Milford Plaza Hotel in downtown New York, I ran into my old friend Wendee Wilson. (If you recall from Chapter One, she was the person responsible for getting me into the airline business.) I then chose to hang out with their crew that night and we ended up riding the Staten Island ferry. It was a fun night and I was glad to be able to catch up with her. I also must have thanked her a dozen times for helping me get this wonderful job!

September 16th, 1995 - Over the last few months, I have been pleasantly surprised and at times completely overwhelmed, by the generosity of my fellow flight attendants. After I had placed the flyers for Mike's fundraiser in the flight crew mailboxes, I was often stunned by the variety and sheer volume of items that my co-workers donated to us. Some of the most incredible items from my flight attendant friends included a signed bat and ball from St. Louis shortstop Ozzie Smith, a signed football from Miami Dolphins quarterback Dan Marino, Presidential cufflinks from former President Gerald Ford, and an autographed drumhead from the Johnny Winter Band. One of my local pilot friends also offered a free one-hour ride in his vintage bi-plane. It was just so heart-warming for my co-workers to help out like they did, especially because most of them had never met Mike, but only heard me talk about him.

I had also decided to take a leap of faith and had contacted my old Eastern Kentucky classmate, ESPN sportscaster Dan Patrick. Evidently, Mike and Dan had competed against each other in several high school sports and had even attended the same church for awhile. After explaining to Dan what we were trying to do, he also graciously agreed to see what he could come up with to donate.

September 20th, 1995 - While on an overnight in Hartford, Connecticut, I contacted Dan and he agreed to stop by our hotel to drop off some items for our charity auction. I had secretly hoped for maybe one or two nice signatures from some of the ESPN jocks, but when Dan and his young son stopped by, I was again completely astonished by his generosity. Not only was there a huge 4'x 6' ESPN banner signed by all the on-air personalities, but there were also a couple of signed NBA jerseys as well!

As I stammered out how appreciative I was and how much these items would help our fundraiser, Dan just grinned and told me that he had one more little thing that he wanted to donate. He then handed me a small round item wrapped in several layers of tissue paper. As I gradually peeled it open, I uncovered a baseball with the logo from the 1995 All-Star game. I told him thanks and that with all the baseball fans coming to the auction, that ball would probably bring in a decent amount of money.

This time he laughed out loud and told me to turn the ball over. As I rotated the ball, I saw a signature appear. It was autographed by Cal Ripken, the guy that I tried to meet after the game in Boston a few weeks earlier! Because this was the hottest sports collectible on the market at the time, I remember profusely thanking him over and over. I even asked if this wasn't something that he wanted to save for his son. He replied no, and that if he did, he could get another one later. However, he did want me to know the history of the signed ball.

It seemed that ESPN had assigned Dan to interview Cal Ripken on the night before he was set to break the major league record for most consecutive games played. Since the gist of the story was going to be about how gracious Mr. Ripken had been with signing autographs, Dan wanted to film him actually signing a baseball during the interview. Evidently, Dan had that 1995 souvenir All-Star baseball rattling around in his desk, so he took it along to the interview and that was what he autographed for Dan's story. The absolutely coolest thing that we had for the fundraiser...just got cooler! Because of his generosity, Mr. Dan Patrick will always have a special place in the hearts of all of Mike Butts' friends!

September 30th, 1995 - Long story short, our "Butts-fest" party and fundraiser was a huge success! The silent auction featured about 65 items which absolutely stunned everyone who showed up. Overall, we raised in excess of $8,000, which in 1995 was a huge amount of money! The Cal Ripken ball was the most bid-on item and everyone at the event couldn't have been more generous. It was a beautiful evening celebrating a great friend and a life well-lived! (Just to let you know, that money was then put into a trust, and over the next 20 years or so it generated enough income to help put all three of Mike's children through college!)

October 14th, 1995 - We had a long Tampa layover tonight, so my sister Cindy decided to drive over and meet me for dinner. In fact, she pulled up to the Sheraton Hotel just as our crew van arrived out front. What was hilarious was that there was also a science fiction convention booked at the same hotel. As I recall, just as my sister got out of her car, a whole slew of outrageously dressed fans walked past her into the hotel lobby. Her stunned expression was priceless, especially as she wondered out loud about the kind of hotels USAir was using to house their crews!

October 15th-17th, 1995 - All week there had been rumors about a possible United Airlines and USAir merger. There was also talk of an American Airlines attempt to buy USAir as well. Even though the chatter seemed to be rather vague, it was still a little unsettling.

October 31st, 1995 - During the past year, my son Brian had transferred to Ohio University and eventually started a band called "Red Wanting Blue." Tonight was their first real gig at a bar in Oxford, Ohio and apparently it went very well. Hopefully they will have as much fun with their band as I have had with mine! (Special note: Although my son left the band around 2006, the rest of the group is still touring, at least as this book goes to press.)

November 9th, 1995 - On my commuter flight home to Dayton, Ohio, I ran into three people I knew. One was Alice Miller, a U.D. law school classmate, one was Bob Mount who I wrestled with in high school, and the last one was a young lady named Debbie Jett who had been one of my students when I taught at Little Miami High School. It really is a small world sometimes!

December 1st, 1995 - An easy two-day trip in and out of Las Vegas. At that time, we were staying at a hotel just off The Strip owned by actress Debbie Reynolds. One of my crew members apparently went to Vegas a lot because everybody at that hotel knew her by name. She also gambled quite a bit which was ironic, considering that her name was (true story) Bette Moore!

December 5th, 1995 - During our New York City overnight, I ran into my old flight attendant friend Stu Burke, who was mentioned in Chapter 4. We then tried to go see the big tree-lighting ceremony at Rockefeller Center, but the crowds were too large, so we settled for a bar instead.

December 7th, 1995 - We had Nicole Brown Simpson's sister Denise Brown, on our flight from Los Angeles to New York. She was so interesting to converse with and she also had some amazing insights into the O.J. Simpson murder trial. That included some very personal stories that I probably didn't need to know about.

December 19th, 1995 - A huge snowstorm over the East Coast really delayed our flight into Philadelphia. We also had a passenger who suffered chest pains about halfway through the flight. When we finally got him to the gate, the ambulance that met us could barely make it through the deep snow. It also took us about four hours afterwards to finally get to our hotel.

December 29th, 1995 - After finishing up my last trip of the year, I got lucky and got the last seat going home to Dayton. However, a very irate USAir Express pilot yelled at me after my seniority bumped him off that flight. I told him that unfortunately, that is how seniority works and that I have had the same thing happen to me many times. Apparently, that didn't seem to make him feel better.

Chapter Eleven

1996- 1997...."Who's" This Guy and Elvis 2.0

January 10th-13th, 1996 - This trip was severely affected by the infamous "Blizzard of '96," which had dumped over three feet of snow on the Northeast last week. There were lots of delays and cancellations and it was incredibly difficult to commute home afterwards.

January 18th, 1996 - Today we had fog delays into New York, so our crew ended up waiting around in Pittsburgh with some onboard through passengers. Eventually, this one big guy in First Class asked me if I was any good at crossword puzzles, and when I replied that "I had my moments," he said that was good enough. We then sat and worked on his New York Times crossword for awhile until I started thinking that this guy looked familiar. It turned out that he was former Yankee first baseman Chris Chambliss who was now working as a coach for the Yankees. He was very nice, and actually pretty good at puzzles!

However, after a little while I got hungry and decided to go check out the newly opened "Steak Escape" restaurant in the Pittsburgh Airport. Because that particular place had been getting rave reviews for their breakfast hash browns and their grilled steak sandwiches, the waiting lines there often extended out into the main terminal. As I took a whiff of the delicious aromas, I decided that the wait would be worth it, so I grabbed a tray and got in line.

As the line continued to grow, I eventually heard a gentleman behind me comment on how good things smelled, but he spoke with a charming English accent. As I very gradually turned to see who was behind me, I spied four, long-haired gentlemen. The guy immediately behind me had white hair, a little white goatee beard, and sort of looked familiar. Not wanting to be rude, I kept sneaking occasional glances at him while I pondered why he seemed so recognizable. Finally, it hit me! We had a poster of this guy on the wall of our band studio!

It turned out that he was musician John Entwistle, the bass player for the rock band "The Who." After debating with myself on whether I should say anything, he actually broke the ice by asking me what was good at this restaurant. I told him that it was my first time there, but I had heard good things about their steak sandwich. After a few minutes of chatting, I leaned in closer and very discreetly asked him if he was indeed Mr. Entwistle. When he nodded and answered yes, I then told him that I played in a little garage band and that we performed quite a few Who songs. I also stammered out that in my humble opinion, I thought that he was "the best bass player...ever!"

His response was rather endearing. He then pretended to dig his toe into the carpet and uttered the word "Aww," while acting sort of embarrassed. I then inquired as to why he was in the Pittsburgh Airport and he replied that since The Who was taking a break from the road, he and the guys behind him (the "John Entwistle Band") were going out on a little ten-city tour. When I asked if they would be performing anywhere close to either Cincinnati or Dayton, he said no, and then indicated that their only stop in the Midwest was going to be in Chicago.

Taking a deep breath, I then politely asked if he would mind signing an autograph, to which he just grinned and said that he didn't mind at all. Because I only had one piece of paper on me at the time, I had him sign the back of my trip sheet that I had in my shirt pocket. It was indeed a wonderful moment, and as soon as I got home, I immediately framed his signature and hung it in our studio, right next to that poster of The Who! However, a few years later, Mr. Entwistle unfortunately died of an apparent drug overdose at the Hard Rock Hotel in Las Vegas. To this day, I always remember his kindness and good-natured personality.

March 15th, 1996 - By this point, you are probably aware that a lot of flight crew members commute before and after their scheduled trips. That extra travel can become a bit of an adventure, especially if those hoped-for flights cancel or they fill up all their seats. While commuting does allow you to live wherever you want, on bad days it can really cost you a lot of time and money.

On this particular trip, I was flying with captain Ed Daugherty, who was also a fellow commuter out of Indianapolis. After our trip had ended at about 3 p.m. in Pittsburgh, we then headed over to check out the TV screens showing all the upcoming flights. It was then that my heart sank. Both of the last two possible flights to Dayton were showing as "cancelled." That meant I was probably going to have to spend the night in Pittsburgh and wouldn't get home until the next day. Just as I was about to curse my bad luck, I heard Ed also muttering under his breath. It seemed that both of his last two flights to Indianapolis had been cancelled as well. We then looked at each other and both shrugged our shoulders as if to say..."Oh, crap!"

I then headed over to the bank of pay phones to begin calling around for an available room for that night. Before I could ask him if he needed a hotel room as well, Ed looked at me and motioned for me to wait a minute. As I hung up the pay phone with a bit of a quizzical look on my face, Ed started dialing furiously on his pay phone. A few minutes later he was grinning from ear to ear and announced that he had arranged for a ride home for both of us.

It turned out that Ed was a part-owner of a small private airplane. The really good news was that his plane had just finished its annual safety check and was parked in one of the hangers at the Pittsburgh Airport. After checking with the other owner, he got the okay to fly it home to Indianapolis that night. He then informed me that since Dayton was right along his flight path, he would drop me off at the Dayton Airport.

Within 30 minutes, we had arranged a ride out to the maintenance hangar. That's where I saw that our ride home that night was a beautiful vintage Mooney 4-seat aircraft. As Ed went through his pre-flight checklist, I stashed our bags in the small cargo area. We then taxied out and took off for the 90-minute flight to Dayton. Along the way, Ed even let me take the controls for a little while, after giving me the tutorial on basic flying. (It was so cool!) After landing in Dayton, Ed even arranged for a ride for me from the hangar out to the parking lot. Because of how it all worked out, this might be my favorite commuting story yet.

May 9th, 1996 - During a Nashville overnight, I got a chance to visit with my high school classmates Jim and Debi Cole. Jim is a very talented singer/songwriter and is primarily a Christian musician who has a style similar to James Taylor. Jim was also the guy who showed me my first few chords when I decided that I wanted to learn guitar. Eventually, he opted to move to Nashville to try to make a living as a musician. By this point, he had produced three CDs of original music and his song "Every Generation" had reached as high as #3 on the Christian charts. He is also one of the funniest people I know.

May 11th, 1996 - Although I was not working today, the big news was the crash of ValueJet flight 592. Evidently, there was a fire in the cargo area that crippled the airplane and caused it to crash into the Everglades soon after taking off from Miami. All on board were killed. Within a few months, investigators found that poorly marked oxygen containers in the cargo area had probably ignited and caused the fire. Once again, this was another reminder to us that anything can happen during a flight.

May 21st-24th, 1996 - A great four-day trip on the MD-80 with a really nice crew. One of my co-workers was a sweet young lady named Patty Leopardi, who was working her very first flight. Our captain was a really nice guy named Chesley Sullenberger, who had been a former PSA pilot. (If that name sounds familiar, you will read more about him in a later chapter.) On the second day of the trip, I got a chance to chat with former Ohio State running back Eddie George who was also a past Heisman Trophy Award winner.

July 17th, 1996 - While in Cleveland on an overnight, I got up early and went to visit the recently opened Rock and Roll Hall of Fame. There were some amazing displays and some great audio/visual presentations of all the wonderful music that I grew up with. After getting back to the hotel, I decided to squeeze in a little workout before we left for the airport. After changing clothes, I had to wait a little bit for the elevator to take me downstairs to the health club.

When the doors finally opened, two other people were already inside: a younger girl and a woman with a sort of "page-boy" style haircut. I nodded and said hello and then pushed the button for the lobby level. After noticing my workout clothes, the woman inquired as to whether there was an exercise room at the hotel. I replied that there was, and that it was actually a pretty nice one. We chatted a little bit more, before I realized that I was talking to the incredibly talented singer Linda Ronstadt and her daughter.

Once I realized who she was, I told her that I had always enjoyed her music and in fact, that I had seen some of her memorabilia on display at the Rock and Roll Hall of Fame earlier that morning. She smiled and replied that a lot of folks had been telling her that she needed to go check out that museum. I also asked whether she was in Cleveland for a performance and she informed me that she was doing a concert the next night with the Nelson Riddle Orchestra. At this point, the elevator doors opened, I pointed out where the workout room was, and wished her good luck with her upcoming show.

July 17th, 1996 - Today we had what was technically considered a "bomb scare" on our plane that had just landed in Buffalo. One of the other crew members spotted a metal box under a seat after everyone had deplaned, so he notified the captain. The captain then asked for security to come down and check it out. After making sure everyone was a safe distance away, the security official discovered that it was just an old stereo boombox that someone had forgotten to take with them. (Whew!)

August 8th, 1996 - On our flight from Baltimore to Charlotte, we had former Baltimore Colts quarterback Johnny Unitas onboard. He was a very nice man with very gnarled fingers, which was probably a result of his long career in the NFL.

October 18th, 1996 - During our flight from Boston to Orlando, we had two really fun guests onboard: Boston morning DJ Amy "Lynn" Hoffman and her boyfriend Los Angeles police detective Mark Warner. They were both so great to chat with and Ms. Hoffman and I had a wonderful time swapping stories about music personalities. (A few years later, Lynn Hoffman would end up hosting a great television series on the A&E Network called "Private Sessions." On that series, she got to interview a number of high-profile musicians who then performed in a closed studio for a very limited audience.)

November 12th, 1996 - We found out today that our new CEO Stephen Wolf wants to give our planes a new color scheme and also change our name from USAir to USAirways. Supposedly this will happen within the next few months. He also announced that we have committed to purchase the new line of Airbus A-319s, A-320s, and A-321 aircraft.

November 13th, 1996 - This was my first trip to the newly opened Denver International Airport. It seemed very futuristic, but the drawback was the fact that it was located way out on the eastern side of Denver in the middle of nowhere. Also, the top of the airport facility was designed to imitate the nearby Rocky Mountains. However, from a distance the very unusual roofing of the buildings made it appear like the circus was in town! The new airport also featured a unique statue of a blue horse with eerie red eyes that greeted drivers at the front entrance of the airport. I also heard stories much later that some people thought it was haunted. Apparently, the statue's sculptor was accidentally killed when the giant horse head detached and then crushed its creator. (I guess someone should have given him a little "heads up!")

December 13th, 1996 - I was randomly selected to be alcohol tested after I finished up my trip in Pittsburgh. I had no qualms about that, until the breath machine malfunctioned and because of the delay, I ended up missing my last flight home. That meant I had to spend the night in a hotel room and not get home for another 16 hours.

February 4th, 1997 - Our "B" flight attendant had been upset today because her boyfriend was apparently missing. However, by that evening she had finally heard from him. Come to find out, he went missing because he had just discovered that he was going to be a daddy with another woman! (Ouch!) She ended up calling off the trip after breaking up with him over the phone.

February 6th, 1997 - My father had been in failing health the last few months, so I made sure to call home tonight to wish him a very Happy Birthday. He is such a good man! My family will tell you that I picked up a lot of my humor, people skills, and storytelling ability from him.

February 18th, 1997 - My first trip with captain Mel Pipes. He was a very interesting guy with lots of amazing stories. According to him, he used to fly charter trips for all sorts of musicians, including Jimmy Buffett and Pink Floyd.

March 3rd-11th, 1997 - A long week with lots of rainstorms over the Midwest. Some river cities like Louisville and Cincinnati had record flooding. In fact, on our approach into Louisville this week, you could barely see the roofs of some of the submerged buildings near the Ohio River.

March 21st, 1997 - I got a very clear view of the Hale-Bopp comet this morning on a very early departure from Greenville-Spartanburg. Supposedly, this was the only time in my lifetime that it would be this close to us. (My logbook note for today was a reminder that I should start packing a camera in my travel bag, just for occasions like this.)

April 16th, 1997 - We had a great night tonight at the legendary "Elbo Room" on the beach in Ft. Lauderdale, Florida. Crew members included longtime friends Sue Peterson, Lee Cunningham, and first officer (and fellow musician) Lou Bailey. The weather was great, the beer was cold, and the bar band was outstanding. After singing along with the band and occasionally hitting the dance floor, we reluctantly had to leave the party when we got close to that 12-hour mark before our departure the next day. I was so glad that we were a responsible crew, because as we were leaving, I happened to look up and saw something I had not noticed before. Hanging from the ceiling was a camera and a small sign that said,

"Smile! You are live on our new www.elboroom.com website!"

If any of our supervisors had been monitoring that site, they would have seen my eyes squinting to focus on that sign, and then my lips silently mouthing the words, "Oh crap" as we left the bar!

April 24th, 1997 - As our crew finished up checking into the very nice Omni Hotel in downtown Albany, New York, a big tour bus pulled up and out came the dance troupe for the show "Riverdance." The dancers were very friendly and they all had those great Irish accents!

May 28th, 1997 - After we landed in LaGuardia, I decided to assist the cabin cleaners with turning our flight around quickly. As I was helping tidy up the cabin, I found a razor blade wrapped up in one of our cabin blankets. Since this was a potential security breach, we had to notify the New York supervisors and then fill out a lot of paperwork.

July 23rd, 1997 - I was lucky enough to run into another friend of mine from my days at Eastern Kentucky University named Mark Watkins. Mark was another member of our college wrestling team and of the 18 total members of that team, Mark is the third guy I've had on my flights. That is an incredible occurrence for such a small group of people. (Even more incredible was the fact that over the next few years, I would indeed run into two more teammates on my trips!)

August 7th, 1997 - A great trip with a fun crew of Patty, Vance, and Melissa. On our flight into LaGuardia, we had quite a few passengers dressed in Western garb, including cowboy hats and boots. After chatting with some of them, we found out that country music star Garth Brooks would be performing a free live concert that night in New York's Central Park. After we got checked in to our hotel, we decided to go to the show. Once there, we also discovered that it was going to be broadcast live on HBO as well. In short, we eventually found some decent seats close to the stage, and it ended up being a wonderful performance.

September 9th, 1997 - On a long overnight in Las Vegas, I went exploring and got to check out the new Hard Rock Hotel, as well as the Luxor Hotel and the new Forum Shoppes behind Caesar's Palace. The Hard Rock had some very cool music memorabilia displays.

September 19th, 1997 - My father fell ill and had to be rushed to a hospital tonight. As his health continued to slowly worsen, he would eventually be moved into a nearby nursing facility. I also made a note in my logbook that since I have some vacation coming up, I will use it to spend some time with him and my mother.

October 11th, 1997 - My father passed away peacefully tonight with his family surrounding him. He was a wonderful man, a terrific role model, and someone who took great delight in hearing the stories of my adventures. I ended up staying home for a few additional days to help my mom with the funeral arrangements.

November 1st, 1997 - On our Nashville-Pittsburgh flight, we had Lulu Roman, who was one of the stars of the old television show "Hee-Haw," up in First Class. She was very sweet and when I asked what she was doing now, she informed me that she was writing and performing Christian music. I then inquired as to whether she knew my childhood friend Jim Cole, who was also a Christian musician based out of Nashville. She then grinned and said that she loved his music and that he did in fact sound a lot like musician James Taylor! Later in the day, I had another Dayton Law School classmate, Nancy Nash, on our Pittsburgh-Dayton flight.

November 11th, 1997 - I have been on another of those unexplainable streaks where I was again running into people from my past. Today I had one of my favorite ex-students and wrestlers, Rick Frommling on from Dayton to Pittsburgh. I had not seen him since I attended his wedding a few years earlier.

November 20th, 1997 - Today we had Elvis' daughter Lisa Marie Presley and her two young children Ben and Riley, on a flight from Tampa to New York City. Ms. Presley was very nice and her children were very well-behaved. However, I was struck by the fact that although she definitely resembled her mother, there were certain ways that she moved and spoke that kind of reminded me of her famous father.

At some point during the flight, I do remember her politely asking me for a bottle of water. Now I sort of hate to admit this, but after I brought it to her, I then waited around for an extra second or two, just to see if her lip would curl up and she would say, (and remember that it is very difficult to do Elvis impersonations in a print medium.)

"Thankya....thankya vury mush!" (She did not.)

November 25th, 1997 - I was alcohol tested after our last flight tonight. This time the machine functioned properly and I passed the test. I also had enough time to catch my flight home, so I was a happy camper!

December 11th-13th, 1997 - This was a nice trip with flight attendant Cindy Newcom, who it turned out was a cheerleader at Eastern Kentucky University about the same time that I was there. I also found out that her sister (who also went to E.K.U.) was a flight attendant for us as well. She also made me feel much better about my commuting difficulties, because Cindy had to commute between Pittsburgh and somewhere in Montana.

December 18th, 1997 - What a long day! Our morning flight from Boston to Philadelphia had to be delayed until they could fix the heater on our airplane. Two flights later, some businessman got mad at me because I had to move his bag in order to store another passenger's suitcase. There was no harm done and he eventually calmed down. Then on the last flight back into Boston, some drunk missed the toilet and urinated all over the floor. The only saving grace was that I ended up winning a trivia contest that night at a local restaurant. With the money I won, I bought dinner for my fellow crew members.

Chapter Twelve

1998 - 1999....I "Almost" Win the Lottery

February 4th, 1998 - Apparently, the great blues guitarist B.B.King was also staying at our hotel in Ft. Myers, Florida. As I was checking out of my room the next morning, I saw a group of maids happily examining a small item. Evidently, one of them had found one of Mr. King's guitar picks in the room he had vacated. As a fan of his music, I was tempted to offer them some money for that pick, but I could see there was no way they were giving that up.

February 19th, 1998 - This morning, we had to abort our takeoff out of Indianapolis due to an engine problem. Although the passengers were fairly understanding at first, after a couple of hours, the company cancelled the flight and they all had to be reaccommodated. We ended up ferrying the airplane from Indianapolis to Louisville later that afternoon.

March 26th-27th, 1998 - For the first time ever, USAirways extended our normal one-day recurrent training to two full days. Despite the fact that there was slightly more material to cover, it still could have been condensed into just one day. Most of the additional information had to do with the new Metrojet service which will be starting up in a few months. (Metrojet was USAirways attempt at running a low-cost, more efficient subsidiary. It only lasted for a few years before it was scrapped.)

April 1st, 1998 - We had professional wrestler "The Undertaker" on our flight from Syracuse to Washington. He was very quiet but was nice enough to sign an autograph for a young fan. Appropriately, it read, "Rest in Peace, The Undertaker!"

May 21st, 1998 - While on an overnight in New York, I got a chance to see actor Johnny Depp and gonzo journalist Hunter Thompson at the Virgin Music bookstore. They were promoting the recently released movie "Fear and Loathing in Las Vegas" about Mr. Thompson's bizarre adventures as a journalist. They were also dressed in exactly the same outfits and were mimicking each other's actions. It was so funny!

June 3rd, 1998 - Today we had young actress Christina Ricci and Senator Elizabeth Dole in First Class from Boston to Washington. Although they were both very pleasant, neither one knew who the other was.

July 7th-10th, 1998 - This was a nice trip with my buddy Ed Flowers. While standing in front of our Atlanta hotel on the third day, we got to watch the Atlanta Bomb Squad respond to an item they found outside the Marriott Marquis hotel. That squad included three officers in full, protective bomb gear. They also brought in the "boom car" vehicle, which could be used to detonate any suspicious items safely. Eventually, they discovered that some hotel guest had driven off and accidentally left a piece of luggage behind. (Fortunately, that guest returned just in time to keep his suitcase from being blown to bits!)

July 28th-31st, 1998 - A wonderful trip with friends Joan Hathaway and Sue Peterson. On the first day, my commute from Dayton to Pittsburgh had a two-hour mechanical delay. Because the Powerball drawing was at a then-record 250 million dollars, (and because Powerball was not yet available in the state of Ohio) I decided to use the delay time to drive from Dayton across the Indiana border to the town of Richmond. There I purchased ten dollars' worth of lottery tickets and then returned to the Dayton airport in time to catch my flight into Pittsburgh.

While in Toronto on the second day of our trip, Sue and I took the "CN Tower" tour. It is one of the tallest buildings in the world and features a clear glass floor on the top level. I didn't mind the sensation of looking down through the floor, but Sue was a little freaked out about it. While on the tour, I remember having the always entertaining "what if" conversation with Sue, concerning how I would spend my winnings if I indeed won the next night's lottery drawing.

That next night, we had a very short overnight in West Palm Beach, so I went right to sleep. The following morning, I got up early and took my shower. As I exited the bathroom with my towel around my waist, I heard a local morning news anchor on the television announce that there had been one winning ticket drawn for the huge Powerball jackpot, and that winning ticket had been purchased in... Richmond, Indiana! They also said they would be back to announce the winning numbers after a short commercial.

Now, I hope I can adequately describe the sensations that I experienced during that commercial break. My brain told me that Richmond, Indiana was a very small town with only a few places to buy Powerball tickets. It also reminded me that I had those tickets stashed in my travel bag and I should retrieve them right away. All this had to be done with only one hand, as I needed the other hand to keep my poorly knotted towel on my waist. Last of all, my mind gradually let the rest of me know that I realistically had a shot at this incredible 250-million-dollar prize! As the news team came back from the commercial, I tried to fan out the tickets on the bed so I could follow along as the numbers were announced.

Now, I have heard it said that some people who have been in life-changing situations, have experienced a feeling like time began to drag, and everything around them was in slow motion. As the news anchor read off the first three numbers of 6,12, and 24, I noticed that one of my tickets also had the first three numbers of 6,12, and 24!

THAT is when I felt like time began to slow down. For a split second, I just knew that I had won the lottery! In those few slow-motion seconds, I also realized that I was extremely excited and that I was now clutching that possible winning ticket with both hands! In addition, I also somehow sensed that my loosely tied towel was yet still in place. (Giving you some idea of HOW excited I was!)

The sad truth was that I wasn't even close on the last three numbers. As the announcer read off those last meaningless digits, a new reality slowly dawned on me. In fact, in a nearly simultaneous succession, my "bubble" burst, my dreams of retiring early crashed...and my towel fell away! The good news however was that the ticket with the first three numbers on it did earn me a whopping seven dollars, and the somewhat accurate sensation of knowing how a Powerball winner might actually feel after a big win!

August 4th-7th, 1998 - Yet another fun trip with Sue Peterson. On the second day we explored downtown Philadelphia, saw the Liberty Bell, and took the tour of the Philadelphia Mint. The next day in New York, we took the Statue of Liberty tour and checked out the Wall Street area. (I love that this job continued to allow me to explore such interesting places.)

August 27th, 1998 - We had NBA all-star Moses Malone on our flight from Houston to Philadelphia. I didn't get to interact with him very much because he was holding a baby most of the flight. At one point he did briefly hold the child out from his body, and I saw that the baby was safely cradled in just one of his huge hands!

September 8th, 1998 - The summer of 1998 had been a memorable time, especially for baseball fans watching stars Mark McGuire and Sammie Sosa battle for the home run title. Tonight, after dinner, I watched the game broadcast of McGuire breaking Roger Maris' record with his 62nd home run! For a baseball fan like me, it was quite a night.

September 23rd, 1998 - While in Las Vegas for a long overnight, I was able to scalp a ticket to the Jimmy Page and Robert Plant concert at the MGM Grand. They did lots of Led Zepplin songs and sounded pretty good. Since I never got a chance to see Led Zepplin when I was younger, this was as close as I probably would ever get to see some of them perform.

October 29th-30th, 1998 - A nice "steel-y" two-day trip. On the first day we had author Danielle Steele on our flight from Pittsburgh (the Steel City) to Orlando, Florida. The next morning, on the way out of Orlando, we had professional wrestler George "The Animal" Steel and his wife on board. (He was not in character then and in fact looked like a regular businessman with a briefcase and a raincoat.) We had a nice conversation during the flight and when he found out that I used to be a wrestling coach, he offered me a job with his side business; selling wrestling mats! (I eventually told him no, mostly because I just wasn't sure if I wanted a boss who might "body-slam" me if things weren't going well that week!)

November 8th, 1998 - On our flight from Las Vegas to Pittsburgh, we had a very sick passenger who claimed she was ill from food poisoning. Because she spent the entire flight in the rear lavatory, we decided to have the paramedics meet our flight. She ended up having to get IV fluids because she was so dehydrated.

November 11th-14th, 1998 - I used my buddy passes to fly my garage band down to our drummer's vacation house in Florida for a "boy's weekend". We took our acoustic guitars and had a great time jamming all weekend. We also all enjoyed the looks from other passengers who saw our instruments and were trying to figure out if we were "somebody famous."

December 7th, 1998 - Today, USAirways started using the new Sabre Computer system for bookings and reservations. It was a total mess. There were so very many complaints and complications, even though our agents had been training for this for quite a while.

January 6th, 1999 - A huge blizzard hit the Northeast this week and caused lots of delays and cancellations. We also heard that the newly installed Sabre system didn't exactly help the situation either.

January 14th, 1999 - We had a very tough flight today from LaGuardia to Tampa. Not only were we short on passenger meals but we were also "short-staffed" and missing one flight attendant. In addition, we also had some F.A.A. check riders onboard who watched and recorded everything we did and how we did it.

January 19th-21st, 1999 - By the end of this trip, I was starting to feel very sick and wondered if it might be the flu. (It turned out that it was indeed the flu and I would end up being off sick for the rest of January.)

February 10th, 1999 - Our crews had recently been switched to a new Day's Inn hotel in Myrtle Beach, South Carolina. Fortunately, it was right next to the "Broadway on the Beach" complex which featured lots of interesting shops and great restaurants. That included the always entertaining bars at the Hard Rock Cafe and the Jimmy Buffett's Margaritaville.

March 25th, 1999 - We took the famous Harlem Globetrotters basketball team from Philadelphia to Boston today. One of the players spent most of the flight practicing spinning a basketball on the tip of his finger.

April 1st, 1999 - (Warning: Despite my weird sense of humor, this story is not an April Fool's Day prank.) With an unusual name like Holtzapple, you just don't run into many others with that same last name. Today, as I was checking in for my commuter flight home to Dayton, the gate agent looked at the seat chart and asked if I was traveling with any family members. I must have looked puzzled because she then told me that there was another person named Holtzapple already on board. She also said she would give me a seat located right behind her in case it was one of my relatives. (Since there are only about a dozen families with the same spelling as ours, I didn't think that would be the case.) It turned out that the lady in front of me did have the same last name as me, and we eventually discovered that she was married to my third cousin.

April 8th, 1999 - While on a two-hour layover in Philadelphia, I grabbed a seat in the waiting area and did some "people watching." Today I saw Bruce Johnson, one of the current members of the Beach Boys, and actor Louis Gossett Jr., who played the drill sergeant in the movie "Officer and a Gentleman."

May 4th, 1999 - Today is the first day that USAirways will start using the new A-330 aircraft for some of our international flights. Initially they will just be used out of the Philadelphia crew base, but there is talk that they might eventually be flown out of Pittsburgh as well.

May 6-7th, 1999 - During a rather bumpy flight from Charlotte to LaGuardia, one of the drink carts fell over onto one of our female crew members. She claimed she was all right but did have some bruises on her leg. Because she was aware of my past law school experience, she eventually asked for my opinion about a possible lawsuit against the company. Despite my desire to stay away from the obvious, but appropriate pun, I did advise her that..."she didn't have a leg to stand on."

June 25th, 1999 - For the second time in my career, I had Senator Ted Kennedy on a flight from Washington, D.C. to Boston. He wasn't very talkative on this flight either.

August 11th, 1999 - During a long layover in Dallas, I took in a Texas Rangers baseball game at the new Ballpark at Arlington. It was a very nice park, but the tickets and the concessions were rather expensive.

September 14th-15th, 1999 - This week, a major hurricane named Floyd was stirring just off the southern coast, and had disrupted lots of flights and caused numerous cancellations and delays. When it did finally come ashore, Floyd caused severe damage all over the Southern United States.

September 24th, 1999 - Today, we had a very drunk lady doctor on our flight from Washington, D.C. to New Orleans. At first, she just loved me and claimed I was the "best flight attendant ever!" However, when we decided to stop serving her alcohol, she then yelled at me and apparently changed her opinion of me to being "just the worst!"

October 7th, 1999 - This was a nice day in Scranton/Wilkes-Barre, Pennsylvania. We checked out an interesting Farmer's Market, as well as a local attraction called Fatima's Grotto. Also, as we were getting ready to leave for the airport, a big tour bus pulled up next to our hotel van. It turned out to be the members and crew of the rock band "Styx."

November 30th, 1999 - At the very end of the boarding process for our Tampa-Philadelphia flight, we had a very angry family of five show up. The mother then started trying to bully other passengers into changing seats so the five of them could sit together. When I checked their tickets, I saw that they all had middle seats, but were generally right behind each other.

Because we were very close to our departure time, I asked them to take their assigned seats for the moment, with the hope that we might re-arrange some seats once we got to our cruising altitude. The mother then started screaming that there was no way they WEREN'T going to sit together and that she thought I had an "attitude problem!" At that point, the gate agent showed up to close the door and told the family to either sit down or get off the plane. They elected to get off the plane.

December 7th-10th, 1999 - Another great trip with one of my favorite crews of Nancy Blake and Mark Wagner. On the second day,

Mark and I took the tour and rode the tiny little tram car up to the top of the St. Louis Arch. There, we checked out the view of the downtown and the mighty Mississippi River. On the next night, we all had a great night in New York City at a bar called J.R.'s. The following day, we also explored Rockefeller Center and St. Patrick's Cathedral.

December 14th-17th, 1999 - A very interesting trip with friends Michelle Coates and Kris Monch. On our second flight, we had a young man who became very agitated and started making threats against USAirways. Although we tried to ignore him at first, after he told Kris that he would "blow up the f***in' plane," we contacted the captain who decided to have him arrested when we arrived in Charlotte. The police then took him away in handcuffs. The rest of the trip was much more relaxing. Perhaps that was because we had stays in Ft. Lauderdale and Orlando, where we had dinner on the beach and drinks by the pool!

December 20th-22nd, 1999 - A fun trip with my old friends from the Elbo Room, Sue Peterson and Lou Bailey. This was Lou's first trip as a captain, so we took him out for a celebratory dinner in Norfolk and even presented him with his first captain's cigar! Because Christmas was coming up, as well as some anticipated Y2K computer disruptions, in the words of Prince, we definitely "partied like it was 1999!"

Chapter Thirteen

2000- September 2001....New Planes and a Near Strike

January 4th, 2000 - This was my first time on one of our new A-319s. Although I was just deadheading, (that is, riding like a passenger) the crew let me check out the front and back galleys. I think I will like working on this airplane.

January 27th, 2000 - A huge ice storm hit central Texas today. After trying for three hours to get into Dallas, the company cancelled the rest of the trip and sent us home a day early...with pay!

February 1st-3rd, 2000 - There's nothing like starting a new year with another of my weird coincidences. On this trip, we had a nice crew including my flight attendant friend Debbie Bodner and First Officer Gregg Wills. We had a short layover on the first day, and it was during that break that I discovered that Gregg was from the very small town of Waynesville, Ohio, the next town over from my hometown. If that wasn't unusual enough, I also found out that his stepmother was a lady named Rhea Guard who coincidentally had been my babysitter when I was young! (What are the odds, right?)

In addition, Debbie's husband Ken was one of my favorite captains. Even though he was off duty, he decided to fly up to Burlington, Vermont with us so he could spend some time with his wife. (For airline couples that really isn't an unusual occurrence.) He even wore his pilot uniform in case we had a full flight, and he had to ride the cockpit jump seat. The overnight was uneventful, but a problem arose the next morning, while we were sitting in the boarding area waiting to board our plane. A passenger claimed that she had seen "that pilot" (pointing at Ken) drinking at the airport bar. Of course, not only was Ken with us the whole time, but the bar wasn't even open yet! However, the station manager had to make a report about the passenger's claim, even though we all knew there was nothing to it. I'm pretty sure that the complaining passenger wasn't even on our flight.

February 10th, 2000 - We had a long overnight in Nashville, Tennessee, so I got a chance to go out and walk the downtown area. I really enjoyed exploring some of the old record stores and I really liked a place called Gruhn's Guitar Shop, which featured lots of beautiful vintage guitars and other instruments. On our flight out of Nashville, we had the country music duo of "Brooks and Dunn" up in First Class. They were both terrific gentlemen and very nice to chat with. They even sent me back to talk with their guitar technician, who ended up giving me a couple of guitar picks from each performer.

February 17th, 2000 - This week we had an overnight in downtown Ottawa, Ontario Canada. It was extremely cold while we were there; so cold in fact that the tears on my face froze while walking down the block to get dinner. The really interesting thing about our stay in Ottawa was watching hundreds of skaters on the Rideau Canal the next morning. (Fun fact: that canal is considered to be the world's longest skating rink.) I saw businessmen with briefcases skating to work, as well as a young couple whose baby carriage was on skates instead of wheels.

February 23rd, 2000 - Our flight attendant union has been without a new contract for almost two years now. Today we heard that talks have broken down and that there is a real possibility that we may be going out on strike within the next month.

March 13th, 2000 - During our long Atlanta layover, I went out walking and ended up taking the CNN studio tour. I was intrigued at what really went on behind the scenes at a major news channel. At the end of the tour, we were invited to sit in the audience of a live broadcast of the CNN show "Talk Back Live." I don't remember the topic discussed, but I remember the guy sitting next to me was pretty agitated about it.

March 22nd, 2000 - It was becoming evident that our flight attendant group would probably be going out on strike effective March 26th. In fact, I had been invited to be part of an informational picket at the Dayton airport on March 25th. There was also going to be a picket line demonstration in downtown Dayton after that. Evidently, our CEO, Stephen Wolf had a history of trying to bust unions and had refused to acknowledge that USAirways was making money again. I recall hoping that it would all work out for the best.

March 25th, 2000 - After a long and chilly day at the Dayton airport, a lot of the Dayton commuter group met up with some other union officials and marched through downtown Dayton. Fortunately, there was a last-minute settlement with the company which kept us from actually having to go out on strike. Apparently, we got a nice pay raise and avoided most of the cuts that the company was pushing for.

April 6th, 2000 - In every athlete's career, there are a few exceptional coaches who really make a difference in your life. When my son, Brian, was playing basketball, one of his favorite mentors was a guy named Lorenzo Romar, who was a former NBA player. He was also the coach of the "Athletes in Action" team at our local YMCA where Brian practiced a lot. After Brian graduated, Lorenzo eventually ended up as an assistant coach on the UCLA team that won a NCAA championship in 1995.

On our flight today from St. Louis to Pittsburgh, I looked up to see a very familiar face which turned out to be Coach Romar. After I introduced myself, he remembered me and immediately asked how

Brian was doing. I told him that Brian was playing in a pretty good rock band out of Ohio University but was no longer playing ball. It turned out that Lorenzo was now the head coach at St. Louis University and he said that if Brian still had any college eligibility left, that he should give him a call. I gave him my son's phone number and they eventually got a chance to get caught up with each other

April 7th, 2000 - I was randomly drug tested at the end of my trip today for the first time in a very long time. I can only attribute that to the fact that the last time I was tested; in protest, I threatened to place the little specimen cup on the floor of the bathroom...and aim into it from across the room! (I can only assume that is why they waited so long to test me again.)

April 24th, 2000 - After some storms over the Carolinas stranded us in Ft. Myers, Florida, I set a new personal record for the category of "flights taken to get home." I ended up riding the jumpseat from Ft. Myers to Charlotte, North Carolina, then to Pittsburgh, then finally home to Dayton. It took me nine hours and I didn't get home until 2 a.m. but I did get home!

April 30th, 2000 - My son's band, Red Wanting Blue, had their release party for their third CD (titled "Model Citizen,") which I thought was their best work yet. In fact, Brian even mentioned his mother and I in the liner notes. (You know that you've got it made when you're mentioned in a band's liner notes!)

May 19-20th, 2000 - Two days of training in Pittsburgh on the new Airbus aircraft. The A-319 will be easy to work, but the A-321 is much larger and a little more complicated.

May 23rd, 2000 - Today United Airlines proposed a possible merger with USAirways. If it worked out, it would create the world's largest airline. However, there seemed to be a lot of opposition from other airlines as well as some possible airline monopoly issues.

June 2nd, 2000 - During my commuter flight from Dayton to Pittsburgh, I managed to curl up in a window seat and catch a little nap. However, while I was sleeping, something happened, and our flight got diverted to Harrisburg, Pennsylvania. (It was a little disconcerting for me to wake up and see the giant nuclear cooling towers of Three Mile Island going by outside!) We then sat in Harrisburg for three hours which made me fifteen minutes late for my trip check-in. Fortunately, crew scheduling allowed me to stay on my trip because our first leg to Las Vegas was also delayed for three hours.

July 5th, 2000 - Today, I ran into former flight attendant Becky Russell Slaughter (mentioned in Chapter 7) on a flight from Pittsburgh to Nashville today. She now has two young sons and is living in Nashville. It was great to catch up with her.

July 18-21st, 2000 - This was a good trip with friends Charlie Welch and Julie Monson. On the third day we had a long overnight in downtown Providence, Rhode Island. When Julie and I went out to find some lunch, we accidentally discovered an extreme-sports festival called the "Gravity Games." There were lots of interactive displays to enjoy and lots of free "swag" such as complimentary photos and free sandals. I was also impressed with how athletic the skateboarders and bike riders were. Some of their tricks were truly unbelievable!

August 15, 2000 - My first trip with my friend Deb Feren. She is a big music fan and also enjoys going to concerts. In fact, her boyfriend at the time was the bass player for the country music band Montgomery Gentry.

August 22-25th, 2000 - A great four-day trip with friends Renee Tate and M.J. Weiss. On our New York overnight we went to the famous TKTS booth in Times Square and got tickets for the Wednesday matinee showing of the Broadway play "Jekyll and Hyde." It was my first Broadway play and the lead role featured Sebastian Bach, the singer from the band "Skid Row." There was one memorable scene where his schizophrenic character argues with himself in two distinctly different singing voices. In short, he was very impressive.

September 19-22nd, 2000 - A nice trip with Chris Sowa and my buddy Ed Flowers. On the first day we had five trainees on the Pittsburgh-Houston flight and they all did really well! On the third day, we rode the New York subway to Canal Street and took in the Festival of San Gennaro in Little Italy. It was a fun atmosphere, and the food was delicious.

September 26th, 2000 - Today we had a layover at the Washington-Dulles International Airport. In a nostalgic "throwback," our plane got parked at a remote gate, so they sent one of those old-style "people-movers" out to pick us up. (I can only describe it as sort of a living room on a set of scissor wheels.) When they got to the plane, they raised the whole room up to the level of the entry door. After all the passengers got in, they lowered us down about ten feet and then drove us over to the terminal. The driver then informed us that we were probably one of the last groups to be transported this way, as those vehicles were going to be "mothballed" the next day.

I then had an intriguing idea and wondered if I shouldn't buy one of them after they were retired. I imagined that I could install a refrigerator and some recliner chairs inside the vehicle and then it could be used for sporting events or music concerts. Instead of buying a ticket, I could just drive it to the venue and park near a fence. After raising it up, I could just relax inside and watch the event over the fence! I still think it's a terrific idea!

October 12-13th, 2000 - An easy two-day trip and my first opportunity to work on the new Airbus-319. If this aircraft has as many good overnights as the MD-80, I will be working this plane quite a bit!

October 19th, 2000 - While on a long overnight in downtown Boston, I got a chance to go see the "Blue Man Group" at the Charles Playhouse with my "Jekyll and Hyde" friend M.J. Weiss. It was a fun show, and the three main characters were all very talented percussionists!

November 7th, 2000 - Once we got to the hotel, I decided that I was going to stay up and watch the presidential election results. However, by 2 a.m. there was still no clear winner, so I went to bed. In the morning there was still no official announcement as to whether George W. Bush or Al Gore was the new President. (As you might recall, this controversy would take several months of legal appeals before it was determined that Bush won the election.)

November 16th, 2000 - We had the doo-wop/soul group "The Drifters" on our flight from Philadelphia to Toronto. After chatting with the band members, I found out that the lead singer was married to one of our Philadelphia-based flight attendants.

December 5-8th, 2000 - This turned out to be one of my favorite trips to date. Our crew included Captain William Mocock, and my great friends Linda Lory and LuAnn Thompson. On the first night in Rochester, New York, we found a fun little Irish bar and spent the evening throwing darts. The next day we had a long overnight in downtown New York City and had way too much fun that night at the Playwright Bar next to our hotel. We laughed all night and even had the bar's Santa Claus sitting with us at one point. I am really starting to like Christmas time in New York!

December 13th, 2000 - Five of us Dayton commuters got stuck in Columbus, Ohio after an ice storm in Dayton forced our flight to divert. Fortunately, one of the other commuter's relatives owned a big limousine, so the next day he drove it to Columbus and then brought all of us back to Dayton. However, before I could get home, I had to spend close to an hour trying to chip the ice off my car windshield.

December 15th-17th, 2000 - This weekend my friend Steve Moore and I used my buddy passes and flew down to Jacksonville, Florida. Fortunately, Steve had discovered a golfing package where we were allowed to golf on the famous TPC Sawgrass golf course in Ponte Vedra, Florida. That Sawgrass course is well known for the iconic par three 17th Hole which features a green surrounded by water. Although I am not a very skilled golfer, I did manage to hit that green with my tee shot, but missed a chance for a par when my putt came up just short. Despite his exceptional golf skills, Steve put his tee shot into the water, but putted well and also bogied the hole. (A little bit of consolation came several months later at the 2001 PGA event, when Tiger Woods also bogied that 17th hole, the same way that I did!)

December 21st, 2000 - During a layover in Washington D.C., I got to meet former New York Knick player (and then U.S. Senator) Bill Bradley in the National Airport. At 6'9", he was still a very imposing figure.

January 2-5th, 2001 - My first trip on the new Airbus-320 aircraft. (I figured that with a new Millennium, I should try out a new airplane.) It is slightly bigger than the A-319 but still relatively easy to work. In fact, it still had that "new plane smell." During the long overnight in Seattle, I got a chance to explore some great antique stores and vintage music shops in the Pioneer Square area.

January 8th, 2001 - We had Georgetown University head basketball coach John Thompson on our flight from Washington D.C. to Orlando. He was a pretty large guy but unfortunately there were no seats available in First Class, so he had to squeeze himself into one of our coach seats. At least he had an exit row seat with a little more leg room.

January 23rd, 2001 - During the boarding of our Ft. Lauderdale to Philadelphia flight, the ground crew accidentally damaged our nose gear wheel while attaching the tug bar. We were delayed over two hours until they could repair it. Our captain and our passengers were not very happy about that.

March 28th-30th, 2001 - This week included three days of training at the old Carnot School in Pittsburgh. The first day we learned all about the new Airbus-321 aircraft, which will be delivered sometime this summer. The other two days were for our annual recurrent training.

April 6th, 2001 - Our arrival into Milwaukee was delayed several hours because President Bush's Air Force One was landing ahead of us. (Apparently, the President was attending the opening of the new Miller Park baseball stadium in Milwaukee.) Since there are a number of regulations that severely limit how and when other airline traffic can proceed whenever the President flies, our arrival time was repeatedly pushed back. Because of those delays, we then had a very short overnight at our hotel.

May 3rd, 2001 - We had a really nice night in West Palm Beach with the entire crew, including my old friend Nancy Blake. After dinner and drinks, we all huddled around the bar television to watch the final episode of a new television series called "Survivor."

May 24th, 2001 - Because of the upcoming Memorial Day holiday, all possible commuter flights home were completely full. However, I got lucky and caught a ride to Dayton on a previously cancelled plane that was being sent to Dayton as a repositioning flight or "ferry" flight. Those types of flights don't carry passengers but can occasionally carry airline crew.

July 3rd-4th, 2001 - This was my first trip on the Airbus-321 aircraft. It was an easy two-day trip to Las Vegas. Generally, it would be staffed with a crew of four, but for a short time USAirways required that it carry a crew of six flight attendants. I was the "E" flight attendant and did all the prep work in the First-Class galley. All of our passengers seemed to really like the new plane.

July 10th-13th, 2001 - A really fun trip with friends Mary Lynn Graves and two of my favorite people, sisters Sue and Janet Grabowski. The "Flying Grabowski Sisters" are fellow Ohioans and two of the sweetest people ever.

July 27th, 2001 - It was announced today that United Airlines was calling off their proposed merger with USAirways. Apparently, the federal government was not going to approve the deal because of antitrust concerns. Most of my flight attendant friends were unsure if they wanted the merger to happen anyway. I just hope that we can survive on our own.

July 31st, 2001 - This was a nice long overnight in San Francisco, so I decided to go see a baseball game at their newly opened Pac Bell Stadium. It was a really cool ballpark that featured a giant-sized baseball glove in left-centerfield. The right field fence was so close that a long home run could actually land in San Francisco Bay. In fact, the seating area there was known as the "Splash Zone", because fans in those seats would get sprayed with water if/when that happened!

August 14th-17th, 2001 - This week I had a really enjoyable trip with friends LuAnn Thompson and Melanie Constantine. LuAnn had been on my "Christmas in New York" trip last December, and Mel was a very talented singer and guitar player. (In fact, she had even recorded a CD of her own original music, which she gave to each of us.) During a two-hour layover in Roanoke, Virginia, the three of us sat in the boarding area and had fun playing a number of songs on Mel's guitar.

August 21st, 2001 - On our flight from Pittsburgh to Miami, Florida, I got a chance to chat with a couple of young fashion designers who had attended Ohio University. It seemed that they knew my son and were fans of his band "Red Wanting Blue."

August 28th, 2001 - During another overnight in downtown Seattle, I got a chance to go through the recently opened music museum called the "Experience Music Project." The E.M.P. had a lot of really cool interactive displays and a great music library. In fact, I liked it as much as the Rock and Roll Hall of Fame in Cleveland.

Now, I would like to pause here momentarily for several reasons. Although I couldn't possibly have known it at the time, but by September of 2001, I was at about the halfway point of my airline career. I was 45 years old; healthy and active, and really enjoying the airline business. My wife and I were happily married and regularly used our travel passes to go exploring. Our son was out of college and was making a decent living as a musician. My house was almost paid off. Overall, things were going well in my life. However, who could have known then that the airline business was about to change so drastically after the events of September 11th, 2001?

As I look back at what I have written so far, I am both pleasantly surprised and mildly amazed at my good fortune. By this point, the things that I had experienced and the places I had seen, had made my work life very enjoyable. On top of that, the remarkable people that I had met and the wonderful crews that I had worked with, had been great blessings as well. If I had stopped flying at this point, my airline career would still have been nothing short of fantastic. However, as those guys on the infomercials say…"but wait, there's more!" Although the second half of my work life will be experienced in a slightly different atmosphere due to the tragic events of September 11th, I still hope that you will find the next few years of logbook stories to be just as entertaining!

Chapter Fourteen

September 11th, 2001

September 11th, 2001 - No history of the airline business would be complete without at least a brief description of the impact of the tragedy of September 11th, 2001. Just as most people from my parent's generation remembered where they were when the attack on Pearl Harbor happened in 1941, my generation will always remember where they were when this day happened. Although I was fortunate enough to not have been personally or immediately affected by those events, it still had a huge impact on our business and very core of our airline lifestyle. Nothing about our job was ever the same after this day.

I was scheduled to work another four-day "extra" trip starting on Tuesday, September 11th. There were going to be a couple of nice long overnights in Orlando and Philadelphia and most of my crews were Pittsburgh-based, which meant I would probably know at least a few of them. The real bonus was that the trip would end early on Friday morning, which would give me a better chance of commuting home easily.

Since my check-in time wasn't until late afternoon, I had the rare luxury of being able to take a late morning commute rather than my more standard 7 a.m. flight. This allowed me to sleep in a little bit and didn't conflict with my wife's morning routine before she left the house at about 7:30 a.m. I did get up in time to kiss her goodbye and then made myself a little bit of breakfast. I also turned on our bedroom radio before hopping in the shower. After drying my hair and shaving, I then put on my uniform shirt and pants before deciding to double check my airline suitcase.

It was while I was packing my suitcase that the radio DJ came on and said that evidently some sort of aircraft had accidentally flown into one of the World Trade Center towers. He also said that his listeners should turn on their televisions because we would probably never again see something like the smoke coming from the tower. I then went and turned on the local news channel and started watching as the events unfolded.

I definitely remember innocently thinking that what I was seeing must have been the result of a private airplane pilot who might have had a heart attack or stroke, and was unable to steer clear of the building. There were just too many regulations limiting air traffic over downtown Manhattan to imagine anything else. Even the news announcers failed to insinuate anything other than what an unfortunate accident it seemed to be.

Along those lines of thought, about ten minutes later I was still glued to the television and it was then that I remember seeing a plane coming into view from behind the twin towers. Again, my first inclination was that it was some sort of news team trying to get closer to the accident scene in order to get some close-up photographs. About that time, I started thinking that they were also violating Manhattan air-space regulations and were also going to be in real trouble with the F.A.A. That's when that second plane hit the other tower!

As I sat in stunned silence, I literally could not form any cognitive thoughts. It was like my brain was stammering or misfiring. Eventually I did manage to start formulating some rational thoughts, but again it was along the lines of how unlucky that news crew had been, and that their pilot should have been paying more attention to how close they were to the buildings. It just couldn't have been anything more than a couple of very unlucky accidents.

Soon after the second crash, when smoke was billowing from both towers, one of the newsmen came on and announced that there were reports of several missing airplanes. There was also breaking news of some other planes that were not responding to radio communications and were possibly in a hijacking situation. For the next 30 minutes, there was all sorts of conjecture about what was occurring, as well as reports of what was happening on the ground around the towers. Around 9:30 a.m. there was a report that some sort of explosion had happened at the Pentagon, possibly due to another airplane crash. That was soon followed by an announcement that the F.A.A. was grounding all aircraft and directing them to land at the nearest available airport. My head was swimming, and my heart was aching.

At some point, I called my wife at work and told her to get to a television and watch what was going on. After the announcement of the grounding of all air traffic, I knew I wasn't going to get to work, so I called off my trip. My initial thought was that I should drive to Pittsburgh because I knew USAirways would need lots of volunteers to help with all the chaos that I was sure would follow. My wife then reasoned that there would probably be no hotel rooms available, so driving to Pittsburgh was going to be a futile gesture. Reluctantly, I agreed.

The rest of the day was a bit of a blur. I received lots of phone calls from family members and good friends; all wanting to know if I was okay. (I can sincerely say that those acts of kindness and concern were the best thing that happened to me on that day.) Many of them had questions about what I thought was happening and what I thought would happen in the future. Since there was only speculation at the time about which airlines were involved, I also tried to make a number of calls to fellow flight attendants who I knew were on duty that day.

I also remember the sad reality that eventually dawned on me as the rest of the day unfolded. I just knew that they couldn't have possibly evacuated everyone out of both towers before they went down. I also strongly believed that everyone on those hijacked planes were probably gone as well. For someone who has always prided himself for not being a worrier, I was very worried.

I stayed glued to the television for the next ten hours as more and more reports came in regarding the day's events. Each seemed more heartbreaking than the one before. Eventually, the hijacked flights were identified as the following:

American flight #11; a Boeing 767 with 81 passengers and a crew of 11. That plane hit the North Tower at 8:46 a.m.

United flight #175; a Boeing 767 carrying 56 passengers and 9 crew members. That plane hit the South Tower at 9:03 a.m.

American flight #77; a Boeing 757 with 6 crew members and 58 passengers onboard. That flight hit the west side of the Pentagon at 9:37 a.m.

United flight #93; a Boeing 757 carrying 7 crew members and 37 passengers. That plane was most likely headed toward the White House when the passengers overwhelmed the hijackers and were storming the cockpit when it crashed into a field near Shanksville, Pennsylvania at 10:03 a.m. Their heroism quite probably prevented another tragic crash and an untold number of casualties.

Even now, I still remember so many vivid images from that terrible day. I clearly recall how the sky over New York was such a bright blue color and that there were no clouds at all that morning. That was soon contrasted with the horrible image of plumes of black smoke billowing from both towers into that once beautiful sky. I also have the incredible memory of watching the first tower collapse and the resulting cloud of thick dust that worked its way through the streets of lower Manhattan. Soon afterwards, as the second tower collapsed, I remember seeing that bundle of radio and cell phone antennas on the roof, slowly slide down into that swirl of construction dust. Then, there was that long distance view of a Manhattan skyline that no longer featured those iconic twin towers. For someone who had regularly flown in and out of New York City, to no longer see those two spires was just so very sad. I went to bed that night emotionally and spiritually drained.

The next day was more of the same. The reality of what had happened was beginning to sink in. There were occasional bits of good news reported, whenever family members or first responders were discovered to be safe. There was a remarkable story of a security guard who was inside one of the towers when it collapsed; only to be found later sitting on top of a pile of rubble relatively uninjured. However, most of the day's news covered the incredible loss of life of civilians and emergency personnel. Maybe the worst story of the day was a video that showed our foreign enemies dancing in the streets, in celebration of what had happened to America. I almost couldn't believe what I was seeing.

Because the F.A.A.'s grounding of all flights lasted most of the week, I just stayed home and tried to keep myself occupied. I heard later from one friend whose flight had been diverted to Wichita, Kansas.

After being unable to contact anyone at USAirways for four days, their captain made a decision to rent a van and drive back to Pittsburgh; dropping off a few crewmembers at their home cities along the way. Another crew got diverted to Aruba and spent five days there before hitching a ride home to Philadelphia on a cargo plane.

We also found out much later, that because of the increased volume of calls from displaced crews, our company's communication system was actually unable to function most of the week. For most of the stranded crews, it unfortunately turned out to be a case of "every man for himself." I was told that it took almost three weeks for USAirways to fully retrieve all of their planes.

From this point on, I will again be sharing stories of my airline adventures, but a number of them will be heavily influenced by the tragic events of this horrible day. Please bear with me, especially over the next few chapters of logbook adventures. It will eventually be fun again.

Chapter Fifteen

September 2001-2002....Life After 9/11 and Our First Bankruptcy

September 18th-21st, 2001 - Flights were gradually allowed to resume around September 16th, so this four-day "extra" trip was my first time back flying since 9/11. Because security was extremely tight, we had been warned to allow extra time to get through the security screening lines on the way to work. Once at work, it soon became apparent that there was a newfound bond between all flight crews that might not have been so noticeable before. Without it being said, we all knew that any one of us could have been involved in last week's events. With rumors circulating that more attacks might happen, there was also a renewed determination to be hyper-vigilant and not let the bad guys strike again.

My first two legs involved a Pittsburgh-Denver-Pittsburgh turn. We only had eight people on the first flight and seventeen on the return trip. Nearly every one of our passengers took the time to let us know that they would be glad to "help out" if called upon. The unusual thing was that for the first time in a long time, every passenger paid attention to the pre-flight safety demo and took the time to scope out each exit. (I had gotten so used to having maybe five people watch what we do during the demo, that I felt a little conspicuous.) It was also good to have my friend "Flyin' Brian" Lindsey on a couple of those flights. He and I made a point to work up a game plan for what would happen if we did in fact encounter any terroristic activity. (Between Brian being a physical trainer and me being an ex-wrestling coach, we figured we could do a lot of damage to whoever tried to get into the cockpit!)

September 24th-27th, 2001 - Another four-day "extra" trip. Security was still incredibly intense and there were still rumors that there may be more attempts to hijack airliners. I did have one small moment of levity though when Pittsburgh security felt the need to confiscate my small, round-tipped moustache scissors out of my shaving kit. (I can only assume that they didn't want me trimming the facial hair of any unsavory characters that week.)

As it turned out, my second and third days were both cancelled and I ended up staying by myself at our hotel in downtown Baltimore for three nights. I tried to make the best of the situation by going out every day to explore the city. In fact, I ended up seeing the Baltimore Aquarium, the Inner Harbor, the Babe Ruth Museum, and the Oriole's Camden Yards ballpark.

However, due to massive passenger cancellations, I soon learned that all airlines were scrapping their schedules and cutting personnel. By the time I got back to Pittsburgh on the last day, I found out that USAirways was going to cut about 20 percent of their workforce in the near future. In fact, my longtime supervisor Diana Darak had already been let go. I understood the business reasons for it, but it was still a shock. I recall hoping that we would survive this change in our airline culture.

October 5th-12th, 2001 - Karen and I had a nice vacation at our friend John McComb's house in Boca Grande, Florida. We also took our son and his girlfriend. With the decreased flight loads, it was one of the few times that it was relatively easy to get on our flights to and from Florida.

October 15th, 2001 - It was officially announced today that USAirways would be cutting back on everything. There would be reductions in flight schedules, staffing, and salaries. The amounts of each cutback would be determined in the near future. The notation that I made in my logbook for this date said it all: "Uh-oh!"

October 23rd-24th, 2001 - Our flights in and out of Orlando were the first full flights in over a month. For dinner in Orlando, three of us took a cab to the recently opened "City Walk" complex. There were lots of themed restaurants and interesting displays. We finally decided on their Jimmy Buffett-inspired "Margaritaville" cafe. It was a fun atmosphere, and the food was very good! After the last few stressful weeks, it was also nice to experience some lighter moments.

October 31st, 2001 - It was officially announced today that USAirways lost $766 million dollars during the third quarter and would probably lose at least that much during the fourth quarter. As I said earlier..."Uh-oh!"

November 12th, 2001 - Another tragic plane crash happened today. American flight 587 had just taken off from New York when it crashed into a residential area on Long Island. All 251 passengers and a crew of nine were killed, as well as five people on the ground. At first, there were all sorts of wild rumors that it was another terroristic act, but eventually it was proven to be a case of pilot error due to wake turbulence from the plane in front of them.

November 27th, 2001 - After promising to work very hard to fix our many problems, CEO Rakeesh Gangwal resigned today. Despite our poor financial situation, he also left with a very big severance deal. That news really upset a lot of my co-workers. Our previous CEO, Stephen Wolf then took over on an interim basis.

December 6th, 2001 - A very interesting day with crew members Joan Hathaway and Chris Sowa. After our Savannah-Charlotte flight, I discovered an orange, plastic capsule under one of the rear seats with what appeared to be a white powder inside. I then rather thoughtlessly took my finger and rolled it over which caused it to break open. Because of the rather tense security atmosphere at the time, I then decided to notify the captain. After he came back to look at it, he then notified ground security. In the meantime, the gate agent walked back, picked up the capsule...and smelled it!

Once security arrived, they took one look at it and decided to quarantine the area in case it might be anthrax. Our crew of five was temporarily isolated in the Chief Pilot's office while they ran tests on the powder. We heard later that the gate agent was taken to a local hospital and quarantined there. After a few hours, the tests showed that it was not anthrax, so we were allowed to continue on our trip. We never did hear exactly what the substance was.

January 25th, 2002 - Evidently, the fourth quarter didn't help us much. Today USAirways announced that we lost a total of $1.1billion for the entire year of 2001. Other airlines were posting similar numbers, so we realized that it wasn't just our problem. Once again, the appropriate term for this situation appeared to be..."Uh-oh!"

February 20th, 2002 - While on a layover in downtown New York, I took the subway to the East Village and saw my son's band perform at a place called the Mercury Lounge. It was a very good show. The guys in the band just couldn't get over the fact that I was "in the neighborhood" and decided to come to the show.

February 28th, 2002 - One week later, while on an overnight in downtown Wilmington, North Carolina, I went out walking and happened to find a local club called "Marrz." When I looked at their schedule of upcoming shows, I saw that Red Wanting Blue was booked to play there...the very next night! Although I had to leave that afternoon, wouldn't that have been great to surprise the band by showing up at another one of their gigs!

March 1st, 2002 - On our Pittsburgh-Tampa flight we had former Olympic gold medalist and current professional wrestler Kurt Angle onboard. On the return trip, a very nervous lady boarded the plane but then couldn't decide if she really wanted to go. Realizing the stressful atmosphere of the current state of flying, we tried to be very patient with her. We ended up delaying our departure for an extra 10-15 minutes until she finally decided not to go and had to deplane.

March 18th-21st, 2002 - A really nice four-day trip with my buddy Jeff Abbott and a young lady named Dawn Vests. They were both terrific to fly with, especially Jeff who has a warped sense of humor. In fact, he and I were both chuckling when we recalled practicing for a pretend water landing during our yearly recurrent training. During that drill, we are required to yell to the passengers to put on their life vests with the verbal command..."Don vests!" We then imagined our co-worker (Dawn) repeatedly turning her head and asking..."What?" (Yes, apparently my sense of humor is fairly warped as well.)

On our overnight in New York City, Jeff and I took a cab to the "Iridium Room" club to see the 86-year-old guitar legend Les Paul perform. For those who don't know, Les Paul was a jazz and blues guitarist and also helped invent the solid-body electric guitar as well as multitrack recording. He was so well respected that every musician passing through New York almost always stopped by to play with him.

(In fact, our waitress told us that the week before, musicians Lenny Kravitz and ZZ Top's Billy Gibbons had both gotten up on stage and jammed with him.) Although, no stars stopped by while we were there, Mr. Paul was still amazing.

March 28th, 2002 - This little story took place on a "red-eye" flight from San Francisco to Pittsburgh. Again, for those who aren't aware, a red-eye flight generally departs late from a West Coast city and flies all night; arriving at an East Coast city early the next morning. They were relatively easy to work because most passengers tended to sleep during the flight. The real difficult part was staying awake when it got quiet and the cabin was dark.

On this particular flight, I was helping out in the First-Class section. About 4 a.m., the only gentleman who was awake in those first four rows, got up and eventually wandered up to the front galley. He then claimed that he could never sleep on red-eye flights and just wondered if he could chat with me. I told him that actually that would be a great way for me to stay awake as well, so he introduced himself as "Pat" and we started up a conversation.

After discussing the current state of affairs in the airline industry, I eventually found out that Pat was from Erie, Pennsylvania, and was in the music business. Although he was then living in San Francisco, he was on his way back to Erie to visit his family. While talking about music, he started to look more and more familiar to me. Eventually the scar on his chin caused me to ask if he was in a band. It turned out that the gentleman was Patrick Monahan, the lead singer of the band "Train." The reason I asked that question was that at the time, they had a video out for their song "Drops of Jupiter" which had featured a close-up of the scar on Pat's chin.

Seizing the opportunity to pick a working musician's brain, we had a nice chat about his creative process when it came to writing songs as well as the history of their band. At some point, I also told him about the relative success of my son's band, but that they had not yet been signed. Patrick then asked about the depth of their song catalog before assuring me that they just needed to be patient. He related that his band had almost quit the music business twice before they eventually got signed.

After a wonderful 90-minute conversation, our flight started slowing down in preparation for our landing in Pittsburgh. As the lights in the cabin gradually started to come up, Pat and I shook hands as he got ready to head back to his seat. However, he suddenly stopped, turned toward me, and quietly asked who the young man was in the seat behind him. I reached up for the seat manifest and showed him that the guy was listed as "T. Brady." It was then that Pat grinned and asked if his "rock star status" would be enough to allow him to make an announcement to the rest of our passengers.

I kind of laughed and then asked, "What kind of announcement?" He said that he just wanted to inform all the other Pittsburgh Steelers fans onboard that the young guy who beat the Steelers in the last playoffs was up in First Class, and they should give him an appropriate "Steelers Welcome!" After assuring him that we just couldn't do that, he told me that our young guest was a relatively unknown second-year quarterback named Tom Brady. It seems that he had entered that playoff game after an injury to the Patriots starter and led them to an upset victory over the heavily favored Steelers. (Of course, no one knew then that young Mr. Brady would go on to have an amazing career and eventually would come to be regarded as maybe the best quarterback in the history of the NFL!)

April 16th-17th, 2002 - We had a really fun crew on this trip which included my buddy Dean Kroh and my favorite hilarious redhead, Jenni LaDue. (Since actress Jennifer Lopez was then familiarly known as "J. Lo," we decided to nickname our Jenni…"J. La!") We also had a great time that night at a New York City bar called "J.R.'s" and even ran into a passenger that had flown into LaGuardia with us that night. The other logbook notation I have is for the next morning, when a lady passenger decided to go into the rear lavatory right before we got ready to take off. I remember that she ignored all of our pleas to go back to her seat and so the captain had to delay our takeoff until she finally returned to her seat. Although we did not say anything more to her at the time, the rest of the crusty New Yorkers onboard loudly booed her for delaying their flight. (With all the razzing she took, I'm pretty sure that she never did that again!)

April 24th, 2002 - While on our overnight at the Marriott Marquis hotel in downtown Atlanta, we encountered a number of Arizona

Diamondbacks baseball players at the table next to us at dinner. They were so funny, especially a guy named Mark Grace. He even slid his chair over to our table when he found out that we were an airline crew, because he said we would be much more interesting to talk to! At the health club the next day, I ended up working out next to their first base coach Robin Yount, who had been a long-time star for the Milwaukee Brewers and is now in the Baseball Hall of Fame. He was also very nice to chat with.

May 2nd, 2002 - Today we had singer/actor Frankie Avalon on our Tampa- Pittsburgh flight. He was nice enough to sign an autograph for my wife who had been a huge fan of his when she was younger. Later in the day, we had a very serious hydraulic leak on our flight out of Harrisburg, Pennsylvania, which caused a four-hour delay. Because of that delay, I had to adjust my commute plans by flying into Columbus, Ohio instead. I then had to rent a car in order to drive to the Dayton Airport. I didn't make it home until 3 a.m.

May 14th-17th, 2002 - To help out my sister Sherri's elementary school classroom, I volunteered to take along a "Flat Stanley" on my trip this week. (Flat Stanley is a children's book about a character who could travel anywhere because he was flat.) For a class project, my sister had her students create and color their own Stanley. I then took one of the Stanley's along with me and took pictures of it in different cities and at well-known attractions. After he was returned, the students would then learn about all the places he went. On this particular trip, my Flat Stanley got to pose with our captain in the cockpit and up in First Class. He also got to see the beach in Tampa and tour the Las Vegas Strip.

May 20th, 2002 - Every summer since 1985, I had played on a softball team back home that included most of the local lawyers and some judges. (It was appropriately known as the "Bar Association.") Unfortunately, on this particular day I suffered a very serious knee injury when I tried to slide into third base on a play. I then suffered tears to my MCL ligament and severe damage to my ACL, and eventually had to have a long operation to try to repair everything. Consequently I had to take a "sick leave" from work for about four months. Fortunately, I had enough sick hours built up which allowed me to still collect a paycheck while I was off. Our health insurance at the time was also terrific and covered almost all costs and the physical therapy afterwards. It was only the second time in my career that I had missed more than a week or so of flying.

August 11th, 2002 - It was announced today that because of the continued downturn of our business, USAirways had filed for Chapter 11 bankruptcy protection. Basically, that meant that all the old rules and contracts were going away, and no one knew what might happen to our company or our jobs. It was very unsettling but not unexpected news.

September 19th-21st, 2002 - Today was my first trip after being off for four months. We had a long San Diego overnight which allowed me to try walking around my favorite nearby neighborhood known as "Old Town". The knee seemed to hold up pretty well.

October 2nd, 2002 - This afternoon, we had a nice flight to Los Angeles and then stayed at a hotel called the Palos Verdes Inn. It was an older but very historic hotel near the Redondo Beach area. After dinner, I got to walk the beach and again my knee seemed to do pretty well.

October 31st, 2002 - This trip included a nice long stay in Scottsdale, Arizona at a beautiful Marriott hotel. While out having dinner and drinks at an old cowboy bar called the "Rusty Spur," we also witnessed a crazy, costumed celebration for a couple who had just gotten married on Halloween.

November 6th, 2002 - Today, I experienced one of the most somber moments of my career so far. Before we could start boarding our Philadelphia-Orlando flight, we were informed that we would be transporting the casket of a fallen soldier back to his family in Florida. In a very solemn and respectful procedure, the entire ground operation in Philadelphia came to a complete stop while the military escort group transferred the soldier's casket from the hearse into the belly of our plane. Both of our pilots, who were also military veterans, went down to the tarmac and saluted the young man's casket as well.

The Army officer who was in charge of the operation, then rode with us to Orlando and once we landed, he then coordinated the transfer of the body from our plane to the waiting funeral home car. Again, in a wonderful show of respect, all ground transportation came to a complete halt and all personnel either saluted or bowed their heads in prayer. As I watched from inside the plane, I was almost moved to tears by the very touching scene.

November 7th, 2002 - While trying to land on the island of Bermuda, we encountered high winds and some serious turbulence on our approach. After two missed approaches, we were just a few minutes away from having to turn back, when the captain decided to try it one more time. This time we got in safely and the passengers gave us a loud round of applause when we finally got to the gate.

November 21st, 2002 - This was a very bad trip for our luggage. During a two-hour layover in the Philadelphia crew room, someone or something ripped the handle off my crew suitcase. If that wasn't bad enough, later in the day, two other crew members who had stored their luggage behind the last row of First-Class seats, had their travel bags "soiled" in flight. (Apparently, a young man who was waiting to use the First-Class lavatory suddenly got sick and vomited behind the last row of First-Class seats...right on their luggage!) Needless to say, despite their best efforts to clean those suitcases, we still made those crew members follow at a "safe" distance behind us for the rest of the trip.

December 21st, 2002 - After months of speculation, USAirways finally refiled for some federal loans in order to keep operating. However, there were still lots of rumors about what else may or may not happen to us.

December 27th, 2002 - I ended the year with an easy redeye trip to Phoenix, Arizona. It was also the final trip for my friend Sherry Snead who has decided to quit flying and try for a more "normal" occupation. With all the uncertainty of our current situation, I wouldn't be surprised if a lot of other flight attendants eventually choose to do the same thing.

Chapter Sixteen

2003-2004....Another Bankruptcy Sucks....
And So Does Arnie

January 6th-8th, 2003 - This was an easy Seattle redeye trip on a newly delivered Airbus-319. I was also working with my good friend Jody Compton. On that particular aircraft, our main cabin service involved two smaller, single-person carts that were used to hand out drinks and snacks. It also meant that we closely followed each other down the aisle; with each of us serving a set number of rows. As of the first of the year, we had also just changed from serving small, 12-ounce bottles of water to using larger one-liter bottles.

On this trip we had a pretty funny interaction with one of our passengers on the way out to Seattle. I was following Jody and her cart down the aisle when a young serviceman stopped her and asked if he could have a small bottle of water. In what would become our funniest moment together, Jody attempted to explain that we no longer had the smaller bottles.

However, in a completely innocent attempt to emphasize that point, she grabbed the two one-liter bottles off the top of her cart and held them chest high while explaining to the young man that,

"I don't have any small bottles. All I have are these two big jugs!"

Without any hesitation, I stifled my laughter; leaned around from my cart, and in my best cigar-wiggling, eyebrow-arching, Groucho Marx voice, told the young man,

"And isn't that really better than a bottle of water!"

He never really got the joke, but Jody did a perfect "spit-take," turned beet red, and laughed out loud for the next twenty minutes! To this day, we cannot see each other without breaking into fits of laughter!

January 28th-30th, 2003 - Another redeye trip, this time with a long layover in Los Angeles. We had a great crew of flight attendants Cathy Lazlo and Maddie Grasso, as well as a fun first officer named Jim Glick. After checking into our hotel, we agreed to meet up for a couple of frosty beverages at a bar across the street called "The Bullpen."

The entertainment that night was a one-man band, featuring a gentleman who either played guitar or saxophone to pre-recorded background music. Since there were only about six other people in the bar, we got a chance to chat with the guy in between sets and eventually my crew told him that I played in a garage band. At that point he asked me if I wanted to get up and perform with him, as well as what song I felt comfortable playing. (We settled on "Mustang Sally" with him on sax and me on guitar.) It went very well, and even though I am not a good singer, I did manage to chime in on the chorus with a robust, "Ride, Sally, Ride", which delighted my enthusiastic crew! I must not have been too bad, because the guy even told me to stop by again the next week, should I be in the neighborhood!

February 6th-7th, 2003 - This "extra" trip had me overnighting by myself for 24 hours at the beautiful Sheraton Resort on the beach in Cancun, Mexico. The hotel was fabulous, and the ocean looked amazing. However, the transportation company that was supposed to pick me up the next afternoon and take me back to the airport, failed to show up. Despite my very limited Spanish and a very strange telephone system, I did eventually secure a cab ride and was only a few minutes late getting to my plane.

February 21st, 2003 - It was 20 years ago today that I started my flight attendant training program in hopes of working for USAir. I am not sure where that time went, but it sure was entertaining! My crew even got me an anniversary card and treated me to dinner!

March 6th, 2003 - Today we had singer Englebert Humperdinck on our flight from Los Angeles to Philadelphia. He was also nice enough to autograph the birthday card that I had purchased for my mom's birthday tomorrow. (In fact, she loved it so much, that she kept that card displayed on her fireplace mantle for the next ten years!)

March 26th, 2003 - Since things were getting a little unsettled at work and no one was sure what would happen in the airline business, I decided to cover my bases and interview at my old high school for a teaching position. I hated to think about possibly leaving the airlines, but I was too young to think about retiring yet. The interview went well, but I was not offered the job.

March 28th, 2003 - Our annual recurrent training had finally been reduced to just one day of classroom education. There were five of us from our initial training class that attended recurrent together and it was great to get caught up with my friends. (And yes, we did manage to squeeze in a few games of Euchre for old time's sake!) Later that night, I caught my son's band playing at a downtown Pittsburgh nightclub. My old friends Tom Kilheeney and Wendee Wilson also showed up to hear them as well!

April 8th-11th, 2003 - For this trip, we had a really good crew that included captain Tom Campbell and flight attendant Celine DeLuca. During dinner down on Rush Street in Chicago, the captain revealed that he had been college roommates with President Bill Clinton while they were at Georgetown University. He told us how intelligent Clinton was and what a phenomenal memory he had. He also told us that he had accepted personal invitations from his old roommate to attend both of his presidential inaugurations.

The next day, I also got to go see a Chicago Cubs game at Wrigley Field. Despite it being an afternoon contest, it was a mere 40° temperature with a very gusty wind, which made for a really chilly day. Even though I wore every piece of clothing that was in my travel bag, I was still absolutely frozen during the game!

May 2nd, 2003 - My supervisor showed me a complimentary letter today from a vegetarian passenger who was on our flight from San Francisco some two weeks earlier. She was most appreciative of my efforts to find her something to eat after her vegetarian meal was not provisioned. As I recall, I gave her an apple and some oatmeal from my crew bag. I was just glad it worked out for her.

May 9th, 2003 - While on a long layover in Anaheim, California, I rode the city bus to Angel's Stadium and took in the Angel's/Blue Jays game. As we entered the ballpark, they handed out a pair of souvenir noisemakers (called thunder-sticks) to every fan. The scoreboard also featured the very unique "rally monkey" that was made famous last year when the Angels won the World Series.

June 19th, 2003 - We had a very long day today. Due to bad weather and runway congestion in Philadelphia, our plane eventually had to get out of line and return to the gate for more fuel. Our passengers were not happy at all about that.

June 26th, 2003 - Another first for my commuting legacy. Every flight to Cincinnati and Dayton all day long was oversold, so I paid for a seat on Delta in order to get home. (I hope I don't have to do that very often.)

July 1st, 2003 - While on a San Francisco layover, I took the subway over to Oakland and attended an Oakland A's baseball game. The stadium wasn't much to speak of, but the game against the Seattle Mariners was terrific. The A's won 3-2 in 11 innings.

August 14th, 2003 - In a very bizarre turn of events, much of the Northeast area of the U.S. and parts of Canada lost electric power this afternoon. Fortunately, we had departed from Washington, D.C. just before everything went haywire. The Pittsburgh airport was not affected, and I was able to catch the last flight home to Dayton. Although there were fears of terroristic sabotage, it was later found that some overgrown trees had damaged a few outdated power lines and some computer program then failed to keep it from getting worse. It took two days for air travel to return to normal levels.

August 29th, 2003 - Due to severe weather in Pittsburgh, we ended up sitting on the runway in LaGuardia for over four hours. During that time, we used up most of the ice and drink provisions, while serving our customers on the ground. That effort probably kept them placated enough to not want to riot. Our captain was also nice enough to keep giving them weather updates while we waited.

September 10th, 2003 - This trip included a great overnight at a unique hotel in Miami, Florida. The company had just started putting us up at the very classic Mayfair House in Coconut Grove. It was an old, established neighborhood hotel and featured lots of beautiful architecture. Also, every room had a hot tub on its balcony which overlooked the water. After a nice soaking while watching the sunset, I had to admit that sometimes I just love this job!

October 26th, 2003 - We had a very angry passenger on our flight from Philadelphia to Orlando who refused to check her bag after the overhead spaces had filled up. Not only did she delay our flight, but she also took a picture of the gate agent who had to come down to remove her from the flight. (For security reasons, rules forbid photography of airline staff without their permission.)

October 29th, 2003 - After checking into our hotel in downtown Albany, New York, I got to have a short conversation with a gentleman in the hotel lobby who said he was waiting for his ride to show up. Once his giant limo rolled up, I figured out why he looked familiar. It was rap star Fifty Cent!

November 11th-13th, 2003 - This was my first working trip on the Boeing 757 aircraft. During our long overnight in Las Vegas, I had dinner at the Hard Rock Hotel and then took a cab down to the Strip. I also ended up winning a whopping $12 dollars at the slot machines, which just about covered my cab rides.

December 13th-15th, 2003 - On the first day of this trip, we had a young lady who told us that she felt bad, right before she passed out. I then assisted with giving her oxygen and relaying her condition to the captain. She eventually recovered enough that we didn't have to make an emergency landing. On the last day, there was a lot of bad weather in the East which snarled air travel in Pittsburgh. To get home, I ended up flying south to Charlotte, then north to Dayton.

December 28th-30th, 2003- Unfortunately, I somehow forgot to bring my wallet on this trip, so I didn't eat much this week. Thank God for the food I had stored in my suitcase and those occasional crew meals!

January 16th, 2004 - USAirways announced today that they want a lot more cuts from all their labor groups. Things could start getting ugly really fast for all of us.

January 24th, 2004 - My logbook notes for today indicate lots of snow everywhere and very cold temperatures. Due to the bad weather, I had to spend two nights at the Pittsburgh Sheraton Hotel because it was impossible to get a flight home.

January 26th-29th, 2004 - This was a decent trip with a nice crew that included my friend Winston. On the Indianapolis-Philadelphia flight, we had a very strange passenger in First Class who wanted Winston to "warm his nuts." We couldn't decide how to interpret that, so we basically just ignored him. At the end of the trip, we encountered more bad weather and I had to stay in Pittsburgh again. I also recall thinking that if I didn't get home soon, my wife was going to forget what I looked like!

February 17th, 2004 - Another amusing logbook note which stated, "I know that I am getting older, but this is ridiculous. Today I hurt my lower back...by moving pillows in the overhead compartments!" (I don't think that I actually told anybody what really happened. It was just too embarrassing.)

March 1st, 2004 - On our flight from Pittsburgh to Providence, Rhode Island we had the University of Pittsburgh men's basketball team, the Harlem Globetrotters basketball team, and my old friend from U.D. Law School, Professor Jeff Morris. I hardly knew who to chat up first.

March 7th-9th, 2004 - A very nice three-day trip with my old housemate Sherri. While in Orlando, we took the new Hard Rock Cafe "Vault" tour. It featured some really interesting music memorabilia and the building itself was built to resemble a giant safe.

On the last day, we encountered the first group of flight attendants who will be working for USAirways' discount airline called Mid-Atlantic. That subsidiary will use smaller and cheaper planes, offer fewer amenities, and will pay their flight crews a lot less than us.

March 23rd, 2004 - While on an overnight in Scottsdale, Arizona, I had a nice visit with one of my ex-wrestlers, Jeff Duermit. We ended up going to a karaoke bar and he surprised me with a great Elvis impersonation when he sang the song "Burning Love." (If I had known he could do that when I was coaching him, I would have had him entertain the whole team!)

April 5th, 2004 - Our captain today had a bit of an attitude/ego problem and he clashed with one of the other flight attendants on several occasions. The real kicker came during our second flight, when he took off with all of us flight attendants still standing in the aisles. He then claimed that it was because of a bad P.A. system. I'm pretty sure that our senior flight attendant wrote him up for that safety violation.

April 8th, 2004 - We had a very "detail-oriented" F.A.A. inspector on our flight from Miami to Pittsburgh today. Not only did he check our Safety Manuals and I.D.s, but he also quizzed us on a number of "what if" scenarios. Although this type of inspection doesn't happen often, I really didn't mind it. It reinforced the mindset that we need to be ready for any safety-related situation at any time.

April 27th, 2004 - Toward the end of our San Francisco-Pittsburgh red-eye flight, the lady in seat 18F came back to the rear of the airplane and told me that she was missing three, $100 bills out of her purse. She described them as having three consecutive serial numbers because she had just received them from her bank. Her purse had been tucked under the seat in front of her and she had not gotten out of her seat during the flight.

Since there was nobody sitting next to her in the middle seat and nobody sitting behind her, I decided to go up front to check the flight manifest and seating charts. It turned out that the young man sitting directly in front of her in seat 17F was a 17-year-old unaccompanied minor. After considering all my options, I decided to put on my best "big brother" demeanor and I motioned to the young man to follow me to the back of the plane where my crew member, JoAnna, was standing.

There, I explained what had happened and informed him that even if he didn't have anything to do with the situation, he would probably be detained by the Pittsburgh police and thoroughly searched as well. That delay alone would also keep him from making his connecting flight. However, if the missing money somehow "magically" reappeared, then probably nothing else would happen to him. Despite his denials, I told him to return to his seat and think about the situation. Nothing else was said.

About 20 minutes before we got ready to land, the lady who was missing the money came to the back of the plane and informed us that when she woke up from her nap, there were three folded up $100 bills (with consecutive serial numbers) laying on her blanket. She then said that she was satisfied with the outcome and would not press the issue. On my way to the front of the plane, I made sure to wink at him and nod approvingly regarding this matter. (As a former teacher and coach, I always wanted to give young people a chance to rethink their actions on questionable issues. I didn't want a bad decision to negatively affect his future.) Because of this incident, I also reminded my wife every time we flew to keep her purse zippered shut and tucked between her feet so that something like this would not happen to her.

May 4th, 2004 - USAirways announced today that they would be joining the rather prestigious "Star Alliance" group. This was an association of several foreign carriers as well as some rather high-end national airlines and was designed to allow easy transfers for international travelers. With the financial mess that we were in at the time, I was a little surprised that we were allowed into that group.

June 20th, 2004 - While on a long layover in Los Angeles, I rented a bicycle and peddled from Redondo Beach to Hermosa Beach. Somewhere along the way, I passed "Late Night" host Jimmy Kimmel who was grilling out on a beachfront patio. Whatever he was cooking smelled fantastic!

June 24th, 2004 - My final trip with my friend Jody Patton, who was going to begin a three-year leave of absence and had said that she probably wouldn't be back. I also had a nice chat in the lobby of the Albany Hotel with a gentleman named Duke Fakir. I eventually found out that he was one of the singers in the band "The Four Tops." According to him, he also had a family member who worked for USAirways.

July 7th, 2004 - I got to fly from Los Angeles to Pittsburgh to LaGuardia today with one of my favorite captains, Chesley Sullenberger. He was still just the nicest guy to work with. Again, he will be discussed more in an upcoming chapter.

July 8th, 2004 - A really interesting night in San Francisco with my buddy Rich Dempsey and a very colorful captain named Arnie. During dinner at a local restaurant, Arnie shared with our crew that he liked to suck on women's toes. After being razzed by Rich and myself, he then finished off his beer and strolled over to a lady sitting at the bar. After chatting quietly with her for several minutes, he turned to us and gave us the "two-thumbs-up" sign, and then disappeared from sight. The next thing we know, the lady is squealing and slapping the bar while Arnie was apparently doing his thing. It was bizarre AND hilarious, all at the same time!

August 13th, 2004 - It was announced today that USAirways would be eliminating about 20 cities from their upcoming flight schedules in Pittsburgh. That was roughly one-third of the available flight time and meant that our work schedules would also be drastically altered. Because of that, and the extreme difficulty in commuting to work, I was then forced to seriously consider transferring to another crew base in the near future. That seemed to be a real shame because I really liked Pittsburgh.

August 21st, 2004 - After mulling over transferring to Philadelphia or Washington, D.C., I finally opted to put in for the Charlotte, North Carolina crew base; mostly because it would be the easiest place to commute to. Charlotte had been the main hub for our merger partner Piedmont, and was actually a very nice city. Today, I was awarded a transfer to Charlotte, effective November 1st. Eighteen other Pittsburgh flight attendants also decided to go there at the same time, so at least I would have a few familiar faces around me to start with!

September 6th-9th, 2004 - A very rough week due to several hurricanes off the Florida coast. Hurricane Frances hit first and severely damaged our hotel in Orlando. Despite the damage, we ended up staying there anyway. Our rooms smelled musty, and the electricity was intermittent, but apparently there were no other options. Hurricane Ivan followed soon after and forced more evacuations and cancelled many more flights.

September 12th, 2004 - USAirways announced today that they will enter into Chapter 11 bankruptcy protection for the second time in two years. The fun just never stops!

September 15th, 2004 - Apparently hurricane Ivan did not want to go away. After devastating several areas of Florida, it looped around, regained its strength, and headed for New Orleans. Along with wreaking havoc with our flight systems, this storm had also inflicted terrible property destruction and tragic loss of life.

September 21st, 2004 - My first trip on a Boeing 767. Although that plane was much larger than the aircraft I normally worked on, I was not that impressed with it. However, it did include a nice, long layover in Las Vegas, which allowed me to finally see the amazing water fountain displays in front of the Bellagio Hotel! What a great show!

October 16th, 2004 - In response to our recent corporate filing, a federal bankruptcy judge today announced 21% pay cuts for our flight attendant group. (The company had asked for a 23% pay reduction and our union had proposed a 15% cut.) That reduction is really going to put a big financial strain on a lot of us.

October 20th, 2004 - I didn't get much rest in Boston tonight. The Red Sox came back in Game #7 against the Yankees and won their playoff series to advance to the World Series. Consequently, the town was celebrating all night and decent sleep was impossible.

October 27th-30th, 2004 - This was my last Pittsburgh-based trip, and our crew included my good friend Laurie Sismour. We had a great time all week, especially during our stay in Orlando. That night we celebrated at both the Hard Rock Cafe and at Jimmy Buffett's Margaritaville. In my opinion, it was a wonderful way to close out my time in "The 'Burg."

October 29th, 2004 - The bankruptcy court awarded our pilots an 18% pay cut today, which really upset a lot of them! There were also lots of rumors going around about possible upcoming work rule changes. Nobody seemed to be happy today.

November 2nd-5th, 2004 - This was my first trip out of the Charlotte crew base. Not knowing what to expect, I commuted in early and then made my way to their crew room on the lower level of the Charlotte airport. Over the years, I had worked with a few Charlotte crews and generally speaking they were terrific. I was also aware that there would be a lot of very thick Southern accents in that crew room, but after having gone to college in the state of Kentucky, I figured I could handle that as well.

That changed quickly. As I was getting settled in at one of the crew-room tables, a very sweet Southern girl came over and stated something like...

"Mah name's Mara-lee. Ah don reck-nize yew!" (Again, it is so difficult to do vocal impressions in a print medium!)

Not sure exactly what had been said, I took a chance and replied that my name was Larry, and that I had just transferred in from the Pittsburgh base. She again sweetly replied,

"Weell... y'all certainly welcome hee-ya!....Hoosier draahver?"

Now I was really stumped. I knew that I had been asked a question, but I wasn't sure how to reply. (I do remember thinking that a "Hoosier driver" was probably a golf club made in Indiana.) Hoping that she was wondering who I was flying with, I answered with...

" Well, I believe my pilot's name is Dave."

She chuckled when she finally realized that I was having trouble comprehending the gist of conversation, so she dumbed it down and restated her question with,

"No, no....What NASCAR team do y'all support?"

Then it dawned on me. The question was the very important issue of regional sports loyalty, and she was asking..."Who's your driver?" I then replied that I hadn't settled on one yet, to which she just shook her head and walked away. I was told later that it was a good thing that I hadn't mentioned meeting driver Jeff Gordon years before. (Mr. Gordon had been nice enough to donate a signed photo for our Mike Butts fundraiser.) Evidently many southern NASCAR fans considered him a "Yankee." Yep, welcome to Charlotte Larry!

November 6th, 2004 - Through some loophole in their bankruptcy agreement, our company announced today that they will be requiring all flight crews to work an extra five hours of flight time this month. That was in addition to whatever flight hours you had already been scheduled for in the month of November. (We later sarcastically inferred that USAirways just wanted to "help" their crews get into a good mood during an already stressful holiday month!)

December 22nd, 2004 - After finishing up my trip, I had to stay in Charlotte for an extra day and a half because of a huge, winter storm over most of Ohio. I finally got a seat to Columbus and then rented a car in order to get home in time for Christmas. Apparently, commuting from Charlotte is going to be just as irritating as it was commuting from Pittsburgh.

Chapter Seventeen

2005....More Storms, Millionaire, and Another Merger

January 2nd, 2005 - Today, I picked up a one-day "holiday trip" that went in and out of Mexico City. That trip then qualified me for two, free "guaranteed passes" which would allow us to travel without the fear of being bumped off a flight. Those passes may be extremely valuable the next time Karen and I try to go on vacation.

January 5th, 2005 - After being threatened with the possibility of permanently losing our jobs, the flight attendant union reluctantly agreed to an awful contract that made our pay cuts permanent and inflicted some painful work-rule changes as well. If that wasn't bad enough, the next day, the bankruptcy judge also threw out our retirement plan and sent it to a government agency to manage. (The Pension Benefits Guarantee Corporation, also known as the PBGC) Apparently, our company will no longer deposit any funds into our retirement system and the government will decide if and when we will get any of that money upon retirement. Ouch!

January 7th, 2005 - While on a long overnight in Tampa, I got to have lunch with my mom, who was vacationing in Florida this week. If that wasn't cool enough, I also got to meet up with my high school buddy, Dan Dotson and his wife Gloria, for dinner that night!

January 12th-14th, 2005 - A really nice, three-day trip on the Boeing 757 with my friend Stacey Mosley. We had dinner at the newly renovated Hard Rock Cafe in Las Vegas and then checked out a McCormick and Schmidt's later for drinks. I also ended up giving her one of my son's latest CDs. On the last day of the trip, I again ran into my law school professor friend, Jeff Morris, who was on his way back to Dayton.

January 18th, 2005 - Today I had a passenger call me by my name, and when I didn't recognize him, he introduced himself. Mark Essex was the younger brother of a guy I wrestled with in high school and he was at Lebanon High School the year that I taught there. He was now a pilot for NetJets, which flies private and charter flights all over the world. He even volunteered to write a letter for me in case I wanted to interview with them for a flight attendant position. (With the current state of affairs at USAirways, I may have to consider looking into that possibility.)

February 12th, 2005 - I was very fortunate today and got to work the inaugural flight between Charlotte and the Caribbean nation of Barbados. My crew included one of my favorite captains, Mike Ryan, as well as flight attendants Katie O'Donoghue and Bernard Epps. There was a very nice ceremony for us when we landed in Barbados, and we even got to meet their Prime Minister. It was also the first time that I got to work the "Duty Free" cart. That program allowed us to sell "Duty Free" items (ie. liquor, perfumes, candy) to our passengers, as part of USAirways' new international service program.

February 15th, 2005 - Our crew had to deadhead from Philadelphia to Manchester today. It was my first time deadheading since the new contract went into effect. What was once a fully paid flight was now worth 50% less AND those flight hours did not count toward your monthly flight obligation. (I also recall thinking that since I was being screwed, I should have at least have been offered a cigarette afterwards!)

February 21st, 2005 - Today, I got to "enjoy" some more contract changes. We spent the whole day in Airbus-330 training, and instead of getting our usual 6-8 hours of flight pay, we were paid a mere $60 total, with no flight hour credit at all. (To use another sexual metaphor, there was again, no offer of a cigarette...and this time, no type of lubrication either!)

March 18th, 2005 - This was a nice, easy day at our annual recurrent training with my old housemates Sherri Perfett and Scott Parks, as well as training classmate, Dave Marchetti. The only sad news was that Sherri had decided to quit at the end of June; mostly because of the reduced flying time in the Pittsburgh base. Because of all the contract changes, I consider her another work-related casualty.

March 31st, 2005 - This evening, we had singer/comedian Dick Smothers on our flight from Charlotte to Buffalo. (He and his brother Tom had hosted a comedy series on CBS in the 1960s.) He was a very nice man to chat with and seemed to be very intelligent.

April 11th-14th, 2005 - A very interesting Airbus-319 trip with my crew of Kim Larson and Donna Barron. On the first day, we had a young man on our Philadelphia-San Diego flight who was completely unresponsive. Because we couldn't seem to wake him up, the captain decided to execute a medical emergency landing in Pittsburgh to get him to a hospital. The paramedics guessed that he may have taken some pills, so they took him off on a stretcher. However, once out on the jetway, he awoke and then became very argumentative when he figured out where he was. He also refused any more medical treatment and then decided he wanted to stay there in Pittsburgh.

If that wasn't enough, when we finally arrived about two hours late in San Diego, the hotel told us their van driver was sick and that we would have to take a couple of taxis to get there. That didn't seem like much of a problem...until one of the cabs took part of our crew to the wrong hotel! It was about 4 a.m. before all of us finally got checked in.

Although we were very tired from that first day, our second day was relatively easy. We then had 32 hours off in Toronto, so three of us decided to rent a car and go see Niagara Falls from the Canadian side. Finally, on our last day, we finished up with my first trip in and out of the Turks and Caicos Islands. The view of the incredibly blue waters and the bright green vegetation made me want to add this place to my list of vacation possibilities.

April 29th, 2005 - USAirways announced today that they lost $791 million dollars during the first quarter of the year. That led to rampant speculation that they may be looking for a merger partner soon. We have heard that either America West or Delta is a possibility.

May 3rd, 2005 - My first trip with a very colorful flight attendant named Shugie. She was sweet and sassy and had some outrageous stories to share. Among other things, she claimed to be personal friends with singer Willie Nelson, and that she had sung on stage at the Grand Ole Opry in Nashville.

May 17th, 2005 - There were more rumors around today of a possible merger with America West Airlines. Some said that we would buy them, and others claim that they would be buying us. As they say on television..."Stay tuned!"

May 19th, 2005 - It was officially announced this morning: America West and USAirways would indeed merge, effective this fall. As I understood it, we would keep the USAirways colors and logo branding, but America West's management team (led by then 39-year-old wunderkind Doug Parker) would actually run the airline. This was the first airline merger since the attacks of 9/11 and would eventually lead a lot of consolidation within the industry. From what we understood, there was also a lot of investment capital from outside sources that funded this transaction. Apparently, no one airline bought the other.

June 1st, 2005 - There were extensive delays in Charlotte today after the Charlotte control tower's radio went out. It took most of the day to get things back to "normal," if there is such a thing in the airline industry anymore.

June 9th, 2005 - There was a near-tragedy this afternoon in Boston. According to the reports, an Aer Lingus flight took off on an intersecting runway and just barely missed hitting our USAirways flight that was taxiing out also. Evidently our plane went under their plane, missing a collision by about 60 feet. It was reported that our first officer noticed what was going on and kept the captain from actually lifting off, which would have caused a terrible crash. We found out later that two different air traffic controllers were unaware of the other's plane.

July 13th, 2005 - I met a very nice passenger today named Michelle, who was a congressional aide to Utah Senator Bob Bennett. She gave me her business card and told me if I was ever in Washington, D.C., to contact her. She also said she could get me a behind-the-scenes tour of the White House and the Senate chambers. Although I never did end up taking advantage of her offer, I still retained her card. Michelle will also be mentioned again in an upcoming chapter.

July 27th-30th, 2005 - On the first night of this trip, I got a chance to take in a baseball game at the newly opened Safeco Field in Seattle. It was a beautiful park and even had one section of seats where you could see five of the seven mountain peaks that were in the area. The next night we had a 24-hour stay in Bermuda at the very chic Hamilton Princess Hotel. On the way back to the airport the next day, our van driver took a little detour and gave us a wonderful, guided tour of the entire island. Finally, on the last day, we finished up with flights in and out of the beautiful Central American country of Belize.

August 1st-4th, 2005 - Prior to starting this trip, I had to really scramble when my Dayton commuter flight cancelled at the last minute, and I was forced to drive like a maniac to the Cincinnati airport to get to work on time. However, once at work, the trip turned out to be a lot of fun. During our long layover in Syracuse, I decided to rent a car and go see the Baseball Hall of Fame in nearby Cooperstown, New York. The museum was amazing and, for a baseball fan like me, it was definitely a great way to spend a day.

August 7th, 2005 - After years of trying to qualify for the game show "Who Wants To Be a Millionaire?" I finally was invited to fly to New York and attend a group tryout. Hopefully, all this trivia that I have stored in my brain will eventually help me make a little money!

August 10th, 2005 - Conveniently, I had most of this week off, so I used my travel passes and flew to New York City to attend my tryout for "Who Wants To Be a Millionaire?" I had to be at the ABC Television Studios by 1 p.m. and ready for auditions by 1:30 p.m. After filling out questionnaires and other paperwork, we started the day with a 30-question, multiple-choice test, that quizzed us on a wide variety of subjects. Afterwards, I recalled feeling pretty good about most of my answers. However, I had to admit that I had no idea what woman's accessory Kate Spade was famous for. (It turned out to be women's purses.)

We were told that there were 240 of us to start with, but after the tests were graded, they dismissed about 200 people. (Apparently, I did well enough to survive that cut.) We then had to take part in a pretend game which I also felt pretty good about. After some deliberation, the panel of judges and producers made some more cuts, and I was fortunate enough be one of the twelve that survived. We then were asked to stand

and talk about ourselves, which after years of teaching and being a flight attendant, was not a problem for me either. In fact, when we were asked about the most interesting person that we had ever met, I had them spellbound with my tale of watching boxer Muhammad Ali levitate.

At the end of the day, out of the original 240, myself and another guy named Kevin were chosen to be in the "contestant pool." That meant that we could be called with very little notice and asked to be in New York within a day or so. (I also think that I made a favorable impression on them when I reminded them that I fly for free, therefore saving them the cost of a ticket.) Additionally, they said that we might not get called right away, and that our eligibility was good for up to two years. The real problem was that for the next few months, I couldn't just read a newspaper or watch a television program without thinking, "Hey, that could be a possible "Millionaire" question. I better remember that." (To this day, my brain is still crammed with a lot of trivial information; much to the dismay of my very tolerant wife.)

August 16th, 2005 - On our flight today from Newark to Charlotte, we had professional wrestler "Nature Boy" Ric Flair and his son up in First Class. Fortunately for us, Mr. Flair was much more low-keyed than his normally effusive wrestling personality. I was also impressed when I found out that his son had been a New Jersey high school state wrestling champion as well.

August 29th, 2005 - Our trip to New Orleans this week was cancelled because of the extremely destructive hurricane Katrina. As you may recall, that storm severely damaged most of the state of Louisiana. In fact, the flooding and destruction was so devastating that our flights were unable to resume there for the next couple of weeks.

September 27th, 2005 - Today, USAirways emerged from bankruptcy protection and officially merged with America West to form the fifth largest U.S. airline. Hopefully that means that things will eventually start to settle down and work will become a little easier for us.

September 28th, 2005 - For the first time since the "Alice Cooper" game in 1994, I had a nice, long overnight in Montreal. That city always had a very European feel to it, and I loved checking out some of the great shops and restaurants. The only negative aspect of the trip was that I purchased a beautiful men's necktie, but didn't realize that the

Canadian exchange rate was much different than the last time I was there. Although I didn't notice it before we left the country, that simple tie cost me over 50 U.S. dollars! (However, some 20 years later, I still have that tie so I may have gotten my money's worth after all.)

October 19th, 2005 - Today we had actress and "Saturday Night Live" alum Molly Shannon on our flight from Charlotte to Newark. She was traveling with her children and was very polite and personable.

October 21st, 2005 - Unfortunately, we encountered another problem with another storm during this incredibly long hurricane season. My friends and I were attempting to have a boys weekend down in Tampa at our friend Dan Dotson's place, but had to cancel at the last minute when hurricane Wilma threatened to hit Florida.

October 30th, 2005 - This trip was originally scheduled to have a long layover in Cancun, Mexico this week. However, due to damage from hurricane Wilma, those flights were canceled and we overnighted in Charlotte instead.

November 1st-4th, 2005 - A really nice, four-day trip with the Newcome sisters: Cindy and her sibling Karin. Because we all attended Eastern Kentucky University at about the same time, we had a lot to talk about. On the second day, we also had a very strange reason for a delayed departure out of Philadelphia. It seemed that we had to wait awhile for our jet fuel to be delivered, because the fuel truck itself (true story) ...ran out of gas!

November 15th-18th, 2005 - A very, very long first day. Due to bad weather, we had numerous delays all day, and I ended up being on my feet for over 21 hours. Fortunately, we had a late afternoon departure from Philadelphia the next day, so I slept in until noon, but I still didn't feel rested. On the third day we had another Philadelphia overnight, which gave me a chance to have dinner with my brilliant law school friend Kevin McNulty. I shared with him that I might be appearing on "Millionaire" and wondered if he would entertain the possibility of being one of my "Phone-A-Friend" options. (He did say he would consider it.) I had also considered adding my 80-year-old mother, a former math teacher, to that list. Despite her reservations about not remembering things, she still knew instantaneously what a dodecahedron was. (It's a 12-sided geometric figure.)

December 7th, 2005 - I had to stay in Charlotte in between trips, so I ended up having dinner with one of my old high school buddies, Scott Flint. Scott is still living in our hometown but is now working a few days a week in the Charlotte area. He and I have known each other since we were 12 years old.

December 14th-15th, 2005 - While the rest of the U.S. was freezing, I got to enjoy the only warm spot around, which was West Palm Beach, Florida. I also had lunch at Pete Rose's baseball-themed restaurant the next day. Unfortunately, we then encountered some lengthy delays while trying to get into Charlotte after a major ice storm hit the city. Because of that icing, I didn't get home for another day and a half.

Chapter Eighteen

2006....A Giant Slice of Meat Loaf

January 13th, 2006 - This was my first trip in and out of San Jose, Costa Rica. Since many of the passengers on board spoke highly of both the city and the country, I may have to pick up a trip with an overnight there, just to see what it's all about.

January 17th-18th, 2006 - We had engine problems on the taxi out from Newark and consequently had to return to the gate. We then had to wait several hours just to get a mechanic to look at it and eventually they cancelled the flight. After another couple of hours, they fixed the engine and then had us ferry the plane to Charlotte. While we were sitting around, I found out that our captain had flown the rock band "Led Zepplin" around the country during a couple of their tours. (He just chuckled and neither confirmed OR denied some of the crazy Led Zepplin rumors that we asked him about.)

March 6th-9th, 2006 - This was a good four-day Airbus trip with captain Ed Terry. He is also a musician who favors old cowboy music and almost always brings his guitar along on his trips. He also showed us a hilarious video of his favorite horse coming over to meet him at the corral gate. That horse then mouths Ed's coffee mug and chugs down the coffee. (Ed calls him his "Maxwell Horse!")

April 5th-7th, 2006 - On the first day of this trip I severely lacerated my ring finger on something sharp in the rear galley. Fortunately, I had a three-hour layover in Philadelphia, so I went to the company doctor and he bandaged me up, which allowed me to stay on the trip. On the second night of the trip, we stayed for the first time at a hotel located in

Tempe, Arizona called the Twin Palms. It was an older building with very poor air conditioning and limited amenities. (In fact, it was so bad that the America West crews had nicknamed it the "Sweaty Palms!")

April 11th, 2006 - Because I needed a little extra flight time this month, I decided to accept a relatively rare (for me anyway) one-day trip and the even more rare "Senior" or "A" position as well. It couldn't have worked out better! The first bonus was that I got to fly with my old Pittsburgh friend, captain John Taylor, who had hosted that great Halloween party mentioned in Chapter Four. Although I had not seen him lately, his humor still made me laugh out loud on just about every flight. The second bonus was what turned out to be one of my very favorite days and one of my very favorite stories so far.

We had started the day with a relatively short flight from Charlotte to Myrtle Beach and had about an hour layover before turning around and heading back to Charlotte. Since I was the "A" flight attendant, the Myrtle Beach gate agent came down a little early to alert me to the fact that my First Class was going to be completely full. He also wanted to know if he could board that group a little bit early. He then informed me that there had been some sort of celebrity golf tournament the day before, and that a lot of those celebrities would be seated in my First-Class area. I told him that I didn't mind boarding early if it helped things go smoother.

Anyway, once our First-Class group started to board, I did in fact recognize a few familiar faces. Among them was actor Anthony Anderson, who would later go on to star in the ABC television series "Black-ish." I also noticed a musician named Travis Barker, who was the tattooed drummer from the band "Blink-182." Additionally, the gentleman who was sitting in seat 1C looked somewhat familiar, but I just couldn't place him at the time.

After we completed the boarding process, I finally got a chance to look at my seating chart and saw my passenger in 1C was listed as Michael Aday. Now maybe it was my recent surge of trivia loading while getting prepared for going on "Millionaire," or maybe just years and years of being a music fan, but for whatever reason, I recalled that Michael Aday was the real name of the actor and singer...Meat Loaf!

What had also stumped me when I first looked at him, was that for most of his career, Meat Loaf had been a very large man with an approximate weight of maybe around 300 pounds. This gentleman was a nice trim 220-230 pounds and consequently his face wasn't as round, which gave him a slightly different look.

Once I realized that it was in fact Meat Loaf, I remember wondering if I should address him as "Meat", or possibly even "Mr. Loaf?" Rather than risk offending him, I just started out with the basic first question,

"Sir, what would you like to drink?" (It was tomato juice.)

After fetching his drink, I decided to break the ice with a simple question that most golfers like to discuss,

"So, how did you do in this golf tournament that you were in?"

His face brightened and he happily replied that he actually played "pretty well this weekend!" What was hilarious was the other First Class passengers' responses upon hearing him say that. Several of them either laughed out loud or booed him, while the guy across the aisle actually threw his drink napkin at him. That passenger also stated that Mr. Loaf's poor golf skills had cost him "a lot of money!"

After delivering the rest of the first-class drinks and enjoying the somewhat jovial atmosphere of this particular group, I decided to try conversing with Meat Loaf. I began with a relatively simple request, and wondered if it would be okay to ask him a "musical question." He laughed and shrugged his shoulders and said "Sure!" I then told him that my son was in a pretty good band and was touring and making some money but hadn't yet been signed to a recording contract. My question then was,

"So how did you get started in the music business?"

Again, he chuckled, and his face lit up as he replied, "It's actually a pretty good story if you want to hear it." After another quick check of my other passengers, I told him I would love to hear his tale!

According to him, Meat Loaf left his hometown of Dallas, Texas, and moved to Los Angeles around 1968. After some occasional work in a rock band and one album that he said was for the most part ignored, he then moved to New York City. It was there that he caught his first real "break" by being cast in the original Broadway production of the the musical "Hair."

Hearing that, I agreed that it was indeed a fortunate break for him. He then looked at me and asked if I had any idea how much money he was making back then. Somewhat surprised by the question, I replied that I had no idea, but I imagined that it was a lot. Meat Loaf then snickered and let me know that his pay for doing six shows a week was a mere $25 per week. He even said that he was so poor that he was forced to share a small, New York apartment with seven other guys!

Mr. Loaf then inquired as to whether I was at all familiar with the play "Hair," to which I think I said something vague like "sort of." He went on to explain that the play was all about Hippies and their music and even featured one scene where all the actors appeared naked. Evidently that made it rather unique, in that full nudity had never been done before in a Broadway play. Meat Loaf then explained that the nude scene was strictly voluntary, but if you did in fact take off your clothes, you got an extra $30 a week in your paycheck. He also admitted that because they were so poor, everyone in the cast usually accepted the offer to sing in the buff!

Now, a few people will grudgingly admit to letting their imaginations wander while hearing a good story. In this case, I was one of those people. Although I continued to smile and nod my head during his tale, my mind did in fact start to picture what that scene must have looked like. (Truthfully, the image of a 350-pound Meat Loaf naked on stage was a little unsettling.) In fact, I even imagined a situation where I was the play director and offered Meat the sum of $40 per week...just to keep his clothes on! (Of course, I never told him that, but it did cross my mind!)

Meanwhile, Meat Loaf continued to entertain us by telling us about life on Broadway in the late 60s and early 70s. At this point, I also realized that he was such a good storyteller, that all other conversations in First Class had ceased and every guest was now listening to this amazing fable. Some were even leaning out of their seats or sitting up on the armrests, just so they wouldn't miss out on any of the details.

After the "Hair" story was completed, for some reason my "history teacher" brain kicked in and I felt compelled to ask him if he was living in Dallas around the time that President Kennedy was assassinated. My intention was only to pick the brain of someone who may have had a bit of familiarity with a very significant historical incident. There was no way that I could have known that my little query would open the door to another amazing Meat Loaf anecdote. In fact, upon hearing my question, his eyes got really wide, and he leaned forward in his seat to seriously inquire if I wanted to hear another of his stories. I could only nod my head and enthusiastically utter the words…"Of course!"

This tale began with Mr. Loaf informing us that in November of 1963, he was a junior in high school. When he and his friends heard that President Kennedy was coming to Dallas, they decided that they wanted to go see him. However, with November 22nd falling on a school day, they also realized that they would have to skip class in order to see any of the parade.

He then explained that what complicated the situation was that he and his friends played football for a "crazy" coach, and should they miss any part of practice, that coach would make them runs laps until they dropped. So, while they didn't care about missing school, it was really in their best interests to be back in time for football practice. With that in mind, they hopped into one of their cars and drove to Dallas' Love Field to see if they could catch the arrival of the president's plane. According to the story, they did get to the airport in time and were even lucky enough to have President Kennedy wave to them!

Apparently, that experience wasn't enough, because they then decided to drive into downtown Dallas to catch the presidential motorcade that would wind through the middle of town. However, as they got closer to the downtown area, the traffic congestion got worse, and they eventually ended up idling in their car while waiting to find a place to park. Meat Loaf then related that it was at that point that… "All hell broke loose!"

According to his tale, suddenly there were lots of sirens going off and people were panicking and running past their car, screaming and crying. Meat and his friends looked at each other and wondered out loud about what was going on. In the midst of the panic, some guy wearing a black suit, a thin black tie, and one of those early versions of a radio earpiece, came running up to their car. He then put some sort of a large, official-looking badge on their windshield and ordered them to,

"Scoot over boys! I need to commandeer your car!" At this point, Meat Loaf said they were rather dumbfounded by all the confusion and merely replied,

"Uh, okay... I guess??"

Meat Loaf then surmised that, based on how he was dressed, the guy might have been either with the FBI, or perhaps the Secret Service. Whoever he was, he then drove like (and I quote Meat Loaf's very own iconic words here) a "bat out of hell" to of all places, Parkland Hospital. No words were spoken during the short drive, but Mr. Loaf did say that there were a lot of worried looks exchanged between the three friends.

Evidently, they arrived at the hospital within a few minutes. After coming to a screeching halt in a space near the emergency entrance, the guy in the black suit then sternly told the boys to not move their car because he might need it again shortly. As he jumped out of the car, he also warned them not to leave until he told them that it was allowed. At this point in the story, Meat Loaf then laughed and admitted again that the best reply they could come up with was the still dumbfounded,

"Uh...okay?"

After a brief discussion about what they could or should do, they eventually decided to turn on the car radio to find out what was happening. It was at that point that they first heard reports that President Kennedy had been shot. About the time that horrible reality set in on them, Meat Loaf told us that the boys looked up in time to see the presidential motorcade, with lights flashing and sirens wailing, pull into the hospital emergency lane.

If you recall, that black limo carried not only the wounded President Kennedy, but also the First Lady Jackie Kennedy and Texas Governor John Connally, who had also been shot. That vehicle then pulled up and stopped...right in front of the hood of the boys' car! Although Meat Loaf said the limo couldn't have paused there for more than 10 or 15 seconds, it was enough time for them to witness the blood stains on the car and on Mrs. Kennedy's iconic pink suit.

Meat Loaf also recalled for us, the very confused and distressed looks on the faces of the security officers that were there at that time. He also said that after what seemed like an eternity, the limo gradually moved closer to the Emergency Room doors and eventually out of their sight.

At this point in the story, I suddenly realized that I was standing in front of the entire First-Class group with my mouth completely open in utter amazement! The rest of my guests were also gasping in disbelief or about ready to fall out of their seats. Someone then asked Meat Loaf about what thoughts were going through his mind at that time.

" Well," he stated rather sheepishly, "Sadly, it wasn't anything like, "Oh my God, our President has been shot." He then indicated that it was more along the lines of,

"Oh my God, we are going to miss football practice and our coach is going to kill us!" (We all just broke up laughing!)

Mr. Loaf then grudgingly admitted that, after all, they were all just 16 years old at the time and really didn't know any better. However, realistically that was indeed what they were most worried about.

Eventually, it was announced on their car radio that President Kennedy has passed away. Soon after that, the gentleman in the black suit came back out to their car. He then thanked the boys for the use of their car and informed them that they were indeed free to go. In fact, he even offered to give them some money to cover the gasoline that they had used getting to the hospital.

Meat Loaf then recalled that although the three friends had not really discussed it, all three answered him at the same time with the same concern. They all told him that they really didn't want his gas money, but instead wondered if he could write some sort of note to their football coach explaining the situation. The boys claimed that there was no way the coach would ever believe what had happened to them. It was only then that the very serious expression on the face of the agent softened somewhat. Apparently, he then told the boys that if they gave him a little information about the coach and the school, he would..."see what he could do."

Well, evidently by the time the three boys had driven back to their high school, the agent had called and talked with the coach about what had happened and how the guys had inadvertently been involved. The coach then must have let that story leak because Meat Loaf told us that as soon as they pulled up to the front of their school, everybody there came pouring out of the building and surrounded their car. (In fact, for the rest of their time at that school, they were considered local heroes!) The coach also informed them that they were forgiven for missing practice and that no "penalty laps" would be assigned!

At that point, I remember looking out the window and realizing that we were getting close to our final approach into Charlotte. I had just enough time to thank Meat Loaf for the wonderful stories, pick up all the drink glasses, and get the cabin ready for landing. Just as I was preparing to get into my jump seat, I saw Mr. Loaf lean forward and peer into the front galley. He then pointed to the paperwork hanging on a galley clip and wondered if that was the seating chart for this particular flight.

When I told him that it was indeed the seating chart, he then asked me to bring it over to him. Since we were really close to landing, I hurriedly handed it over, and said I would retrieve it from him after we got to the gate.

After I made the arrival announcement and eventually opened the front door, Meat Loaf got up out of his seat and handed the seat chart back to me. It was then that I noticed that he had autographed the page to my son with the inscription, "Brian, Keep on Rockin'! Meat Loaf." He told me to be sure to give it to my son and also offered his best wishes to him for a successful music career. What a great guy!

I then decided to keep the autograph secretly hidden from my son until I could get it framed up for a birthday present. On his birthday, I remember him carefully unwrapping the gift and after realizing what it was, uttered the words, "Meat Loaf...Cool!" He then leaned over and quietly asked me, "So, who exactly is Meat Loaf?"

I then chuckled and related my unbelievable interaction with him, as well as his two wonderful stories. (Brian was open-mouthed as well by the end of the tale.) To this day, he still has that framed seat chart hanging in his room. It became even more poignant after Meat Loaf passed away in early 2022 as I was working on this book.

May 10th, 2006 - This was a really nice day in Las Vegas, because I got to watch an episode of the HBO series "Entourage" being filmed inside the Hard Rock Hotel. I also got a chance to check out the brand new Palms Hotel that had recently opened.

May 15th-18th, 2006 - A really fun trip with my new flight attendant friends Connie Agee, Earl Bunn, and Karen Patrick. We had a great lunch at a rooftop restaurant on the pier in St. Petersburg, Florida. Later, we also enjoyed drinks and dinner by the hotel pool.

Evidently, the local high school seniors were also celebrating their last day of school, because every car that passed by us had kids chanting, "2006! 2006!"

August 8th-10th, 2006 - A very nice three-day trip with my musician friend captain Ed Terry and a hilarious flight attendant named Lyn Smith. After getting checked into our hotel in Tempe, Arizona, (the previously mentioned establishment known derisively as the "Sweaty Palms") the three of us agreed to meet up in the hotel bar for a few frosty beverages. When we saw there was no one else in the place, Ed decided to go back upstairs and bring down his acoustic guitar. We then ended up sitting around that bar for a time while he and I played quite a few songs. The highlight was Ed performing the most beautiful version of the Eagles' song "Desperado" that I have ever heard. It was a very fun night!

Also, after a couple of months of ignoring the Company's offer to hand out applications for their new USAirways credit card, I finally relented and agreed to give it a try. Apparently, we will earn $50 dollars for every application that gets approved. Some friends of mine have been making an extra $1,000-$2,000 a month by doing it. That would be very nice, but I still feel it would be an imposition on our passengers.

August 10th-11th, 2006 - During this trip, a lot of delays were posted because of a huge change in security procedures in England. Due to some very severe restrictions on what English officials allowed in passenger carry-on baggage, (i.e., no fluids, creams, or pastes) there were delays of up to six hours posted for some international flights. Consequently, that ripple effect had spilled over into some of our domestic flights as well.

September 29th, 2006 - Today, we had a bit of a problem with a passenger on our Raleigh-Durham to Philadelphia flight. The guy claimed I rudely poked him in the shoulder when in reality, I only lightly touched his shoulder in order to get his attention. It seems that he decided to ignore the rule about cell phone usage during the safety demo and the taxi out to the runway. After he ignored me twice, I touched his shoulder to remind him that unless he ended his call, we were going back to the gate. He finally turned his phone off and stowed it, but not before he uttered some obscenities at me under his breath. Throughout my career, I had always tried to stay "above the fray" and not take bad passenger behavior personally. (However, when a fellow crew member coined the term "ass-hat," regarding our problem child, I couldn't help but snicker, mostly because it just seemed appropriate.)

October 31st, 2006 - For the first and only time in my career, our crew members were allowed to dress up in Halloween costumes for the day. I opted to go with a pirate costume; complete with an eye patch and chocolate gold coins for the kids.

November 1st, 2006 - While in Washington, D.C. on our overnight, I finally got to go check out the Vietnam Veteran's Wall Memorial. What an amazing (and somewhat solemn) historical display! It really caused you to appreciate the sacrifices those soldiers made for our country. If you have never seen it, please take some time while in Washington to experience this exhibit.

November 8th, 2006 - On our flight from Los Angeles-Philadelphia, we had singer Engelbert Humperdinck (again) and actor Billy Dee Williams up in First Class. They were both very nice. I also made sure to thank Mr. Humperdinck again for signing my mom's birthday card a few years back. (He just laughed when I told him that she still had it up on the fireplace mantle!) Mr. Williams had just had knee surgery and I got a chance to chat with him at the end of the flight while waiting for his wheelchair to arrive.

November 15th, 2006 - USAirways announced today that they want to buy Delta Airlines for something like a gazillion dollars. Delta, of course, scoffed at the idea. We shall see what happens.

December 18th-20th, 2006 - This trip was my first time on an America West route. We flew from Phoenix to Las Vegas to Ft. Lauderdale and everything went very well. On the second day of the trip, I had another unbelievable coincidence happen to me.

Just before leaving for this trip, I had been assembling a shadow box of memorabilia from my son's favorite band "Metallica." It was going to be a Christmas present, and it looked pretty nice after I got it all finished. However, I had lamented to my wife that what it really needed was some autographs of the band members to make it complete.

Well...strangely enough, on our flight to San Francisco, who should be in First Class but former Metallica bassist Jason Newsted! Once I got a chance to speak with him, he was nothing but gracious, and agreed to provide an autograph. When my son finally opened his gift on Christmas day, he then just shook his head in amazement, especially after I related this particular story to him. (I still can't believe it either!)

December 19th, 2006 - Today, Delta formally rejected USAirways' offer to purchase them. Apparently, a gazillion dollars just wasn't enough money!

December 28th-30th, 2006 - While on a long layover in Albany, New York, I got a chance to take in their annual Winter Festival. It was a terrific event and featured ice sculptures, a planetarium show, several Elvis tribute artists, and a great fireworks display! It was also my final trip of 2006.

Chapter Nineteen

2007-2008....Big Dudes, Blair, and Bowie

January 10th, 2007 - USAirways announced that they have increased their bid for Delta Airlines from 8.5 billion to 10 billion dollars. For a company that claims to be losing money, that seems like an awfully extravagant offer!

January 31st, 2007 - After careful consideration, Delta once again turned down our bid to purchase their airline. One of their lower-ranking officials was even quoted as saying that she wouldn't be caught dead in a USAirways uniform. (Ouch!)

February 6th-8th, 2007 - I worked a three-day "extra" trip with 34 hours off in Hartford, Connecticut. Since I was on my own, I ended up renting a car and driving to a nearby casino which was about 20 minutes away. Although I am not a gambler, I did win a few dollars at the slot machines. I also got to see a free concert by blues guitarist Johnny Winter. Even though he was by then almost totally blind, he still played well and sounded terrific. (Unfortunately, my friend Jody's ex-husband was not playing drums on that particular night.)

February 22nd, 2007 - While in Charlotte, I got a chance to see a presentation of some possible new flight attendant uniforms. I don't remember exactly what they looked like but the notation in my logbook for that day just says, "Yuck!" (Evidently others felt the same way because management only tweaked the current uniforms and basically kept them the same for the next few years.)

March 3rd, 2007 - Today we had a full day of "Merger Integration Training." It was a rather boring class built around a few procedural changes and a look at a new reservations system. I attended with my friend Shawn Hallmark whose great sense of humor at least kept me entertained all day!

March 5th, 2007 - The new reservations system started up today and it created quite a mess. We had lots of disgruntled passengers who complained to us about previously delayed or cancelled flights. My own crew personally experienced two delays while waiting for additional passengers to arrive, as well as one cancelled flight. I hope this situation gets better soon.

March 23rd, 2007 - Hmm...maybe this credit card application thing isn't so bad after all. I handed out over fifty of them in just two days, and ended up making an additional $1,200 for the month of March. (Woo-Hoo!)

March-May 2007 - Looking back on my logbook notes, I see that it was an absolutely horrendous three-month stretch for commuting to and from work. Four weeks in a row, I had to fly into Columbus, Ohio and then rent a car to get home. There were also five occasions that I had to ride the spare jump seat on a flight because all seats were full. Additionally, I also had to spend several nights in Charlotte because no flights were available to either Cincinnati, Dayton, or Columbus. (I must not be the only commuter experiencing these problems, because I have noticed other fellow commuters in our crew room having the same spasms and twitches as me!)

May 31st, 2007 - On our flight from Charlotte to Chicago we had to deal with two drunk women who started screaming at each other. Fortunately, my old teaching trick of separating them by re-seating them worked again. (I also then wondered if our potential new uniforms shouldn't include some sort of black-and-white striped referee's shirt, that could be worn just for situations like that!)

June 5th, 2007 - This afternoon, we stayed at a nice new Radisson Hotel near Santa Monica, California, which gave me the opportunity to walk on their beach. I also eventually made it over to nearby Venice Beach and checked out all the colorful characters that were there. It was a very entertaining day.

June 28th, 2007 - While trying to depart from Phoenix today, we twice had to return to the gate because the extreme heat (110°) kept us from safely taking off. The captain then had to explain to our customers that the heat interferes with getting the proper amount of lift under the plane's wings. We were delayed a little over four hours.

July 12th, 2007 - I worked the same trip this week and we had the same problem while trying to leave Phoenix again. Although it was hotter than the last time (112°) it cooled off faster and we only experienced a two-hour delay.

July 30th, 2007 - While working a through flight that was originally supposed to fly from Jacksonville, Florida to Washington, D.C., to Providence, Rhode Island, we experienced a series of air-traffic delays which made us a few hours late. The problem was that because the Washington National Airport is in the middle of a large residential area, it has a very strict 10 p.m. curfew for arriving flights. Because we were so late, we were not allowed to land in Washington. Instead, we were forced to do what is known as an "over-fly" and instead of stopping in Washington, we went straight to Providence. A lot of our passengers were not very happy about that.

August 15th, 2007 - Well, my two-year eligibility for being on "Who Wants To Be a Millionaire?" is up and sadly, I never got the call to be on the show. I can only assume that either they thought I was just too smart and would have won the million-dollar prize...OR maybe it's that I am just too pretty for television?? (It will be tough, but I can live with either of those stigmas.)

August 24th, 2007 - While on a short layover on Grand Cayman Island, I went into the Duty-Free shop and ended up purchasing a bottle of local rum. It was named after an escaped slave named Richard who later became a well-known local pirate. It was called "Big Black Dick." Although the rum itself was just alright, the humorous moniker made it worth having in my personal home bar; just so I could fluster my wife's friends when they came over.

September 20th, 2007 - Because of some sort of union issue with the combined pilot's seniority list after the merger, the USAirways pilots have been pushing for a walkout or a short strike. (Apparently some court ruling gave more junior America West pilots a chance to advance faster than more senior USAirways pilots.) If anything does happen, it could be as early as tomorrow.

September 21st, 2007 - Again we were fortunate because the pilots decided to postpone their walkout. Therefore, we experienced no disruption to our flights today. However, in a way, I wished we had been cancelled. On our last flight of the day, while simply pushing the drink cart up the aisle, I felt a painful, sizzling sensation in my surgically repaired right knee. My knee immediately became swollen and I was barely able to limp back to the rear galley.

It turned out that I had torn the meniscus. Although I was barely able to finish the flight, I did eventually make it home. After a series of X-rays and MRIs, the doctors concluded that no more surgery was needed. However, I would be off work for the next several months to let it heal. The really embarrassing part occurred when my friends asked about how I was hurt. Rather than admit to being damaged while pushing a cart, I led some of them to think that I was actually grappling with a terrorist up in First Class when I was injured.

December 4th-6th, 2007 - My first trip back after being off for ten weeks. The knee seemed to hold up pretty well, but there was a little swelling, so I did have to ice it up every evening.

December 12th, 2007 - In another strange coincidence, I was surprised to see my old high school friend Terry Bussell and his wife on our flight from Las Vegas to Charlotte. He and I had worked together on my father's farm and also wrestled together our senior year. I believe he is the fifth or sixth fellow classmate that I have had on my flights over the years.

December 19th, 2007 - Oops, I spoke too soon. Today I ran into another high school classmate and fellow wrestling alumnus, Duane Pandorf. He is now a captain with NetJets and was just passing through Charlotte when we met up in the Charlotte Airport food court. He also said he could put in a good word for me with his company if I ever felt the need to look for work somewhere else.

December 20th, 2007 - Today I got to work my first professional-sports charter flight. Part of my crew included my Dayton commuter friend Lisa Hertlein, who was always so much fun to work with. Our crew started out by flying an empty Boeing 757 from Charlotte to St. Louis. We then picked up the Pittsburgh Steelers football team after their Thursday night game against the St. Louis Rams. Fortunately, the Steelers won, so they were all in a good mood on the flight back to Pittsburgh.

That flight also operated a little differently than our regular flights. You see, other than being buckled in for takeoff and landing, those guys were allowed to do pretty much whatever they wanted. Because of the amazing size of some of these players, they were all assigned to either a window or an aisle seat. Even though there was no one seated in the middle seats, some of the huge offensive and defensive linemen still had their shoulders touching because of their sheer girth! (Steelers quarterback Ben Roethlisberger's size was also mind boggling. At 6'8" and at least 270 pounds or more, I just couldn't imagine how a "regular-sized" defensive player could ever tackle him!)

Once we were airborne for the two-hour flight, our job was to continually pass through the cabin with crates full of food, such as sandwiches, fresh fruit, desserts, and a variety of sports drinks. The guys were allowed to have as much as they wanted, and it was astounding how much some of them consumed. (I saw one guy, who's hand was as big as my head, pick up five large sandwiches with that one huge paw!)

Although we were not allowed to interact with the team during the flight, we were, however, encouraged to go up to First Class and introduce ourselves to Steelers president Dan Rooney and his family. Mr. Rooney was absolutely the nicest man. He greeted us by name and thanked each of us personally for taking care of "his guys." While up there, I was also introduced to offensive coordinator Bruce Arians (who would later go on to win a Super Bowl as head coach of the Tampa Bay Buccaneers) and quarterbacks' coach Ken Anderson, who had taken my favorite team (the Cincinnati Bengals) to the Super Bowl in 1982. Overall, it was a great experience and a fun way to end the year 2007.

February 12th-15th, 2008 - A really nice four-day trip with my friends Donna Dent (who will be mentioned again in an upcoming chapter) and Susan Linner. While on our layover in Las Vegas on the second night of the trip, we got caught outside during a sudden sandstorm. Although we were able to duck into one of the casinos after a few minutes, I had granules of sand in every orifice (yes, THAT one too!) for the next few hours. It was amazing how quickly it hit and how bad it was for anyone who happened to be outside at the time.

March 22nd, 2008 - My 25th anniversary with the company. Although things have changed a lot since I started, I still have a sense of awe regarding how lucky I am to be able to fly for a living. For the most part, I still look forward to going to work!

April 18th, 2008 - Because the pilots were still dissatisfied with their seniority issues, today they formally voted out their old union and will install a new union soon. I am not sure how that will help the situation, but I hope it does.

April 23rd, 2008 - While on a layover in Toronto, I went to have lunch at a nearby restaurant called Mother Tucker's. As I was leaving, I ended up holding the door open for a group of young ladies who were just arriving. Since they were all wearing sashes, I eventually asked who they were. It turned out that they were all contestants in the Miss Canada pageant that was going to be held that weekend. There must have been about 30 of them and they were all very polite.

May 29th, 2008 - While on the last day of my trip, I got a call from my supervisor that my father-in-law had passed away that morning. We were just getting ready to leave for a Nassau, Bahamas turn, so rather than delay or cancel the flight, I first checked with my wife and then finished the trip. My father-in-law was a great guy and was a wonderful influence on his entire family.

June 20th, 2008 - USAirways announced earlier this year, that they would be adding a new airplane to our fleet. The Brazilian-made Embraer E-190 can only seat 99 customers and was designed for some smaller market routes. Today I attended the E-190 training class with my old housemate Scott Parks. I am not sure if I will want to work this plane much. After flying on some of our larger planes, this one frankly seems a little claustrophobic.

June 30th, 2008 - There were lots of storms and bad weather over the East Coast today which caused many delays and cancellations. After missing out on three previous commuter flights home, I got lucky and caught the only seat to Cincinnati. I can only say that it was a seat not normally available to me, but the captain was a very cool guy who apparently felt sorry for me and let me on his full flight. I just couldn't tell him enough, how much I appreciated the ride home!

August 5th-8th, 2008 - A four-day trip with one of our best flight attendants, Bunny Haase. It was a good thing that she was there because it was also the first trip involving USAirways' latest service change. It seemed that our company now wanted passengers to pay for ALL drinks, not just alcoholic beverages. The passengers hated it and we spent most of the trip trying to explain to our incredulous guests why USAirways felt it was necessary. Needless to say, we barely sold anything this week.

August 27th, 2008 - In the middle of this week's trip, we had an unexpected plane substitution and were forced to work one of the new E-190's from Chicago to Charlotte. It wasn't as bad as I had thought, but it was definitely a much smaller plane than what I have been used to.

October 19th, 2008 - Two of my crew members this week were old friends who spent most of the trip catching up with each other's lives. Unfortunately, during the wee hours of our redeye flight from Los Angeles to Charlotte, they got a bit chatty. Apparently, this infuriated one of our passengers because she came to the back galley and screamed at both of them about all the noise. Sadly, crew members sometimes forget that passengers are indeed listening to everything we say. I myself have overheard several embarrassing stories while commuting that definitely should not have been aired! (One included the best ways to cheat on your taxes.)

October 23rd, 2008 - This was the last day of a trip with my friend Mike Nicholson and old pal Tony Shimkonis. On that day, we had "The Exorcist" movie star Linda Blair up in First Class from Phoenix to Charlotte. She was very nice and actually a lot of fun to interact with. Because we didn't have a lot of passengers, we were able to spend a little time chatting with her.

When Tony revealed to her that I had been preparing to go on "Who Wants To Be a Millionaire?" she then wanted to play trivia. I did pretty well and answered most of her questions. However, she seemed the most impressed after she created the category of "Linda Blair trivia."

I think I may have stunned her by naming about 10 movies that she was in, as well as remembering that she had once been on a National Equestrian team. She eventually informed us that she now sponsors a large animal, rescue facility and was in fact, on her way to do some fund-raising for that group. She also said that she loved our crew and wondered why we couldn't be on all her upcoming flights!

October 28th-30th, 2008 - This was a really nice trip with my old Pittsburgh colleague Janet Renda and one of my new favorites Jeannine Dalton. During a long limo ride to our hotel in Indianapolis, we found out that Jeannine had been a former "Miss North Carolina" and that her daughters were still competing in a number of pageants.

November 4th, 2008 - I flew the same trip again this week. However, this time we discovered that we would be landing at the brand-new Indianapolis International Airport. (In fact, I believe we were just the third flight to land on the new runways.) The new terminal was very spacious and because of that, it took us awhile to get to the area where the hotel vans were parked. Since the facility had just opened, the van driver was even a bit confused and not sure how to get out of the airport parking area.

December 4th, 2008 - I worked a nice trip to Las Vegas with my old friend Nadine Freeman. Once we got to the hotel, we decided to get a cab and go check out the Christmas light displays on the Vegas Strip. They were very impressive and the decorations at the Bellagio Hotel were especially beautiful.

December 21st, 2008 - Today I completed and turned in all the preparation materials for a new piece of technology called the H.H.D. (short for Hand-held Device) This equipment will allow us to better process credit card payments for charges on the flights. It will also allow for better communication with the company as well as giving us more information on passenger seating, weather updates, and flight delays.

December 25th, 2008 - I worked a Christmas Day trip for the first time in a long time; mostly because they offered extra "holiday pay." Fortunately, my trip had an early evening departure, so I was still able to open a few Christmas gifts with the family before having to leave for the airport. However, the coolest gift was yet to come.

On our flight from Charlotte to Ft. Myers, Florida, I noticed a very tall gentleman and his family crammed into the last row of seats. The guy was obviously uncomfortable, especially since it looked like his legs were in different time zones. However, once everyone boarded, I saw that there was one empty seat near my jumpseat, that had a little extra legroom. When I went back and offered it to him, you couldn't imagine the look of gratitude on his face.

After he thanked me several times, we got to talking and I discovered that my tall friend was none other than former basketball star Sam Bowie. (He had attended the University of Kentucky a few years after I was at Eastern Kentucky University.) He was such a nice guy that he even offered to pay for my dinner that night. I told him that I appreciated the thought, but I was just glad to help him out. After all, that is what Christmas is all about. (Trivia note: Did you know that Sam Bowie was chosen by the Portland Trail Blazers as the second pick of the 1984 basketball draft? That was just ahead of some guy named Michael Jordan.)

Chapter Twenty

The Miracle on the Hudson

There have been two incidents in my airline career that really freaked out my friends and worried my family. The first of course were the harrowing events of September 11th, 2001. The second one was just as unforgettable, but not as tragic. That was January 15th of 2009, or the event that became known as the "Miracle on the Hudson." What could have been an absolutely horrendous airline accident instead became a symbol of what is good and honorable about our profession. Here are my recollections of that day and of that particular crew.

January 14th-16th, 2009 - This was a nice three-day trip with another all-guy crew which included my buddies Gary Vinceguerra and Dale Landefeld. We had a relatively easy day on the first day followed by a nice long layover in Pittsburgh. On the morning of the second day, I decided to get up early and go downstairs for some breakfast. Since we didn't leave the hotel until mid-afternoon, I was also going to squeeze in a little workout as well.

As I got off the elevator, I saw another USAirways crew getting ready to board the hotel van to the airport. It was then that I recognized several members of that crew. The first officer was a guy named Jeff Skiles who I had flown with a few years before. There was also my flight attendant friend Donna Dent, who I had worked with just a few months back when we got caught in the sandstorm in Las Vegas. The other familiar face was one of my favorite captains, Chesley "Sully" Sullenberger. As crews usually do, we exchanged greetings as they got ready to leave. I remember the conversation going something like this:

Me: "Good morning, guys! Y'all have a busy day coming up?" (Since I had been in the Charlotte base for almost five years, I now considered myself "bi-lingual.")

Them: "Not bad. We just have to go to LaGuardia and back to Charlotte. You?"

Me: "Meh....an afternoon flight to Las Vegas, then out to L.A."

Them: "Okay. Nice to see you! Have a good trip!"

Me: "You too! Safe travels!"

I really didn't think about this conversation again until a little later on. My breakfast was delicious and I had a good workout, so my day was starting out well. My crew eventually met up in the hotel lobby around mid-afternoon. Because the weather outside was fairly cold, the driver had let the van idle so we would be nice and toasty for our trip to the airport. However, it was during that 20-minute ride that suddenly, all of our cell phones started ringing at about the same time.

I recall seeing that my call was from my best friend, Steve Moore. Being curious about why he was calling, I started the conversation with...

"Hey man, what's going on?"

Steve: " So, did you get your feet wet?"

Me: "What? Why would my feet be wet?"

Steve: "So you are safe? It wasn't your crew that went into the Hudson River?"

Me: "Hudson River? No, we're fine."

My cell phone was now beeping with several other incoming calls, so I told Steve I would call him back. As I paused to see who else was calling me, our captain interrupted us with the news that one of our airplanes did in fact make a crash landing into the Hudson River just a few minutes earlier. However, there was no word yet of what flight it was or what crews were involved. We could only imagine the worst, but we all were hoping for the best news possible.

Well, that news turned out to be so good that it was almost unbelievable. An Airbus-320 with a full cabin of 150 passengers and a crew of five, all survived a "ditching" or water landing in the freezing-cold Hudson River in the middle of January! There were only four or five people with injuries that were considered serious. Everyone else was shaken, but relatively unharmed.

I am sure most people remember that particular day. After seeing them in our hotel lobby that morning, Sully and his crew had flown into Charlotte and then into New York LaGuardia. After they arrived in LaGuardia, they then boarded Flight #1549 to Charlotte for what was supposed to be their last leg. My friend Donna was the "senior" flight attendant. The other two crew members were Doreen Welsh and Sheila Dail.

Again, as generally happens, the flight started out in a normal manner. The takeoff was apparently going well for the first minute or so, until the plane encountered a flock of Canadian geese. The subsequent bird strikes then caused both engines to fail, which essentially turned the plane into a giant, metal glider. At that point, they had only attained about 3,000 feet of elevation.

According to the reports, both pilots immediately began their emergency procedures and tried to re-start the engines, but to no avail. Although it was Jeff's turn to be in charge of the takeoff, Sully then assumed command while Jeff started going through their emergency checklist. After notifying the control tower of the situation, they then had to make some split-second decisions about how and where they could land. After considering a return to LaGuardia and/or the Teterboro airport across the river in New Jersey, Sully realized that neither one was a realistic option. He then made the hard decision to try for a water landing in the Hudson River. This option also involved the fewest obstacles and structures, and therefore lessened the chances of other human casualties on the ground.

Meanwhile, the flight attendants reported that they heard the "thumps" and felt the plane shudder during the bird strikes. Since they weren't sure what was going on, they surmised that they might possibly be returning to the airport. Passengers also reported hearing and feeling the bird strikes, as well as noticing a burning smell as the geese were ingested into the engines. The flight attendants reported some concern from the passengers and recalled trying to calmly explain that at worst, they may be headed back to LaGuardia. That is, until they heard Sully's command to "Brace for impact".

Most everyone knows the rest of the story. Sully and Jeff managed to execute a perfect water landing on the Hudson River. The flight attendants up front (Donna and Sheila) managed to open the doors and inflate the slide rafts. Passengers in the exit row managed to open the window exits which then allowed others to go out onto the wings. Doreen, in the back of the plane, had to immediately deal with a panicked passenger who cracked open one of the rear doors which started letting water inside. She had also been injured by a piece of metal that came up through the galley floor which severely lacerated her leg. Still, she managed to direct people toward the front of the plane as the water continued to rise.

Perhaps the most incredible part of this incident was the fact that a number of water taxies and a Coast Guard ship just happened to witness the splash-down and were at the scene within minutes. They were then able to pluck the passengers off the wings and out of the slide rafts. Considering that the temperature of the water in the middle of January was a mere 38° degrees, it was very critical that only a few people chose to actually enter the water. Hypothermia would have probably killed multiple swimmers.

In short, this could have easily been an absolutely horrible situation. However, the combination of highly skilled pilots, a well-trained, veteran cabin crew, and the close proximity of the rescue boats allowed this to become a celebration of good fortune. For the battered airline industry, there was some long-awaited positive praise for the crews and for the handling of the passengers afterwards. For the city of New York, it was a chance for them to finally overcome the stigma of September 11th, 2001, and show everyone that they were still a world-class city.

Over the course of the next several months, it was eventually proven that Sully and Jeff performed heroically under incredible pressure and that any other options would have led to probable tragedy and loss of life. The entire crew was featured on the news for weeks on end. Their grace and humility with the press afterwards only cemented their status as heroes and heroines. For those of us who knew them, it was a joy to have them representing our profession.

I do have to share one lighter moment with you. About three or four days after the accident, I was watching a morning news show and they were interviewing a panel of four passengers from Flight 1549. One of the ladies was recounting her version of what she had seen and heard during the short flight. She first went out of her way to praise the actions of the flight attendants, especially their reactions to Sully's command to..."Brace for impact!" She then went on to describe how Donna and Sheila yelled to the passengers in unison to "duck and tuck" until they had landed.

Now as I watched this interview, I became a little confused. Throughout my entire career, we had always been instructed to use the command "Brace, Brace! Heads down, Stay down!" in that type of emergency situation. (The subsequent investigation would later prove that they did in fact use this correct phrasing.) I then remembered something that I had learned from my law school days; that "eyewitness" accounts are sometimes inaccurate, especially during stressful circumstances.

Therefore, I humorously consoled myself with the fact that perhaps in her mind, she did hear something like those words. However, it was not coming out of the mouths of Donna and Sheila, but instead it was emanating from under the front cockpit door. Also, instead of hearing the words "duck and tuck", it may have been the voices of the pilots cursing those Canadian geese with a few choice semantics; possibly... "f***ing ducks!" (A few years later, I shared this story with Jeff while on a deadheading flight. He laughed out loud and warned me that he might have to re-tell that version later on!)

In the end, most of the crew of Flight 1549 eventually went back to work. Doreen, however, elected to retire and never put on her flight attendant uniform again. Sheila worked a few more years and eventually retired on the 10-year anniversary of the "Miracle on the Hudson." I had the great pleasure to work with Donna several times over the next few years. However, she was always a little reluctant to discuss most of what happened that day, and consequently, I never pushed her on that issue. She was (and still is) a class act.

Sully and Jeff were eventually cleared to resume flying. Jeff has since assumed several advisory positions with a number of aviation-related companies. As of 2021, I had heard that he was a captain again for American Airlines. (He eventually retired in late 2024.) Sully only flew for a few more months after returning. He retired later that year with 30 years of service with PSA and USAirways. He is also in a number of advisory positions within the airline industry as well as the author of two books. In addition, he was an advisor for the 2016 movie "Sully." That film was based on his first book "Highest Duty," which detailed the events of that fateful day. The Airbus-320 aircraft that was flown that day, was eventually cleaned and restored and was originally on display at the Carolinas Aviation Museum located near the Charlotte-Douglas International Airport. Fittingly, that museum was recently re-named the Sullenberger Aviation Museum, in honor of Captain Sully.

Before I close out this chapter, I want to point out a few incredible factors that may have helped make this day what it was. First, if Flight 1549 had made contact with the geese any sooner than they did, they would not have attained enough altitude to have avoided the George Washington Bridge which spans the Hudson River. As it was, they only cleared that structure by about 900 feet.

Secondly, from what I remember, Sully at one time may have been a glider pilot. Gliders are planes with no engines that are towed up to a certain altitude and then released. They are then dependent on the wind currents and updrafts to allow them to descend gradually. Throughout the flight, glider pilots must continue to make judgement calls as to when and where to bank the plane and to recognize places where they may eventually have to land. Although I never heard any interviews that mentioned this as a factor in Sully's success that day, I wonder if that skill didn't subconsciously come into play.

Thirdly, the weather in New York that day was about as good as one could have hoped for. Despite it being a very cold January day, it was clear and sunny. If it had been any colder, there might have been ice in the river which would have complicated the ditching even more. If there had been thick clouds or snow in the area, visibility would have been hampered which may not have allowed the pilots to clearly see their landing options.

Finally, from what I have heard from other pilots, their training in the flight simulators covers just about any emergency situation that has ever happened. However, this particular scenario had never even been imagined. Therefore, Jeff and Sully had to be somewhat creative with what they did and how they did it. (I was tempted to use the phrase "they made it up on the fly," but that pun may be a little too obvious.) After the investigations were completed, most airlines added a similar scenario to their pilot simulator training program. I believe it is now known as the "Sully Situation." Talk about an appropriate honor!

Chapter Twenty-One

2009....A Munchkin and a Little Sweet

January 19th-21st, 2009 - This was a good three-day trip with friends Billy Walton and Teresa Lea. On the second night we had a nice layover in Cancun, Mexico. However, the strangest thing happened when Billy and I went to get a few beers at the Hard Rock Cafe near our hotel.

While seated at the bar, a young lady came over and wanted to show us a picture. It was a photograph of her and some guy from a few years back. Although her English was broken, she wanted to know if I was the guy in the picture. While he did sort of look like me, the guy in the photo was missing a finger. (I still have all of my digits.) We never could figure out exactly what she wanted, but after she left, we double-checked to make sure we hadn't been pick-pocketed.

February 17th, 2009 - On our Charlotte-Ft. Lauderdale flight, we had a very angry woman with a huge bag that obviously wouldn't fit in the overhead compartments. After loudly arguing with every one of the flight attendants, she then started swearing and even pushed another passenger. After she delayed the flight, the gate agent eventually removed her from our plane. A couple of flights later, on the way to Denver, we had a very upset older man who claimed that "Everyone at USAirways is rude" and that we owed him some free drinks! Fortunately, he dozed off before the drink cart came out, so we quietly worked around him and didn't have to fight that battle.

February 24th-27th, 2009 - This was a really great four-day trip with captain Mike Ryan, first officer Roger Payne, and friends Lyn

Smith and Joy Baker. On the first night, we had a great time on our Cancun layover. In fact, we returned to that previously mentioned Hard Rock Cafe again, but this time there were no girls with photos. On the third night, we had a fun night out in San Francisco at a place called Tommy's Joynt. I don't think our crew stopped laughing for the entire four days!

March 4th, 2009 - While boarding our flight from Philadelphia to Los Angeles, I noticed a young man with a guitar case. After he stashed his instrument, I discovered that he would be sitting right across from my jump seat in Row 9. We had a chance to chat a little bit during the boarding process, and it was then that I found out that he was a musician. After talking about what kind of acoustic guitar he was playing, we also had a chat about his new computer program which was designed to assist with song writing. Once we finished boarding and performed the safety demonstration, I then settled into my jump seat and we continued our conversation.

It was only then that he finally decided to remove his ski cap for the flight to L.A. At that point, a massive amount of curly hair unfurled and after he brushed it away from his eyes, only then did I recognize his face. It turned out that my new friend was a gentleman named Justin Guarini. For fans of the television talent show "American Idol," Mr Guarini was the runner-up on the very first season to eventual superstar Kelly Clarkson. I then very discreetly leaned forward and whispered that I now recognized him; mostly because of his very familiar curly locks. I think he appreciated that, because we continued to have some very nice conversations throughout the flight. (Here's a fun fact about Justin. A few years ago, the Dr. Pepper company came out with a very recognizable character named "Little Sweet" who was used to promote Diet Dr. Pepper. Although it took me a little while, I finally figured out why that character seemed so familiar. Justin Guarini played the part of "Little Sweet!")

April 13th-16th, 2009 - This was an interesting four-day trip. On the third day, I got to fly in and out of Cabo, San Lucas, for the first time. The water looked amazing, and I am pretty sure that I saw some whales breaching off the coast as we came in to land. That evening, I also got to fly into Salt Lake City for the first time as well. It was so beautiful to look out the plane windows and see all the snow-capped mountains on our approach to the airport. Incredibly, after the trip was over, I ran into another high school classmate on the flight home to Cincinnati. Mike Carpenter and I were both on the wrestling team, as well as a trivia team for a quiz show called "It's Academic." (It was back then that I first realized that I was pretty good at trivia.)

April 29th, 2009 - For a good part of the spring, there had been a highly contagious sickness called "swine flu" making the rounds. Many people had fallen ill for long periods of time, and some had even died. Before our trip started today, I made some calls to the company office and to our flight attendant union to see what they were doing to protect us from exposure to this disease. I got a lot of reassurances, but very little specific information on what they were going to do for us. I was told that if a lot of us got sick and had to miss work, they would "deal with it then." (Somehow, I didn't exactly feel "reassured.")

April 30th, 2009 - Here is another really great story of a chance meeting with one of our passengers. We were flying from Phoenix to Pittsburgh and I was working the back half of the coach cabin. After our service was completed, I took a little break and sat down on my jumpseat in the rear galley. It was soon after, that a very sweet (and very tiny) older lady with a cane, came back to the rear lavatory. She then wanted to know if I would hold her cane while she was in the bathroom. I told her that was fine and said that I would have it ready for her when she came out.

After she exited the lavatory, I handed her cane back to her and she thanked me several times. As I often did, I then asked how her trip was going and whether she was from the Pittsburgh area. She then replied that she was on her way to a reunion in the nearby town of Cadiz, Ohio. She also wondered if I knew how far that was from the Pittsburgh airport. Having once taught geography in high school, I knew that it was just over the Ohio/Pennsylvania border and probably no more than an hour's drive away.

When I asked whether she was going to a family reunion, she said no and that it was with some people she once worked with. She then opened up and revealed that she had been an actress when she was younger and in fact had been cast in the movie "The Wizard of Oz." It turned out that she was attending the 70th anniversary party for the release of the movie and that she had been one of the "Munchkins."

When asked why it was being held in Cadiz, she told me that they were also meeting up with the few surviving actors from the movie "Gone with the Wind" which was also released in 1939. (Evidently, Cadiz had been the hometown of actor Clark Gable, who portrayed the famous character "Rhett Butler" in that film.)

She then introduced herself as Olga Nardone and continued on with a wonderful tale of how she had started out in Vaudeville as a ballerina. She also said that she was about 16 years old at the time she went to audition for "The Wizard of Oz," and because of her dance training, she was then cast as one of the members of the "Lullaby League." For those of you who remember the movie, she was one of three ballerinas, dressed in pink outfits, who greeted Dorothy after she landed in "Munchkinland." Ms. Nardone then indicated that since she was the smallest of the three, she was positioned in the center of that group.

I wished I could have had more time to chat with her, but since we were getting close to our final approach into Pittsburgh, she went ahead and returned to her seat. However, before we got ready to land, I made a point of stopping by her row, to tell her how much I enjoyed hearing her wonderful stories and to wish her a safe trip. She then made me chuckle when she sort of blushed and said that I was a "nice boy." Once again, meeting interesting passengers like Ms. Nardone, was truly one of the best perks of my job.

May 28th, 2009 - While on a short layover in San Diego, I had $240 of liquor money stolen from the change bag that was inside my rolling suitcase. Whoever it was, knew that the crews often got off the plane for lunch while it was parked at that particular gate. They also must have been in a hurry because they ripped open the zipper on my suitcase, and left the empty change bag. Since the only people allowed on the plane are other airport workers such as cleaners and/or caterers, it may have been one of them. I reported it to the San Diego station manager, who didn't seem to think it was that big of a deal. She also hesitated when I told her I wanted to fill out a full, written report to send to our security office. I also had to send reports to my flight attendant supervisor as well, which took the better part of two days to complete.

June 4th, 2009 - Since I had the same trip again this week, I took the time while in San Diego to track down that same station manager to see whether any progress had been made, regarding last week's theft of my liquor money. Sadly, she just rolled her eyes at me and wondered aloud why I was bothering her again. Her reaction not only disappointed me but made think that she may have known something about the situation. I also found out much later that other USAirways crews had experienced similar thefts while in San Diego. (Hmmm...)

June 25th, 2009 - During a late-afternoon lunch with the entire crew in Tempe, Arizona, we found out that pop star Michael Jackson had passed away earlier in the day. We were all in shock at the news. In fact, one of the girls on our crew was so upset that she started crying. It was a rather sad day.

July 10th, 2009 - After trying for about 10 hours to commute back home to Cincinnati, I finally had to use one of my precious SA-1 passes (a guaranteed seat) to get home. It was a good thing that I did, because there were no more open seats for the next two days.

August 5th, 2009 - Our company had recently moved us to a rather sketchy hotel for our Las Vegas overnights. I don't want to disparage it too much, but the actual name of the place was "Terrible's." (And yes, that name fit.) The only good thing about it was that it was just down the street from the very cool Hard Rock Hotel.

September 1st, 2009 - As I mentioned earlier, airline crews sometimes get to see amazing things while peering out of the airplane windows. Tonight, we were scheduled for a late-evening arrival into Los Angeles. During our approach, I could see the wildfires that had been burning around the L.A. area during the previous week. Although it was dark, I could clearly make out the burning silhouettes of the mountains and unfortunately some of the homes as well. I felt so bad for the people involved in this tragedy.

September 29th, 2009 - Another long Las Vegas layover; this time with my buddy Mark Moses. Perhaps in an attempt to try to improve their image, the staff at Terrible's Casino offered our crew an invitation to their "VIP" party out by the pool. Mark and I were curious about what type of "VIPs" might be staying at this facility, so we accepted the offer. I can only describe that gathering as an "interesting mix." You see, the soiree' around the pool included a lady in her own well-worn bathrobe and slippers, and a bearded gentleman with no shirt or shoes, but clad in his finest denim bib overalls. We didn't stay long.

November 5th, 2009 - During the boarding of our Charlotte-Atlanta flight, a very angry couple were the last ones allowed to board the plane. When they couldn't find room for their luggage, the husband got in my face (twice) and yelled obscenities at all of us. I then calmly told him that I would "see what I could do." What I did do, was go up front and alert the captain, who then chose to remove them from the flight. After all these years of flying, I still don't understand why some folks feel the need to rant and rave like that. It never ends up getting them what they want, and it also makes everyone around them uncomfortable.

November 16th-19th, 2009 - This was a really nice trip with my friends Willie Whitmore and Katie O'Donoghue. On the second day we had actor/rapper Flavor Flav on our Phoenix flight. He was in full regalia including the sunglasses and the signature clock around his neck. He was just so much fun to chat with. He even laughed when someone (me) facetiously asked if he knew what time it was!

On the next night while in Las Vegas, I managed to scalp a ticket to the "Santana" concert at a newly opened venue called "The Joint." That theater featured great acoustics and had a smaller and more intimate feel to it. Their lobby also offered a very unique display of framed concert t-shirts; some of which I had owned over the years.

December 7th, 2009 - A big winter storm hit Southwestern Ohio this week and consequently it took me over three hours just to get to the Cincinnati airport in order to commute in to work. I then managed to get safely into the terminal; only to find out that I had forgotten to pack my airline ID. Because I couldn't fly without it, I had to take a "personal day" off. That cost me two days of pay.

December 12th-15th, 2009 - I had a few days of vacation scheduled this week, but through a new company program called "Vacation Flyback," I was able to pick up a trip and make up for some of the lost time from last week.

December 15th, 2009 - Well, maybe I shouldn't have picked up that trip after all. According to my logbook notes it was "The Day from Hell." On our flight from Tampa to Charlotte, a young man passed out in his seat. After seeing us scramble to give him oxygen and making an announcement for any doctors on board, his parents only reluctantly came forward to ask what was going on. They didn't seem to care much about his welfare and, in fact, had purposely chosen not to sit with him during the flight. They also didn't want us to divert the flight because that would have made them miss their connections in Charlotte.

Later that day, on our flight into Boston, we had a drunken, one-legged man who chose to ignore all of our announcements and decided to try putting on his prosthetic leg in the rear lavatory during our landing. He was then angry at USAirways...because they couldn't provide larger restrooms! My only rationalization was that there must have been a full moon on the rise.

My final logbook notes for 2009 seem to indicate that it was a pretty good year and that I was happy to be flying better trips with fewer legs (no pun intended) each week. However, I then wondered how long that was going to last. As I have said before...we shall see!

Chapter Twenty-Two

2010....The Year of Breathing Dangerously

January 12th, 2010 - Our plane incurred a flat tire in Ft. Myers, Florida today that took over eight hours to fix. Eventually they sent us back to our hotel to wait things out. When they couldn't find a replacement tire, they then cancelled the flight. We finally ended up ferrying the flight back to Charlotte and then staying there for the night. (It's a good thing too, because I was really "tire"-d!... this time, pun intended!)

January 16th, 2010 - We heard that there was a USAirways flight in Philadelphia, that encountered what the company called a "fume event." Apparently, some engine fumes filled the cabin and afterwards, a lot of folks were taken to the hospital, including some of the crew. I will be very interested to find out what happened to them.

January 27th-28th, 2010 - Our company had recently created a few redeye trips with very short layovers between flights. Because most of our redeyes normally travel to and from the West Coast, the crews also have to adjust to a three-hour time zone difference. That can sometimes interfere with sleep patterns and make it hard to rest. Therefore, crews would normally have about 12-24 hours off before heading back East. However, with these new redeye flights, a person might only get 10-12 hours at the hotel and maybe manage about five or six hours of actual sleep. Today was my first "short redeye" and it was horrible. I only got four hours of sleep and felt really exhausted on the way home. I definitely won't be working these very often!

February 15th-18th, 2010 - This was a really nice trip with my friends Jewel and Barrington. At some point, I found out that Barrington was on the USAirways investigative team that researched what happened before and after Flight 1549 went into the Hudson River last year. His descriptions of the plane and the damage afterwards amazed us and only solidified my respect for that crew. I also found out that USAirways exercised some extreme measures to locate, repair, and eventually return nearly every item left behind on that plane to its rightful owner.

March 10th, 2010 - In another of my unbelievable coincidences, I accidently bumped into my nephew, Scott, in the Philadelphia Airport food court. He had just started working as a pilot for the PSA commuter group and like me, was just passing through. He is a good kid and it sounded like he was enjoying the airline business.

March 23rd-26th, 2010 - Another family member (my niece, Casey) who is an elementary teacher, asked me to take another "Flat Stanley" along on my trip this week. Apparently, she had one student who didn't have anyone to help her, so I agreed. Hopefully that student got the best grade, because "Uncle Lar" managed to get that Stanley into a New York Yankees spring training game, as well as the Tampa Bay Buccaneers football stadium. Stanley also got to tour the Sea World park in Orlando and have his picture taken in the cockpit and up in First Class. (It was actually fun for me, because as a former teacher, I have found that I still enjoy helping young minds learn new things!)

April 8th, 2010 - I had been having a lot of success lately with handing out those applications for the company's credit card. In fact, in the last two months, I had made over three thousand dollars in commissions. Although, I still disliked the thought of pushing credit cards on our passengers, occasionally the credit card offers were so good that I seriously considered getting one of them.

May 21st, 2010 - On our Phoenix-Charlotte flight today we had a couple of our flight attendant supervisors who were performing a "check-ride." One of them was my old Pittsburgh colleague Tom Kilheeney. He apparently thought that we were doing a great job because he gave us the highest marks possible. I hadn't seen him in awhile, so it was great to catch up with him as well.

June 18th, 2010 - During the last day of our trip, our plane had a major mechanical problem while at the gate in Philadelphia. It seemed that all the toilets stopped working and the mechanics couldn't seem to figure out why. Because it was required that you have at least one working lav, we eventually had to cancel the flight and ferry the plane back to Charlotte.

June 23rd, 2010 - We had a very strange male passenger on our flight from Los Angeles to Philadelphia today. Not only did he refuse to look at anyone directly, but he spent part of the flight trying to read a book that was upside down. He also took off his seat belt just as we were landing and despite our pleas to "remain seated," he stood up for the taxi into the gate.

July 20th, 2010 - We had a long layover in Nashville, so I got to spend the day hanging out with high school buddy, Jim Cole. He is still doing well in the music business and in fact, may get to play the fabled Carnegie Hall venue in New York City this Christmas. Since Carnegie Hall is a dream goal of many musicians, I was just so very happy for him!

July 26th-29th, 2010 - This was a really nice four-day trip with friends Lisa Fussell and Ivy Murray. On the first night, we had a long layover in Orlando, so I got to have dinner and catch up with my sister Cindy. (Her big news was that my nephew's girlfriend had just won the Miss Florida pageant!) The last part of the trip included a very long San Francisco overnight, so the girls and I went exploring. We first checked out the old hippie district of Haight-Ashbury and found some interesting vintage clothing stores. We also walked part of Golden Gate Park and then had dinner at a great seafood restaurant on Fisherman's Wharf. I also discovered that Ivy's husband worked for us, and was one of my favorite gate agents in Orlando, Florida.

August 4th, 2010 - On our flight to Orlando today, we had an "extra" flight attendant named Jeff, who also encountered fumes on the same Boeing 767 plane that suffered that "fume event" in Philadelphia earlier this year. He said the company was generally denying that anything serious happened, despite the fact that the rest of his crew had been sick and/or off work since it happened. He also said that similar "situations" had occurred since then. That made me sad. I didn't want to think that our management wasn't concerned with what happened. I just hoped that it didn't happen again.

August 16th-19th, 2010 - Well, I spoke too soon. On this four-day trip, we had jet fumes in the cabin on five of our eight flights. We informed the captain each time it happened and generally it didn't last long. I also made a note in my logbook to "start carrying a surgical mask" with me.

August 23rd-26th, 2010 - A four-day trip on the A-319 this week. The good news was that I was flying again with my friend, captain Ed Terry. The bad news was that we encountered jet fumes again on eight of our 10 flights. I told Ed every time it happened and again it generally only lasted a few minutes each time. When asked to explain what was happening, Ed informed me that it was called an "air bleed," and it occurred when cold outside air was directed over the warm engines, and then pumped into the cabin. (This allowed the passengers to breathe fresh air and it also kept the cabin pressurized and at a reasonable temperature.) He said that sometimes that air gets polluted with synthetic oil or hydraulic fluid from the engine and the resulting intake causes a "dirty sock" smell that can be pulled into the cabin. I am going to file a report about each incident with my supervisor and see what happens.

August 30th, 2010 - I had to call off "sick" from my trip this week. I had congestion, chest pains, and nausea. I am now wondering if it isn't some sort of reaction to all the fumes I have ingested over the last couple of weeks.

September 21st-23rd, 2010 - On our flight out to Los Angeles, we had ESPN reporter Chris Meyer and former Los Angeles Laker All-Star James Worthy up in First Class. They were both very nice guys. The next day, I got to enjoy a beautiful morning while walking the Marina Del Rey area near our hotel. We then flew cross country to Boston, where I had one of the worst hotel rooms ever. Evidently, the hotel elevators were located just on the other side of one of my walls and caused rumbling noises all night long. When I complained to the manager, he said there were no more rooms available, but he did offer me a free breakfast the next morning and a free Boston Red Sox hat. (The breakfast was just okay, but I did end up wearing that hat for the next year or so!)

September 28th-30th, 2010 - I did the same trip this week. However, I had a much better room in Boston. In fact, the manager remembered me from the previous week and offered me a pass to take the Boston Fenway Park tour. It was a great tour through arguably the most iconic baseball park in the Major Leagues. We even got to sit in the seats that are perched on top of the famous 40-foot-tall outfield wall known as the "Green Monster." It was a wonderful experience for a baseball fan like me. Also, I was wearing the Red Sox hat that I got last week, so I at least looked like a Boston fan!

October 18th-21st, 2010 - This started out as a very good trip, and I got to work with a husband-and-wife team named Gray and Pepper Coleman. However, on the second day we had bad fumes on all four flights. On the last day we had fume problems on three more flights. We all said we would write reports to our supervisors, especially since this is rapidly becoming a real health and safety issue. Lots of other flight crews are also complaining of similar occurrences.

November 2nd, 2010 - I heard today that one of my Dayton commuter friends had been working the Philadelphia flight that suffered the massive "fume event" last January. I learned too that her entire crew of five flight attendants and two pilots had been hospitalized off and on since the accident.

I also discovered much later, that there were in fact, a total of 12 "incidents" on that very same airplane. (That Philadelphia crew was involved in the third event.) My friend Kim was the only one who managed to return to work, even if just sporadically. She also suffered seizures and even lost her speech for a little while. Also, at one point, she was on something like a dozen different medications, just to try to cope with her body's reactions to the fumes.

It was only much, much later that USAirways would finally admit that there was indeed a problem, and would eventually spend around four million dollars to "rehab" that particular Boeing-767 airplane. I was also informed that the problematic right engine that was suspected of causing all the damage, somehow was mysteriously "misplaced." Although a lot of us suspected as much at the time, it was disheartening to eventually know what really happened.

October 25th-28th, 2010 - This was a very enjoyable trip on the Airbus-321. On the third day, we had singer/guitarist George Benson on our flight to Los Angeles. I really wanted to tell him that back when I was single and dating, I often played his 1976 album "Breezin'" as my favorite "make out" music. However, I resisted that urge and simply told him how much I liked his work. He seemed to appreciate that.

November 16th, 2010 - During our long layover in New York City, I walked over to Carnegie Hall and discovered a large poster advertising their upcoming shows. Sure enough, my friend Jim Cole was listed as one of the performers for their upcoming Christmas show in early December. Again, I am just so happy for his success.

December 6th, 2010 - I was surprised to again see my high school buddy, Scott Flint, on my commuter flight tonight into Charlotte. We managed to get seats together and had a great time catching up with each other.

December 27th-30th, 2010 - I was off sick this week with some sort of upper respiratory infection. After all the bad fumes that I have had to endure recently, it made sense that my body might eventually react like that.

Chapter Twenty-Three

2011....Man Caves and a Mobile Museum

January 2nd, 2011 - A memorable commuter flight into Charlotte, this time in the company of former outfielder George Foster, a key member of those famous Cincinnati Reds teams from the 70s. He was so very nice to converse with, and he still looked like he could crush a baseball into the upper decks!

January 10th-13th, 2011 - The first of a series of wonderful four-day trips; many of them with my good friend Jeannine Dalton. On the first night, the whole crew had drinks and dinner at a fun place called the Riviera Bar near our hotel in Los Angeles. The following day we had an enjoyable chat with actress Jackee' Harry who was on our flight to Las Vegas. Once in Vegas, Jeannine and I checked out the Forum Shoppes near Caeser's Palace and then I gave her the rock-and-roll memorabilia tour at the Hard Rock Hotel. At some point, Jeannine also modestly revealed that her oldest daughter had been crowned Miss USA a few years earlier.

However, after this trip was over, I was unable to get home due to a very bad winter storm in Ohio. Since my mom was vacationing at the time in Florida, I asked her if she wanted some company for the weekend. When she said yes, I commuted to Pensacola instead and spent the weekend on the beach. (As a flight attendant, you just have to learn to be flexible with your plans!)

January 17th-20th, 2011 - Same great trip, same great crew! Also, in keeping with the consistency of last week's trip, I again could not get any flights home because of the lingering snowstorms. Therefore,

I ended up back in Pensacola for another weekend visit with my sweet mother.

February 8th-11th, 2011 - An absolutely incredible four-day with Jeannine and another favorite crew member, Bunny Haase. After dinner in Boston at McCormick and Schmidt's, we went exploring and discovered an open auditorium at our hotel. While I sat in an opera box seat, the girls took over the stage. Since they had both had dance training, each one gave a fabulous recital of their favorite routines. (It was so cute. I recall it was like watching kittens play!) My job was to cheer enthusiastically and occasionally use my "announcer's voice" to introduce the next performance. The three of us still laugh about this, even many years later.

The next day, we got back to the reality of our jobs. On our Los Angeles flight, we had a family with a very angry (and very stinky) cat board the plane. However, after assuring us that the cat would not be a problem on the five-hour flight, it got sick on the taxi out to the runway. That made the smell even worse, and the family finally agreed to go back to the gate and get off the flight. It was probably for the best, because our five-hour flight eventually turned into a seven-hour flight due to strong headwinds. Despite the shortened layover, we also celebrated Jeannine's upcoming birthday that night as well.

February 15th-18th, 2011 - Just when I thought that my trips couldn't get any better, I end up flying with Jeannine (again) and my old friend Tony Shimkonis, who is also good friends with Jeannine. Although it was the same trip, we sadly discovered that the auditorium in Boston was closed and locked this time. (However, on the plus side, there were no stench-ridden felines on any of our flights this week.) We still had a great time catching up with each other during the trip. Jeannine was especially amused at Tony's re-telling of our drunken adventures years ago in Buffalo and of playing trivia with actress Linda Blair.

April 5th, 2011 - My wife and I had been planning a trip to the New York area during the summer, so while on our LaGuardia overnight, I secured tickets for both a Mets' and a Yankees' game for that week. I also found tickets for the Broadway production of "The Lion King" that my wife wanted to see.

April 12th, 2011 - I did the same trip this week, but had a much different adventure while in New York City. After we had checked into our hotel, I decided to go out for a walk and a late lunch. As I got a little closer to the Times Square area, I saw what appeared to be a number of white pop-up tents and also some television trucks. Being curious, I walked up to the barricades and struck up a conversation with one of the production people. It turned out that they were filming an episode of the cable show "Man Caves," which aired on the DIY home improvement channel.

Having seen the show a few times, I knew that the hosts were construction guru Jason Cameron and former NFL defensive tackle Tony "Goose" Siragusa. The theme of the show was to give a deserving guy his own specialized space. They often accomplished this by renovating a garage or basement, based on whatever hobby or team the guy was interested in. I had in fact just seen a segment where they surprised an overworked father with his own Pittsburgh Steelers-themed "man cave."

Anyway, while I was chatting with the assistant, I found out that they were getting ready to start work on a room for the owner of Madame Tussaud's Wax Museum, which was located on 42nd Street. At that point, the show's host Jason Cameron, came out and walked over where a few of us were standing. After introducing himself, he wondered out loud if any of us would be interested in "helping him out." It seemed that he needed some people to stand in the background while they taped the beginning of the show. Four or five of us eventually agreed to participate.

Jason then explained that he and Tony were going to present the owner with a design board that would show what the room would look like after they finished. His instructions to us were to smile and nod our heads "like this was the greatest thing we had ever seen!" Sure enough, once the cameras started rolling, we all enthusiastically listened and nodded approvingly. It was great fun.

At the end of taping that segment, Jason apparently appreciated our involvement and personally came over to thank us. In fact, he told us not to wander off because he had a little something for us. Within a few minutes he returned and handed each of us a small, beveled plaque with the show's logo etched into the wood. After we all thanked him for the gift, he even autographed them for us. With that really cool experience under my belt, I pocketed my souvenir and walked off to get lunch.

About two hours later, I was heading back to the hotel, and I chose to wander by the "Man Caves" set to see how things were progressing. As I got a little closer, I could see that Tony Siragusa was lobbing items into the crowd. As I looked up, one of whatever he was throwing was heading my way. I reached up and made a nice over-the-shoulder catch of what turned out to be a small rubber football with the "Man Caves" logo on it. In order to "complete the set," I then worked my way up to

where Tony was standing and he happily signed it for me. I couldn't wait to get home with my new treasures, just so I could display them in my own personal "man cave"!

By the way, when I finally did get to watch that segment air on the DIY network, I found out that it was the milestone "100th episode" of the series. It also featured a very interesting ending to the show. Apparently, the staff of Madame Tussaud's decided to surprise Tony with a wax likeness of himself inside the museum, and he seemed to be very happy to be immortalized in such a way. (I hope his statue is still there, because Mr. Siragusa was definitely a larger-than-life personality! Sadly, I heard that he too passed away recently.)

May 3rd-5th, 2011 - A bad trip with horrible fumes on five of eleven flights this week. On the first day, we had a particularly bad plane that produced jet fumes twice on the same flight. While on our overnight in Albany, New York, I woke up so congested that I could barely breathe. My throat was also incredibly sore. Eventually, I decided to go to the nearest emergency room and get checked out. Unfortunately, the doctor couldn't find anything obviously wrong, but their tests did rule out strep throat. Again, I continued to file safety reports for every incident, and again, nothing seemed to be improving.

May 11th, 2011 - Today we had actress Jane Seymour on our flight from Los Angeles to Charlotte. She was rather quiet, perhaps because she was so incredibly busy. In fact, she worked non-stop the entire flight on some sort of designer jewelry project.

June 9th, 2011 - This was the last day of a four-day trip, which had included a long layover in downtown Seattle. That morning, I had gotten up early and ended up walking around the waterfront and Pike Market areas. After a nice lunch, I started to head back to our hotel to begin getting ready for our last flight back to Charlotte.

As I was coming up the hill from the waterfront, I noticed a big tractor-trailer rig parked across the street. On either side of the rig were large signs advertising the 40th Anniversary of the Hard Rock Cafe. It turned out that it was their mobile music museum. Inside were numerous displays of some of the most iconic memorabilia from some of their biggest restaurants.

It was then that I noticed a guy leaning up against the rear of the trailer, so I wandered over to talk to him. Come to find out, his name was Jeff Nolan, and he was the main curator for all of the Hard Rock empire. I introduced myself and then asked what time the exhibit would be open. When he said that it wouldn't be open for another hour or so, I must have looked really disappointed. After I explained that I was a flight attendant and had to leave soon to fly home, he wondered if I had a few minutes to spare. He then opened up the trailer door and invited me to "take a look around."

For a music fan like me, it was like I had died and gone to heaven. Inside were numerous glass cases containing some important pieces of music memorabilia. I recall seeing the dress that Madonna wore when she debuted the song "Like a Virgin" at the MTV Music Awards. There was also Jeff Beck's favorite Seafoam Green Stratocaster guitar that Mr. Nolan even let me take out of the case and strum a few times. He and I also enjoyed swapping stories of meeting rock music stars over the years. I remember he was especially impressed with my Alice Cooper and Meat Loaf tales.

My favorite story of his was how the Hard Rock Cafe began to collect and display musical items. According to him, the two original owners opened up their first restaurant in London near Hyde Park Corner in 1971. Because it was close to a number of famous London music venues, artists and musicians started dropping by after their shows. One of their favorite performers was Eric Clapton, who seemed to really like the food and the atmosphere. Since they apparently took such good care of him whenever he showed up, he eventually decided to thank them with a special gift.

Apparently, one day he surprised them with one of his many guitars. The owners were so appreciative that they decided to hang it on the wall near where he usually ate. According to the story, guitarist Pete Townsend of "The Who" stopped by sometime afterwards and then inquired as to why Clapton's guitar was so prominently displayed. After explaining that it was there to "mark his spot," Mr. Townsend appeared both amused and annoyed. Several days later, the owners received a package in the mail. When they opened it, they found an autographed guitar from Pete Townsend, with a note that read, "My guitar is as good as his! Love, Pete." They then joyfully mounted it on the wall next to Clapton's, and their iconic decoration theme began.

Mr. Nolan was also kind enough to share that, like me, he too had once been a teacher, and had started out playing in a garage band as well. He also informed me that he was a guitar smith who often worked on the many vintage instruments that were used as displays.

After looking at my watch and realizing that I was running late, I profusely thanked Jeff for the wonderful stories and the personal tour. I then wondered if he wouldn't mind hiring me as a trainee after I retired from the airline business, because apparently his position was actually my "dream job." He just laughed, handed me his business card, and told me to stay in touch.

July 6th, 2011 - We had the famous horror-film director M. Night Shamylan (and his entire family) up in First Class on our flight to Orlando. Despite how strange his movies are, he and his family seemed very nice...and normal!

July 24th, 2011 - After my trip was over, I had a terrible time trying to commute back to Dayton. Since all the Dayton flights were full and two Columbus flights cancelled, I had to fly into Cincinnati and have my wife pick me up at the airport. I then had to promise her a nice dinner (and possibly some jewelry later) to get her to drive me up to the Dayton airport in order to pick up my car. Being the wonderful person that she is, she consented.

July 28th, 2011 - On our Philadelphia-Los Angeles flight, we had a very nice, but very nervous, passenger in the last row. She really wanted to get off the plane, but after I patiently answered all her questions about how the plane worked and exactly what causes turbulence, she finally agreed to stay on the flight. She did pretty well during the taxi and takeoff, and by the time we had finished up with the meal service, she appeared to be much calmer. Toward the end of the flight, she even came to the back galley to thank me for being so kind to her. Come to find out, she was a British actress named Juliette and was on her way to start work on a movie. She was so sweet, and I absolutely loved her charming English accent.

August 17th, 2011 - This was an "extra" trip with a long layover in Las Vegas. Part of my crew was the very fun Teri Kirkland. Once we got to our hotel, she and I decided to go catch the matinee show of the always entertaining "Blue Man Group." Our original seats were about halfway back on the aisle, and just before the show started, one of the directors came up to us and asked if we would be interested in having a small part in the show.

Now I had seen the show a few years back in Boston, and knew that some participants got "decorated" or otherwise embarrassed on stage. However, Teri had never seen the show and wanted to take part, so I relented. Fortunately, our roles in the show were relatively benign. In exchange for much better seats closer to the stage, all we had to do was act like we were arriving late and let the actors quietly pause and stare at us while we settled into our new seats. (Teri was really good at acting. I just pretended to avert my eyes and not look at anyone.) We got a big laugh from the audience, so we must not have been too bad.

August 23rd, 2011 - Every once in a while, you forget that flight crew members sometimes have issues in their personal life that just have to wait until they are done flying. My friend Gayle, who is normally really fun and outgoing, was very quiet on our first two flights today. Once we had a few minutes to talk, I found out that her husband wanted a divorce and also wanted to sell their house. On top of that, she just found out that her mother had terminal cancer. When I wondered why she came to work at all, she just shrugged and said she needed the money. So, for all you passengers out there, the next time your flight attendants aren't smiling, please remember that some days we are "human" too.

September 19th-22nd, 2011 - After a lot of complaints from our crews about Terrible's Casino, we were finally given another hotel to stay at in Las Vegas. The Palace Station was kind of isolated off the north end of the Strip, but at least the air conditioning worked. Also, on the last day of this trip we found out that our last leg from Seattle to Charlotte was cancelled. They then sent us back to the hotel for one more additional day off.

September 26th, 2011 - Today, I had my old flight attendant Supervisor Diana Darak on our flight from Charlotte to Pittsburgh. It was so nice to get caught up with her. I also found out that her daughter was going to be a flight attendant for us as well.

November 1st, 2011 - There was some sort of security breach today in Charlotte, which created all sorts of problems. Our Charlotte-Ft. Lauderdale flight was delayed for over four hours and we didn't get to our hotel rooms that night until 3 a.m. I never did hear exactly what happened, but security officers were all over the airport.

December 1st, 2011 - After my trip was finished, I grabbed a quick flight home, then jumped on a plane to LaGuardia so I could see my friend Jim Cole perform again at Carnegie Hall. He sounded great, and we had a wonderful time swapping stories afterwards.

December 19th, 2011 - A really great trip with 36 hours off in San Juan, Puerto Rico. Although there was a hard rain most of the day, we still managed to get out and explore a little of Old San Juan. Apparently, a damp day in the Caribbean is still better than a cold day up north!

Chapter Twenty-Four

2012....Pestilence and the O'Hare Explorations

January 4th, 2012 - It was really cold in New York City today. However, I did end up having drinks and dinner with my old pal Sue Burns at a hockey bar called the "Flying Puck" near Madison Square Garden. She is so funny. I always enjoyed flying with her because it seemed that we had the same twisted sense of humor.

January 20th, 2012 - Our new credit card applications are now featuring 40,000 free miles which is enough for two free round-trip tickets. Apparently, that must be a pretty good deal because I can't hand them out fast enough to our passengers.

February 15th, 2012 - I worked an "extra" trip with my old friend Stacey Mosley. On our short overnight in LaGuardia, it took a very long time to get to our hotel because of icy roads and lots of traffic. However, once at the hotel, we got a chance to chat with basketball broadcaster Dick Vitale who just happened to be in the hotel lobby. He was just as animated in person as he was on television.

March 5th, 2012 - This trip had a long layover at a very nice resort in Montego Bay, Jamaica. One of my fellow flight attendants was a guy named Harold. Eventually I found out that he is a cousin to long-time Springsteen guitarist "Little Stevie" Van Zandt. Harold then shared some pretty cool stories about his cousin's time with the "E Street Band"!

March 7th, 2012 - While on a long overnight in Denver, I got to stay at a very unique hotel that featured a board-game-themed interior. Apparently, each floor featured a different game like "Boggle" or

"Trivial Pursuit." My particular floor was based on the game "Scrabble" and each sign on that floor was made from old Scrabble letter tiles.

While in Denver, I also finally got a chance to get caught up with a buddy of mine named John Taylor, who was an old college friend from E.K.U. (Not to be confused with my previously mentioned captain friend with the same name.) He had always been so much fun to be around, and in fact had even dated my little sister for a while. Over the years, he had become very successful as a corporate executive, and consequently his work had taken him all over the United States. Because he had finally settled in the Denver area, we now had a chance to meet up for the first time in over 20 years. We had a great lunch and eventually promised not to wait so long to meet up again!

March 12th-15th, 2012 - This trip was similar to last weeks, but not as much fun, mostly because we encountered three different fume events and one serious medical emergency. The only good thing this week was the chance to chat with NASCAR driver Rusty Wallace on our flight into Charlotte. When I noticed him looking at a livestock magazine, I commented on his unusual choice of reading material. He laughed and said that he was thinking of buying some cattle but didn't know much about them. After I revealed that I had grown up on a dairy farm, he perked up. We then had a nice conversation about cows and what to look for in selecting good ones. He was a very nice guy.

March 20th, 2012 - Today was another example of what flight attendants sometimes have to deal with on the job. Soon after we took off for Philadelphia, the captain called our "A" flight attendant up to the cockpit to inform her of a message that would be waiting for her when we landed. We found out later that her brother had been robbed and beaten after he stopped to assist another motorist during an apparently "staged" accident. Because her brother had ended up in intensive care, she decided to get off the trip. I only heard much later that he survived, but never fully recovered.

March 29th, 2012 - On my commuter flight home to Cincinnati, I had the good fortune to sit next to a very nice, and rather talkative, passenger named Jim Anderson. After we swapped stories for a while, I eventually found out that he was a coach for the Cincinnati Bengals football team. He told me that if I ever wanted to come and watch a practice, that I should look him up. (Sadly, I never got around to it before he retired from coaching.)

May 8th-11th, 2012 - This was a nice "extra" trip with some long layovers. While in Phoenix, I got to catch up with my friends Dan and Gloria Dotson, who were now living outside the Phoenix area. We had a great dinner and then did very well in a trivia contest at a pub called the "Crown and Rose". (Apparently, I was still retaining lots of information from my preparation to be on "Millionaire" a few years back!)

May 15th, 2012 - I found out today that our USAirways gates in Cincinnati, had been moved to the newly opened Terminal #3. While waiting to get my seat assignment on the Charlotte flight, I was interviewed by a reporter for the local Cincinnati Enquirer newspaper. It seemed that she wanted to know how the flight crews liked the new building. When I told her that I was with the mainline part of USAirways and not the commuter group that was based there, she seemed much less interested in my opinion.

May 31st, 2012 - Because our new hotel for the long Boston overnights is now located in the Harvard University area, I decided to go explore the famed campus. It ended up being a really nice day. I especially enjoyed checking out the world-renowned Harvard Law School and reveling in all the history there. I believe I counted something like 18 Supreme Court Justices (including five on the current Court) that had attended Harvard Law School. It also made me wonder what my life might have been like had I decided to finish law school back in the early '80s.

June 22nd, 2012 - Although we had been warned about a recent uptick of bedbugs by our union, I had not encountered them, until today. After spending the night at a Holiday Inn in Los Angeles, I woke up with some itchy red spots on my legs. Sure enough, when I looked closer, I could see what looked like some dark-colored spots on the bed sheets. It was indeed bedbugs!

After furiously showering and then coating my legs with anti-itch powder, I first reported it to the hotel manager, and then called our union. Basically, all I got was a few apologies and some tips on how to not bring them home. (i.e., always store your suitcase in the tub or shower area, put all affected clothes in a very hot dryer, etc.) The itching persisted for a couple of days and I remember hoping that it wouldn't happen again.

July 3rd, 2012 - Well, it did happen again. This time it was at the rather seedy Hotel Pennsylvania in New York City. However, since my first encounter with them, I have been hyper-vigilant about checking the sheets and bed area when first entering my hotel room. This time I noticed the dark "pencil points" on the bed sheets right away and backed out of the room immediately. Fortunately, they gave me a different room, but I still alerted my crew and our union.

July 4th, 2012 - The same thing happened the next night at the LaQuinta Inn in Pittsburgh. Again, I was able to secure a different room, but I still felt restless that night. We have been told also that if there are no other rooms available, we have the right to request a room at a different hotel.

July 31st, 2012 - Today I got to work with a really fun Philadelphia-based crew that included my old friend Jeff Wagner. Unfortunately, just as we were about to close the door in Las Vegas, there was a big fuel spill. Because of the dangers involved with the fuel odors, we then had to deplane the passengers and endure a two-hour delay. Fortunately, the passengers seemed to be okay with the situation because we had very few complaints. Many of them just went over to the slot machines in the lobby area and continued to gamble. One guy was actually happy about it, because he apparently won over $400 during our little delay.

August 1st, 2012 - Because of our late arrival due to that fuel spill, I was not contractually legal to fly the next day due to "insufficient crew rest." That meant that I got to sleep in the next morning and then just deadhead to Dallas, Texas. However, in another one of my unusual "coincidences," I got to have a nice long chat with my van driver on the way to my Dallas hotel. It was then that I found out that he was originally from Mansfield, Ohio, which is where my mother's family lived.

Even more interesting to me was that his brother used to have a business that promoted and produced rock concerts. Back in the 1970s, most major shows in Ohio were connected to his family's "Ross Todd Productions." My driver then modestly related some great stories about his favorite concert events and his favorite bands. One that I vividly recall was a tale about them promoting a young three-piece rock band from the Cleveland area by the name of "James Gang." It seems that one of their first gigs was at a water park. Things were apparently going well until the guitar player got mad because some kids were splashing water on his favorite amplifier. My driver claimed to have talked that guitarist out of quitting the band and then persuaded them to continue. That guitar player was one of my favorite artists, the incredible Joe Walsh!

August 9th, 2012 - Because there was a lot of bad weather in the Midwest, we ended up sitting on the runway in Philadelphia for over three hours. Due to the length of the delay, we went through the cabin several times with drinks and a few snacks to keep everyone happy. At one point, the captain even admitted that he had no idea how much longer it would be, and then asked us to hand out the "emergency cookies." (Those cookies had been recently placed on all of our aircraft for just such an occasion.) I don't know if it actually made any of our passengers feel better about what was happening, but it did seem to mollify the crowd.

September 20th, 2012 - This was a nice day with a long layover in Phoenix. Part of our crew then decided to go catch the Arizona Diamondbacks game which was just down the street from our hotel. Our first officer Todd Daczkowski, and old friends Dave Brown and Chris Young and I, ended up scalping some outfield seats from a guy on a bicycle for a mere five dollars each. Those seats were also close to a really unique ballpark perk; a swimming pool! (In fact, we ended up having as much fun watching the fans swim as we did watching the game.) Afterwards, we walked down the street and had dinner at the previously mentioned "Cooperstown" restaurant owned by rocker Alice Cooper. What a good day!

October 10th, 2012 - Today was my 25th wedding anniversary. Although Karen and I had originally planned to celebrate with a fabulous return trip to Hawaii, those plans changed when my wife broke her foot last week. With her foot in a big cast, she wouldn't have been able to make the long flight or to walk on the beach. Therefore, we shifted gears and settled for a "road trip" instead. This week, I got to push my wife's wheelchair through the Rock and Roll Hall of Fame in Cleveland, the Pro Football Hall of Fame in Canton, and her favorite place in Ohio, the Columbus Zoo. While it might not have been as glamorous as Hawaii, it was still a lot of fun!

October 23rd, 2012 - Here's a logbook notation that I had forgotten about. It said that "Today I was accidentally punched by a passenger"! As I recall, we were deplaning the San Francisco-Philadelphia flight, and a young man was trying to slip his backpack up onto his shoulder. As he passed by me, he swung his left arm around to secure the pack and accidentally struck me in the jaw. We were both really shocked when it happened, and he immediately started apologizing over and over. Once I knew that I wasn't injured, I started razzing him about how bad our service must have been. We both ended up laughing about it eventually. However, just to be sure, I did file a safety report with the company.

October 29th-November 1st, 2012 - On the first day of this four-day "extra" trip, we had our Boston turn cancelled because hurricane Sandy was devastating the East Coast. Eventually, the only flight I worked was from Charlotte to Chicago O'Hare. Because this was an "extra" trip where I was on my own, I was sent to a nearby hotel to wait for further instructions from our crew schedulers. Because of the size of the storm and the fact that my trip consisted mostly of East Coast flights, the schedulers kept telling me to be patient.

That wait ultimately turned into a three-day stay at the Airport Sheraton Four Points hotel. Unfortunately, since the hotel location was in a mostly residential area, the front desk staff informed me that they couldn't take me anywhere except back to the airport. So, as flight attendants are accustomed to doing, I adapted to the situation. On the second day, after hearing that I probably wasn't going to fly that day, I put on my uniform and went back to the airport to go exploring.

On that excursion, I eventually discovered a couple of nice food courts that would sustain me for the next few days. I also found a vintage neon light display in the tunnel between Terminals 2 and 3. In addition, I checked out the historical display of Medal of Honor winner Butch O'Hare, who was the Navy pilot and World War II hero that the airport was named for. On the third day, I continued my exploration and found a 40-foot-high dinosaur skeleton near the United Airlines gates. I also discovered what eventually would become my very favorite snack food.

Based on the recommendation of a fellow crew member, I decided to try out a flavored popcorn from a place called "Garrett's." I can only say that after just a few bites of that deliciousness, I think my eyes rolled back in my head and I had drool on my chin. I also had to seriously control my urge to do a "face plant" right into the bag and not come up for air. It was absolutely incredible. I ate the entire first bag in under two minutes, then purchased the biggest container available to take back to the hotel with me. I can only surmise that if they had not made me go fly again on that last day, I would have purchased a 55-gallon drum of the stuff to ship home.

November 7th, 2012 - After months of reassurances that the company was attempting to fix the fume problem, we were again exposed to another fume situation. This one happened on our New Orleans flight during our pushback. Although it didn't last long, the bad air actually seemed to be worse than usual. Again, I notified my supervisor and filled out the appropriate reports afterwards. (After all these repeated exposures, I am mildly surprised that I am not sporting some sort of added appendage, or at least glowing in the dark!)

November 28th-29th, 2012 - This is a rather strange story of another of my unbelievable coincidences. Apparently, there is a game called "Seven Degrees of Separation", where any two people can be connected by seven or fewer acquaintances. A variation of that game, where any two actors/actresses can be connected, is known as "Six degrees of Kevin Bacon." On our flight into New York LaGuardia today, we had that well-known actor Kevin Bacon traveling with us up in First Class. Although I did not get to interact with him much during the flight, he seemed to be a very pleasant person.

The really weird part of this tale actually took place the next morning as we were leaving LaGuardia. As I was passing through the main cabin with the drink cart, a young man stopped me and wanted to purchase a beer. Because he looked so young, I thought that that it would be wise to ask for his ID. When he presented his driver's license, I saw that not only was he old enough, but that he was another...Kevin Bacon!

I then informed him that I had just had the most famous of his namesakes on my flight, not 12 hours earlier! The young man then replied that although it was a surprisingly common name, he had never met anyone who had actually encountered the most well-known Kevin Bacon before! He also seemed glad to know that his namesake appeared to be a good guy.

December 9th-12th, 2012 - Now that my wife was somewhat recovered from her foot injury, we managed to sneak away for a delayed anniversary celebration in Orlando. Although it wasn't quite as exotic as Hawaii, it was still great to spend some time with my sweetie!

December 21st, 2012 - Although there had been all sorts of dire predictions of the world coming to an end, (at least according to the Mayan calendar) today was a pretty good day. I even got a seat on a commuter flight back to Cincinnati, despite the usual holiday crowds. It seemed like a good way to end a difficult year.

Chapter Twenty-Five

2013....A Flight Full of Stars and the American Merger

January 3rd, 2013 - While on a long layover in downtown Atlanta, I walked over to the Centennial Park area and took the tour of the Georgia Aquarium. It was a fabulous facility with lots of interesting displays. My favorite was the huge saltwater tank in the middle of the building that contained thousands of fish. It was supposedly the largest saltwater tank in the world. In fact, it was so big that it contained several whale sharks, which are the largest species of shark.

January 22nd, 2013 - This was another of those weird weather days that really aggravate my sinuses. We started off in Minneapolis where it was a chilling -13° degrees when we left. By the end of the day, we had worked our way across the country to Las Vegas. There it was a robust 85° degrees and warm enough to go out for dinner with no jacket. However, my nose was running the whole time.

In addition, we have also started hearing rumors that American Airlines and USAirways may be in talks regarding a possible merger. After years of hearing many variations of this subject, I still don't think that it will amount to anything substantial.

February 11th-14th, 2013 - Another good four-day trip with my friend Nadine Freeman. Our senior flight attendant was a very nice 70-year old who was just hired last year. Her only drawback was that she was so slow with her First-Class service, that we had to go up front to help her finish up on several flights. Later that evening, Nadine and I also played trivia at the Crown and Rose Pub in Phoenix. Fortunately, we got lucky and won first place on a bonus question about types of dairy cows. (My farming background finally came in handy!)

On the last day of this trip, we found out that the potential merger of American Airlines and USAirways was not only happening but was now considered "official." It was also announced that the two airlines would merge by the end of the year. Apparently the USAirways brand would disappear, and we would then operate under the American banner. My first reaction to this news was disbelief and then sadness; mostly because American had a reputation of not treating their people very well. They also had a different flight attendant union and very different pass privileges. Once again, the phrase "we shall see" seemed appropriate here.

February 27th, 2013 - We showed up at the LaGuardia Airport this morning only to find that our plane was full of fumes. We then had to delay our departure to Charlotte by more than two hours in order to clear the cabin air and fix the problem. Strangely enough, that actually turned out to be beneficial because our "extra" flight attendant failed to show up on time and we would have had to wait on her anyway.

March 18th-21st, 2013 - A nice four-day trip with my friend Nadine Freeman again. Once we got to Las Vegas, Nadine and I rode the city bus north and took in the "Fremont Street Experience." If you have never seen it, the overhead canopy show featuring thousands of lights is amazing!

March 22nd, 2013 - Today was my 30th anniversary as a flight attendant with USAirways. As I have noted previously, I still am in awe of what I get to do for a paycheck. Despite lots of changes and adjustments, I still love this profession!

April 11th, 2013 - After we had parked our plane at the gate in Las Vegas, the entire crew was asked to step off the plane and onto the tarmac during some sort of security check. While down there we decided to take a group photo in front of the left engine. (Of course, after I recalled what was left of the "pureed" Golden Eagle a few years back, I made really sure that those engines were not running!)

April 26th, 2013 - This weekend I drove to Pittsburgh to attend a big reunion party for anyone who had worked for old USAir. It was a great time and I got to reconnect with lots of old friends. There was a lot of concern expressed about the American merger as well.

April 30th-May 3rd, 2013 - A really good trip with a great crew. The highlight was a 24-hour stay at the beautiful Riu Resort in Punta Cana, Dominican Republic. While we were checking in, we were informed that our crew would have unlimited free access to all bars and restaurants. We were also greeted by a hostess who presented us each with a free banana daiquiri.

If that wasn't enough, just as we were getting ready to go up to our rooms, the concierge informed us that he had authentic Cuban cigars behind the counter, and that we could each have one to take with us. (Although I am not a smoker, I do like an occasional cigar.) Since Cuban cigars were still prohibited at the time in the U.S., I decided to accept the offer. I also fondly recall that about an hour later, I was walking on the beach with a free Scotch in my hand, smoking a very smooth Cuban cigar, and wondering why all of my layovers couldn't be like this one!

May 9th, 2013 - This story is another of my very favorite passenger encounters. On this day we were flying from Los Angeles to Charlotte and I was working the "extra" position on an Airbus-321. I was stationed at the third set of exit doors for boarding, and we had a completely full flight. Unfortunately, my jump seat area can sometimes get a little congested during boarding, so I occasionally have passengers standing right next to me while waiting to take their seats.

After about five minutes, I found myself in that situation, and was almost nose-to-nose with a young man who sort of looked familiar. I broke the tension with some off-the-cuff remark about "the joys of air travel" which made him chuckle. Once we started chatting, he seemed even more familiar, so I wondered out loud if he might have been on one of my flights before. When he replied that he often flew because of his job, I then inquired about what he did for a living.

It turns out that he was an actor. After I heard that, my trivia brain kicked in and I told him that for whatever reason, the name "Rabbit" was coming to mind. He actually laughed and complimented me on knowing that. He then introduced himself as Sean Whalen and clarified that he had played the role of "Rabbit's driver" in the movie "Twister" with Helen Hunt and Bill Paxson. In that movie, Mr. Whalen was one of a group of storm chasers who were following a line of tornadoes. I then welcomed him on our flight and told him if he needed anything, to just let me know.

Eventually we completed the boarding process and then took off for the four-hour flight to Charlotte. Since we were completely full, our crew had a lot of preparation to do for the upcoming meal and drink service. Once we leveled out, we then began pulling out the service carts in the rear galley and started setting up. It was then that a passenger with a very deep and distinctive voice came up to us in the rear galley. He apologized for disrupting our preparations, and then wanted to ask a favor of us.

The gentleman proceeded to explain that he had a bad hip and wondered if there was some place in the rear galley where he could stretch out a bit. He then promised he would "stay out of our way" after that. Because he seemed sincere, I explained that there currently just wasn't any space in the back galley because of all the carts, but perhaps my friend working First Class might be able to let him use the front galley. I then told him to follow me up to the front of the plane.

While working our way up to First Class, we managed to have a little bit of a chat. However, the more we talked, the more his voice seemed familiar. Although it took me a few minutes, by the time we got up front I finally realized that he was veteran actor Ernie Hudson. (Mr. Hudson is possibly most well-known for his role as Winston Zeddemore in the famous 1984 movie "Ghostbusters.") Once my friend okayed him using the galley area for a few minutes, I asked if he was in fact Mr. Hudson. He then laughed and admitted that it was true. He also thanked me for helping him and then wondered aloud about..."How you flight attendants manage to do this job?"

I must have given him a quizzical look, because he then went on to explain that his wife had been a flight attendant when they first got married. However, he admitted that he didn't like her being away all the time and eventually asked her to quit flying. I recall telling him that there were a lot of jobs where one has to be away, (like acting) and that you just get used to it after awhile. After he finished with his stretching, he asked if he could borrow the pen that I had in my shirt pocket for a few minutes.

After I agreed and handed it over to him, he then grabbed a napkin and proceeded to write something down. After returning my pen, he also handed me the napkin and again thanked me for helping him out. It was only after he left to go back to his seat, that I took a look at the napkin. It seemed that Mr. Hudson had been nice enough to jot down a short note that read, "Larry, Great flying with you! Ernie Hudson." On my way back to the rear of the aircraft, I made sure to wink at him and silently thank him for the nice souvenir.

The next hour or so was pretty busy with us trying to get everyone a meal and some beverages. After we had most of the service completed, I decided to pass through the cabin with a trash bag and continue picking up what was left over. Around row 12 or so, a very nice lady stopped me and wondered if we had any forks left. It seemed that she had purchased a salad in the Los Angeles airport but had neglected to pick up any utensils. I told her that I didn't think so but would double-check just to be sure.

Unfortunately for her, I discovered that we had used all the plastic silverware that had been boarded, so when I returned with the bad news, she humorously pretended to pout by sticking out her lower lip. That made me laugh, so I then volunteered to see if my friend working First Class had any utensils left over. She did in fact have one metal fork left over but was hesitant to hand it out. (At the time, our flight crews had been cautioned about allowing any metal objects into the main cabin that could be used as a weapon in a hijacking attempt.) I told my friend that the lady seemed very nice and probably wasn't a threat, so she reluctantly agreed to let her use it.

After returning to her seat, I then knelt down in the aisle and quietly informed her that there was in fact one fork left. But, due to safety regulations about potentially dangerous metal objects, before I could give it to her, she had to promise me something. She giggled and asked what that could possibly be. I then said she had to agree to return the fork AND to not go "crazy" or try to stab people she didn't like. That made her laugh out loud and as soon as she started laughing, she appeared to be very familiar to me. It turned out that my passenger was the well-known actress, Dee Wallace. (Ms. Wallace is possibly best remembered for playing the mother of the three kids in the popular 1982 film "E.T.") When she finally agreed to try to "control herself", I then presented her with the fork and told her to enjoy her salad.

About 20 minutes later, I was again passing through the cabin when Ms. Wallace stopped me. She then thanked me for helping her out and gleefully returned the metal fork with the announcement that,

"As you can see, I didn't kill anybody!"

That made me laugh out loud, so I told her that I was "so very proud of her" for controlling her urges. She also wanted to know my name and how she could thank me. After introducing myself, I told her it was my pleasure to assist her and left it at that.

I then went up to First Class to return the fork. However, as I was returning, Ms. Wallace flagged me down and handed me a folded-up piece of paper. As I opened it up, I saw that she too had signed a nice little note, along with her autograph. However, after I read it I started laughing again. I then recall telling her that I was so very glad that she had "good penmanship," because her note could have gotten me in trouble with my wife. When she looked a bit confused, I pointed out that her note read, "Larry, Thanks for the fork! Dee Wallace." When it slowly dawned on her that a poorly written "fork" could have been interpreted as something else, she turned beet red and began apologizing profusely. That made us both laugh out loud...again! She was just so sweet and so much fun to have onboard!

To begin wrapping up this story, by the time we landed in Charlotte, I was already considering this flight to be one of my best ones yet. When we finally got to the gate and the passengers got up to leave, Dee Wallace waved goodbye to me from row 12, Ernie Hudson patted me on the shoulder as he walked by, and Sean Whalen nodded and told me that it had been a great flight. However, once again the phrase, "But wait, there's more!" seems appropriate here.

You see, as the crowd in the back of the plane was again bunching up around my jump seat area, a gentleman standing right next to me turned and asked me what I knew about the weather in Wilmington, North Carolina. I told him that I wasn't sure, but I thought it was supposed to be a little rainy that particular weekend. He then replied "crap" and indicated that he had left his jacket back on his seat in the next-to-last row. He also said that he had a very short time to make his connecting flight to Wilmington and was debating as to whether he should leave the jacket or not. I then told him that if he would step out of line and wait just a second, I could retrieve his coat and he would still make the flight. It was then that he started looking familiar as well.

As it turned out, I was speaking with another actor. His name was Louis Mandylor and I remembered that he had played the sympathetic younger brother in the movie "My Big Fat Greek Wedding." As I returned his coat, I then asked him why there were so many actors on this particular flight. He replied that most of them were going to attend the annual Wilmington Film Festival that weekend. I then wished him a safe flight before he hurried off the plane.

As you can see, there were times where my job was just so enjoyable. On just this one flight, I got to interact with not one, but four actors and actresses and was even presented with a couple of autographs. The biggest takeaway was that they were all very nice and all of them seemed like really good people.

June 6th-12th, 2013 - My wife and I took a little vacation to Texas during this week. The highlight was being able to watch a baseball game at both the Texas Rangers and Houston Astros ballparks. After that trip, I had then seen games at 28 of the 30 Major League stadiums. That left only Milwaukee and Kansas City to go on my "bucket list" of seeing all the teams home parks.

June 24th-27th, 2013 - This was an absolutely horrendous week of flying, mostly due to bad weather. On the first day, we had long delays in both Charlotte and Phoenix and didn't get into our hotel rooms that night until 5 a.m. On the third day, we had a major mechanical problem with one of the plane's tires and again arrived very late in Newark with a very minimal overnight stay. We were finally replaced on the last day because of crew fatigue issues.

July 29th-Aug 1st, 2013 - A very interesting four-day trip. On the second day, we had a young male passenger who claimed he was worth "millions and millions" of dollars and would have our jobs if he didn't get a drink right away. We basically ignored him, until he left his seat and then lit up a cigarette near the rear lavatory. We then sternly admonished him and told him to get back in his seat or he would be arrested when we arrived in Charlotte. After (again) telling us his dad would have us all fired, he returned to his seat and eventually went to sleep. However, once we landed in Charlotte, we couldn't wake him up. We then called the paramedics who thought he was intoxicated and eventually took him off the plane. The last we saw of him, he was still mumbling about suing the company...and now all the medical personnel as well!

On the third day, during our long overnight in Atlanta, I walked up to the local passport office and renewed my passport for another 10 years. Although we are required to carry a valid passport with us at all times, the office said they had to keep my old one, but they gave me papers showing that I was still covered for any international travel. That didn't sound right, but a quick call to our union office confirmed that it was permissible, at least until my new passport arrived.

On the final day, we finished up in Charlotte and I then had a chance to explore our newly renovated flight attendant crew room. It appeared to be a much nicer facility than our previous digs. There was a much larger space for all the crew computers and mailboxes and it had more room to relax before and after our trips. It also featured a sleeping room with reclining chairs that I suspected would get a lot of use.

August 5th-8th, 2013 - This turned out to be a really nice four-day trip with my friends Sue Burns, Mary Hardy, and Kim Shaver. The highlight was a nice long layover in San Juan, Puerto Rico. However, before we left there was some real contention regarding my not-yet-expired passport. Our schedulers did not want to accept my temporary passport documents and tried to take me off the trip. Fortunately, our union came to my rescue and finally got it straightened out. I was glad I got to stay on the trip because the whole crew had a great time in San Juan!

September 17th, 2013 - What a way to start your day. Apparently, our hotel in LaGuardia had some plumbing problems and there was no running water or working showers in the morning. I tried to deal with the situation by filling the sink with some bottled water and then washing up as much as possible. I was also able to slather on an extra layer of deodorant before we left. Fortunately, we only had to work two flights today, so none of our passengers passed out from the crew stench and blamed it on us!

September 25th, 2013 - We encountered really bad jet fumes on our Charlotte flight today. When we complained to the captain, he informed us that the "outflow valve" was not working. It eventually cleared out, but I had a headache the rest of the day.

November 1st, 2013 - We were informed by the company today of a major change of policy that becomes effective next week. Apparently, passengers will now be able to listen to their electronic devices during takeoff and landings. Although I disliked having to remind our passengers about removing their earphones and/or headsets during those crucial phases of flight, I always felt better that they were at least kind of aware of what was happening around them.

November 12th, 2013 - Today, the government gave their final approval and cleared the way for the upcoming USAirways/American Airlines merger. According to the reports, it would probably be completed by early December. While I hated to be too pessimistic, I was really dreading this huge change in our work lives.

December 9th, 2013 - Today the American merger became "official" and was the beginning of lots of policy and cultural changes for us. As in past mergers, I wanted to keep an open mind and hopefully let things work out.

December 27th, 2013- In another unusual coincidence, I had one of my favorite college fraternity "Little Sisters" on our flight today. I had not seen my friend Connie Upton for a long time; maybe since our graduation day. It was great to catch up with her. We even took a photo of both of us up in First Class.

December 28th, 2013 - There's nothing like ending an unusual year on a humorous note. After checking in at our Holiday Inn in San Francisco, I entered my room and began doing all my normal room assessments, like checking behind the shower curtain and looking under the bed. However, when I opened the storage room door, I discovered that my closet was full of women's clothes! (This included several nice cocktail dresses and strangely enough, two vastly different sized brassieres!) Because I was a Gold-level member of the Holiday Inn frequent customer club, I called the front desk to thank them for the "welcoming gifts" but informed them that I couldn't accept them. When the manager came up to see what was going on, he couldn't apologize enough...but he also couldn't explain it away either.

Chapter Twenty-Six

2014....Missing Vans, Irish Beer,
and Leaking Butt Stitches

January 1st, 2014 - Over the last month or so, my family has had to make some difficult decisions regarding our mother. While she had generally done very well with living on her own since our father passed away in 1997, she had also gradually exhibited increasing signs of dementia. My sisters and I finally got her to agree to try out a nearby Assisted Living facility to see if she felt comfortable there. We moved her in yesterday, and so far, she seemed to be adjusting pretty well. I now hoped that I wouldn't worry as much about her welfare while I was out flying.

January 6th-9th, 2014 - This trip was with one of my favorite pilots, captain Rick Aarnes. (He and I had started out at USAir in Pittsburgh at about the same time, and had flown a lot of trips together over the years.) Eventually, he shared with us that he had decided to retire in about six months, which made me a little sad. He was always so easy to fly with. The trip itself was okay, but very cold and snowy. (Pittsburgh was at -27°, Indianapolis was at -14°, and Minneapolis was at -20°!)

February 11th-14th, 2014 - Another trip with lots of weather problems. We managed to get to Boston on the first day before snowstorms in the South and Midwest cancelled the rest of our day. On the second day, our Charlotte flights cancelled, and we ferried an empty airplane to Pittsburgh. By the time we got to our hotel in downtown Pittsburgh, the snow had increased, and we were pretty sure we weren't going anywhere anytime soon. In fact, there were several other USAirways crews stuck there also.

On the third day, we were eventually sent to the Pittsburgh airport, but after six hours of snow and ice storms, our crew schedulers opted to send us back to the hotel. On the last day, we again tried for several hours to work a flight to Charlotte, but to no avail. After we were told that our trip was finished, our schedulers then confessed that they weren't sure exactly when we would be getting home. Basically, they told us that we were on our own and wished us good luck. After hearing that, I decided to rent a car in Pittsburgh and drive very carefully for eight hours to get home. What a tough trip!

March 8th, 2014 - Today it was reported that a Malaysian Airlines Boeing 777 airliner was missing somewhere over the South China Sea. There were over 200 passengers and a crew of 12 on board when it disappeared. Eventually, some debris from the plane was recovered, but no credible explanation has ever emerged (so far) as to what happened to it.

March 10th-20th, 2014 - I had to call off two consecutive trips because my wife slipped on some ice while I was home, and severely fractured her ankle. Fortunately, my emergency training kicked in and I was able to calm my wife and stabilize the leg. (The fracture was so severe that even the EMTs who responded to the call, looked at it and went "Ewww!") We got lucky and had a terrific surgeon who successfully repaired the damage, but she was laid up for several months.

March 26th, 2014 - This was a crazier-than-usual commute home to Dayton. Because of all the full flights, I was forced to fly from Charlotte to Philadelphia. For a few minutes I even had a seat on a small commuter plane to Dayton. But in a highly unusual situation, I was taken off that plane for a paying passenger, even though the door had been closed and we had been cleared for pushback. I was then forced to take a flight to Cincinnati and then rent a car for the drive up to Dayton. In total, it took me over ten hours just to get home.

April 23rd, 2014 - The "A" flight attendant on this trip told me that I had some great stories and wondered if I would allow her to use one of them in a book that she was considering writing. I replied that I was flattered that she liked my stories and to check back with me later when she actually started putting it together. I never heard back from her. (Hmm...a book about airline related tales? Interesting idea...)

April 30th, 2014 - We had "American Idol" finalist Kellie Pickler on our flight to Nashville tonight. She was just as pleasant as she seemed to be on television.

May 8th, 2014 - Our crew had a 34-hour layover in San Diego today, so I ended up having lunch with my old training classmate Cyndi Veronesi. She had remarried and was living just north of the city. She seemed to be really happy and it was so much fun to get caught up with her!

May 22nd, 2014 - For the first time in my career, we had an airplane that had no trash cans installed in any of the galleys. After checking with the captain and our catering department, it was decided that for sanitary reasons, we could operate that flight, but could not serve any food or beverages until the trash cans were in place. The passengers were a little upset until the captain made a nice announcement explaining the situation.

June 10th-16th, 2014 - My wife and I took some vacation time and drove to Milwaukee and Chicago to see baseball games at two new parks. I now have seen games at 29 of the 30 Major League stadiums, with just Kansas City left to go. In addition, my wife has now seen 22 of the 30 teams' parks.

June 19th, 2014 - Here's a new one. Today we were stuck at the gate in Boston for over an hour. It seems that the jetway bridge suddenly lost power and could not be detached from the plane. Eventually, one of the mechanics figured out how to energize the boarding bridge for about 30 seconds, which gave us just enough time to safely push the plane off the gate.

June 23rd-25th, 2014 - I was finally awarded my first European International trip, so this week I worked a 757 trip to Dublin, Ireland. The serving procedures were different from my usual domestic trips and took a little while to pick up. I tried my best, but it didn't help that the "B" flight attendant was a little "anal-retentive" about everything. However, the rest of the crew was very nice and getting to see the beautiful green island come into view during our approach made the whole trip worthwhile.

After checking into our hotel, a couple of the other crewmembers (Karen and Amy) invited me to go with them into the downtown area.

We started off taking the "On again/Off again" bus tour around Dublin which gave me a much better understanding of the layout of the area. We then opted to take the Guinness Brewery tour which detailed their long history and informed us about how their beer was made. The best part of the day was after touring through seven floors of the facility, we then got to enjoy a free pint of Guinness in their rooftop bar and solarium. The views of the city were amazing and despite not really favoring dark beer, I really enjoyed tasting my first Guinness.

On the way back to the hotel, we also checked out some cafes and an authentic Irish pub. There, we listened to an Irish band, watched a little soccer on the television, and enjoyed another pint of Guinness! Overall, I really liked the trip, but dealing with flying six time zones away will take some getting used to.

July 8th-11th, 2014 - This was a nice four-day "extra" trip with some good crews. On the first day, we had comedian Tommy Davidson on a flight out of Montego Bay, Jamaica. He was very personable and even invited me to attend his upcoming show in Cincinnati next month. On the second day, I had a great crew who asked me to join them for dinner in Denver that night. In a nice "throwback" to the old days of flying, the captain said he really enjoyed our company, and then picked up the tab for all of us that evening. I had not seen that happen in a long time.

The real frustrating part of the trip came at 2 a.m. on the last night, when I came downstairs for my redeye flight to Charlotte and there was no Super Shuttle van to take me to the airport. After trying to call the Shuttle directly and getting no answer, I called our crew schedulers and they had no luck either. I again "adapted" to the situation and called for a taxicab which took another 30 minutes. Eventually, I did get to the airport and was just a few minutes late for boarding. However, because of some new corporate procedures, it took me a long time to get reimbursed for the cab ride that I paid for. Some co-workers have said that is just how American Airlines operates.

July 15th, 2014 - This was my first layover in Long Beach, California, where I discovered that we would be staying on the old "Queen Mary" ocean liner that had been turned into a hotel. Although the amenities were a little outdated, our rooms were comfortable, and my window was actually a working porthole that looked out over the ocean. Our entire crew met up later for drinks and dinner in the old dining hall and afterwards a few of us took the walking tour of the ship. Again, because of all the history associated with the ship, I really enjoyed my stay there.

July 16th, 2014 - The next night, I had a long layover in downtown Pittsburgh and had a chance to catch up with my old friend Laurie Sismour. After a late lunch, we ended up walking across one of the pedestrian bridges to the Pittsburgh Pirates stadium for a look around. As chance would have it, they were having a classic-car show in one of the parking lots and we ended up running into our flight attendant friend Mike McCloskey. (Mike was displaying his beautifully restored Isetta automobile.) Overall, it was a very enjoyable day.

July 21st-24th, 2014 - This was a really good four-day trip with a terrific crew of Carter Lawrence and Peggy Godfrey. On the first flight into Los Angeles, we had two members of the band "Alter Bridge" in the last row. (Singer Myles Kennedy and drummer Scott Phillips.) Both of them were very nice to chat with. On the third day, we had a long overnight in Ft. Myers, Florida, but it was rainy and overcast. So instead of going to the beach, I went to a nearby movie theater and saw the film "Rise of the Planet of the Apes."

August 5th, 2014 - We recently started staying at a really nice hotel in Miami for our shorter overnights. The EB Hotel was brand new and had every amenity you could think of. The new technology included floor-level lights that automatically illuminated when you got out of bed. Additionally, the bathroom featured a walk-in shower area that was so big, it had an island in the middle of it! In the shower, there were four different shower heads, two handheld sprayers, and a wall of pulsating jets that almost reminded one of a car wash. Consequently, my shower today lasted over 30 minutes, just so I could try out all the different options!

August 14th, 2014 - We had well-known, game-show hostess Vanna White on our flight to the Turks and Caicos Islands today. She was dressed casually with very little makeup on, and she was still stunningly attractive. She was also very sweet to everyone around her.

August 20th, 2014 - In a repeat of last month's debacle, our scheduled Super Shuttle van again failed to show up to take our crew back to the Denver Airport. This time the hotel arranged for alternate transportation, but I still filed another report with the company, just to make them aware of the problem.

September 1st, 2014 - We had a flat tire in Cancun, Mexico, that took over three hours to repair. Because we ran so late getting into Charlotte, our crew schedulers replaced us with another crew. After clearing Customs, we were then allowed to go home early!

September 16th, 2014 - During my career, I have experienced a total of four mergers. (PSA, Piedmont, America West, and American Airlines) Depending on which side you worked for, many of us had to adjust to some new (and seemingly illogical) workplace rules. Well, in my opinion, some really disastrous corporate changes occurred today. American Airlines decided to forego our time-honored tradition of seniority-based commuting privileges and stay with their "first-come, first-served" system of pass riding. That essentially meant that whoever can check in the fastest 24 hours beforehand, gets to be at the top of the list and therefore has a better chance of getting on a flight. Although American Airlines said they have always done it that way, no other airline has such a system.

For example, if you wanted to get on a 5 a.m. flight, you now had to get up early the day before that flight and hope your computer would allow you to "click on" quickly as the clock rolled over to 5 a.m. Only after checking in would you be able to see if you were successful, and who it was that might be ahead of you in line for that open seat. The really sad part of this was that my 31 years of seniority now played no part whatever in the process. For example, that very junior employee who had just been hired last month (and had a much quicker computer) now got to enjoy my hard-earned seat on the flight that I wanted. Although I have stated several times throughout this book that one has to be very flexible while working in the airline industry, this particular change seemed so very disheartening!

October 14th, 2014 - This trip had a really good crew, including my old friend Tracy Muskal. Our captain was a veteran pilot named Connie who eventually informed us that she would be retiring soon. She also revealed that she did historically-based "female aviator" reenactments for schools and museums. She even had her vintage pilot skullcap (with the goggles and earflaps) with her, and really entertained us when she wore it in the cockpit during one of our boardings. She was very interesting to fly with!

October 20th, 2014 - Today we got our first look at a new, tentative flight attendant contract. Without going into too much detail, it was pretty bad. There would be many changes to our work rules and even some severely punitive measures for certain minor infractions. The only saving grace was that we would get a pretty sizable increase in pay. I knew after looking it over, that I would be voting "no" on it!

October 21st-22nd, 2014 - This trip had a nice long layover in Milwaukee, Wisconsin. Since the weather was very mild, I got a chance to go out walking in the downtown area. I eventually discovered some interesting antique shops and a number of storefronts that were used in filming the television show "Laverne and Shirley." I also found a statue dedicated to the Henry Winkler character Arthur Fonzerelli; better known as "Fonzie." (Once I saw it, it was all I could do to not imitate his character by going..."Ayyyy!")

Unfortunately, in what is becoming a reoccurring trait of American Airlines management, there was (again) no transportation for us the next day back to the airport. We waited in the hotel lobby for over an hour before the captain called for a couple of cabs that he said he would pay for. Based on my previous experience in Denver last month, I warned him about how long it took to get reimbursed, and for him to be sure to get receipts from the taxi drivers.

October 30th, 2014 - We had a rather bizarre medical situation today on our Charlotte to Houston flight. A very pregnant young lady apparently went into labor about 30 minutes before our landing. Although her water never broke, her contractions were about seven minutes apart by the time we landed in Houston. In trying to get some basic medical information from her, we discovered that she was also dealing with a brain tumor as well. Once the paramedics came on board in Houston, she claimed that the contractions had completely stopped, which seemed a little odd. I never did hear what happened to her.

November 4th, 2014 - While on a long overnight in downtown Phoenix, I went out walking and happened upon an event that was billed as "The Firefighter Olympics." There were teams of fire stations from six different states, with each team competing in a variety of events such as ladder climbing and an obstacle course. Some of the participants were tremendous athletes, especially one female firefighter from California who won two different events in the short time that I was watching.

November 17th-20th, 2014 - This was a wonderful four-day trip with a great crew that included my friends Kerri Duffy and Jayme Steckley. On the second day, we had a really easy flight from Philadelphia to Nassau, Bahamas with only 15 people on board. To pass the time, I entertained my crew with a few of my stories. On the third day, we had a really fun night in Miami, Florida. Over drinks and dinner, I then shared a few more stories with the group. Both Kerri and Jayme then urged me to start writing them down and/or publishing them.

November 28th, 2014 - We heard reports today that a female passenger had tried to take her "emotional support pig" on a USAirways flight. However the animal apparently defecated in the aisle before takeoff, so she and her pig were then removed. It is amazing what some folks try to get away with on our flights!

December 21st, 2014 - This was a very eventful redeye flight from San Diego to Charlotte. As I mentioned earlier, redeye flights are rather easy to work because you usually perform one drink service and then turn down the cabin lights so the passengers can go to sleep. The real difficult part for us is then trying to stay awake all night. However, on this night, we had plenty of things to keep us occupied.

As I recall, about an hour into the flight, a passenger call-bell went off, so I went to see what was going on. An older lady then told me that she was having trouble breathing, so I put her on an oxygen bottle and then started asking some medical questions about her health. Come to find out, she was taking about a dozen medications, but had not taken any of them in the last 24 hours. After I got her bags down from the overhead compartments, we found most of her pills. She then took them with some water and soon said she felt better. Eventually she went back to sleep.

About an hour later, while sitting in the rear galley, I noticed a younger girl in the next-to-last row who started to get up out of her seat. However, her knees buckled and she passed out, falling back into her seat. I then jumped up to check on her while one of my crewmembers retrieved another bottle of oxygen. Once she came to, I asked about her health and medical history and discovered that she had not eaten anything in quite a while. We then got her some crackers and some juice and eventually her color improved, and she also felt better.

Although I have used the phrase, "But wait...there's more" several times already, it really couldn't be more appropriate than in this situation. About an hour from landing, as I was busy filling out the medical report forms for the first two incidents, another call-bell went off. This time, it was the middle-aged woman in sweatpants, who we had seen standing around the mid-cabin lavatory earlier in the flight.

After I arrived at her seat, the lady motioned for me to lean in closer, so she could whisper in my ear. She then told me that she wanted the paramedics to meet our flight when we landed in Charlotte. When I asked why, she quietly informed me that her "stitches were leaking." Seeing that she was serious, I then inquired as to what procedure or operation she had undergone.

She eventually admitted that she had traveled from San Diego into Mexico for some cheap cosmetic surgery several days earlier. She then pointed to her backside and quietly mouthed the words "butt implants." According to her story, the recovery time was supposed to have been just a couple of days, but there had been some complications and she had to stay for over a week. The lady then told me that she had run out of money that morning, so she had checked herself out of the facility...and now her butt stitches were leaking!

At this point in my career, I had encountered quite a few medical situations onboard my flights, some of which I have written about already. Additionally, every year we spend significant time to review and practice handling medical emergencies at our annual recurrent trainings. Therefore, I thought I was fairly well prepared for any scenario. However, I had never even imagined the possibility of a passenger with faulty fanny stitches. Fortunately, my ability to adapt would again come in handy in this situation.

After searching through our emergency medical kit and not really finding anything that I thought would help, I had a sudden burst of insight. I then asked the lady if using some "sanitary napkins" from our lavatory supply kit might help her, at least until we landed. Once I showed her that they were clean and absorbent, she agreed and then placed several of them over her stitches and under her sweatpants.

Once we landed and finally arrived at the gate, I made an announcement for all the passengers to remain seated, because there would be some EMTs coming on board. I then went up to the front galley to brief them on the multiple medical situations that we had encountered. As I recall, the conversation went something like this:

EMT: "So, what's going on with this flight?"

Me: " Well, seat 18-C didn't take her medications, seat 31-D didn't eat for 24 hours; oh, and seat 26-F has leaking butt stitches!"

EMT (stepping back so the passengers wouldn't see him trying not to laugh): "Whaaat?"

Me: "I'm not kidding. Good luck with that examination!"

After turning in all the paperwork, I eventually got a call from my supervisor who just wanted to make sure he was reading my incident report correctly. He was not the only one amused. A few months later, I also had my entire recurrent training class chuckling as well, when they asked us to describe any recent unusual medical encounters. What an interesting way to end the year!

Chapter Twenty-Seven

2015....Family Trees and a Double Rainbow

January 5th, 2015 - On this four-day trip I worked the "extra" position on an Airbus-321. Usually, that would mean working with a few different crews throughout the week. However, for the first time ever, I worked with 10 different crews on 10 different flights. All I did all week was to introduce myself, over and over.

January 19th-22nd, 2015 - While on another "extra" trip in Philadelphia, there was no van to pick me up at our hotel, so I once again had to call for a taxicab and pay for my own transportation to the airport. This is becoming a very disturbing trend for the new American Airlines management, which ironically is still our old USAirways management.

Once I finally got to San Francisco that night, I did have a chance to meet up with my old college fraternity brother Harry Saurer, who lives in Sacramento, California. We had a great time catching up and probably told way too many stories about our college days to our poor bartender, who just kept nodding and smiling. (At least we left him a nice tip!)

On the final night of the trip, I had a chance to walk around downtown Phoenix after dinner and check out all the displays for the upcoming Super Bowl XLIX. The interactive booths were really amazing because the technology was so advanced. At one display booth, I was seemingly able to kick the "winning" field goal of 35 yards in Super Bowl XLIII. (I figure that accomplishment will always look good on my resume'.)

February 4th, 2015 - Once again, no van was available to take our crew from our hotel back to the Atlanta airport. I later contacted our union to let them know, and they said that with us changing over soon to a different union, there was really nothing much they could do.

February 9th-10th, 2015 - I had to attend two days of training in Charlotte this week. The first day was called S.O.C. (Single Operating Certificate) training which dealt with all the changes of our upcoming merger. One of my classmates had us all snickering when he guessed that S.O.C. actually stood for "Same Old Crap."

On the second day, we learned how to operate our new, updated H.H.D. (Hand-Held Device) which would allow us to better access current flight information, weather delays, and product sales onboard our flights. Although I didn't really consider myself a "tech guy," it was still great to have access to all the new electronic technology. However, if we lost it or damaged it, it would cost something like $300 to replace.

February 12th, 2015 - I worked a flight into Ft. Lauderdale tonight that ended up being just a few minutes late arriving. I then notified my hotel that I was running just a little late and they said they would have the van driver wait a few minutes for me. By the time I worked my way out to the area in front of the terminal, the van was already gone. After waiting an hour for the next van, the returning driver confessed that he had been willing to wait for me. However, some American flight attendants told him that they were NOT going to wait for "anybody from USAirways" and made him leave on schedule. When I finally arrived at the hotel, the front desk refused to give me their names or room numbers. In hindsight that was a good thing, because I would have probably left 3 a.m. wake-up calls for all of them.

March 3rd, 2015 - This was my first trip from American Airlines' new bidding program. Their system was known as PBS (Preferential Bidding Systems) and was much different from our previous setup. As of this month, there were fewer four-day trips (which had become my preferred trip length) and the trips were not as commutable. But like everything else with this particular merger, I had to keep telling myself to adapt to the changes.

March 12th, 2015 - At the end of this four-day trip, I got lucky and not only got a seat on my commuter flight home to Cincinnati, but I also got upgraded to an open First-Class seat as well. My seatmate was a lawyer and after we talked for a while, he asked me about some of my most interesting passenger experiences. After sharing the Muhammad Ali and Meat Loaf stories, he said I should definitely start writing them down. In fact, he gave me his business card and said if I ever turned them into a book, he wanted a copy.

April 7th, 2015 - Today was our last official day operating under the USAirways banner, which made it a bittersweet day. The government had finally granted us the Single Operating Certificate, which was effective tomorrow, and officially made us all American Airlines employees.

April 16th, 2015 - In another example of crew scheduling miscommunication, I had showed up on time in Tampa to meet my outbound crew. However, they had been severely delayed inbound the night before. Therefore, they had to delay our flight over two hours, so the crew could get sufficient rest. When I called our crew schedulers to see what was going on, they seemed surprised that no one had let me know about the delay. By then it was too late to go back to the hotel, so I just hung around the airport.

April 22nd, 2015 - Tonight, we had a long layover in New York City at a brand-new Club Quarters hotel. Since it was right down the street from the newly opened 9/11 Memorial and Museum, two of my crew members and I went down the next morning and took the tour. I can only tell you that it was one of the most solemn and sobering experiences of my flying career.

The museum contained hundreds of artifacts from that fateful day and was located adjacent to where the World Trade Towers once stood. Among the displays was the fire truck from the Ladder 3 firehouse that was crushed when the towers fell, and the bundle of cell phone and radio antennae that were on top of the second tower. (I had mentioned earlier in my chapter about September 11th, that I vividly recall those antennas being the last thing I saw slip into the swirling dust cloud as that tower collapsed.)

The most heart-wrenching exhibit was a small inner room where the walls were covered with photos of every human casualty from that terrible day. As part of the presentation, you would also hear voices constantly doing a "roll call" of each person's name while you gazed at the photographs. I found out later that if you knew someone who perished that day, you could arrange to have your voice recorded while speaking their name at the next "roll call." I thought that was an incredibly cathartic way to express one's feelings for the victims of that tragedy.

While the museum was a wonderful way to remember that particular event, I was in a very subdued mood for the rest of the day. However, it was also good for me personally, because whatever problems I thought I had, seemed to be less important now. After touring this museum, one cannot come away with anything less than great appreciation for what our country and people have gone through.

May 13th, 2015 - Today we had well-known golf commentator Gary McCord on our Phoenix-Charlotte flight. He was very pleasant to chat with. Also, as a guy who has worn a moustache most of his adult life, I would have to argue that Mr. McCord has what might be the world's coolest moustache.

May 14th, 2015 - Over the course of my airline career, I was able to bring home quite a few paperback books to my wife, who was an avid reader. Many of them had come from passengers who occasionally left books in their seat pockets after they finished reading them. On today's flight from Los Angeles to Charlotte, we had actor Kirk Cameron on board. He spent most of the flight quietly reading and at the end of the flight, he in fact left his book in the seat pocket. As I was passing through the cabin after our deplaning, I saw it and knew that it was his, mostly because his name was on the ticket stub that he had used as a bookmark. What I also found amusingly ironic was the fact he left behind the book titled..."Left Behind!"

May 21st, 2015 - I had dinner and drinks tonight in Minneapolis with captain Mike Grieco who was also a guitar player. I found out later that one of his friends was a guitar player for well-known musician Dave Mason. Mike mentioned that he will try to get me one of Dave Mason's guitar picks for my growing pick collection. (At this point, I have over 100 picks, from lots of famous musicians.)

June 2nd-4th, 2015 - This was my first trip to London, England, and my first trip on the huge Airbus-330 airplane. Fortunately, my friend Sherri Fogelman was on the same trip and she was very helpful with clarifying some of the differences with the international services and procedures.

Since our hotel was centrally located in downtown London, I was able to do a little sight-seeing after we got checked in. In one afternoon, I managed to see the changing of the guard at Buckingham Palace, the Royal Albert Hall, Kensington Palace, and some of Hyde Park. I then rode the famous red double-decker city bus to Hyde Park Corner and made a pilgrimage to the very first Hard Rock Cafe. It was an exhausting but rewarding day and it just made me want to come back later for more exploration.

June 8th-14th, 2015 - My wife and I enjoyed some vacation time this week and took in baseball games at Kansas City and Denver. After seeing the Kansas City Royals play, I was able to finish my "bucket list" goal of seeing a game in every Major League stadium. (It took me about 30 years to do, but it was so much fun to accomplish!)

We also managed to see the band "Bare Naked Ladies" play a concert at the beautiful Red Rocks amphitheater outside of Denver. If you have never been there, it is one of the most iconic venues in the United States. The stage and the seating areas have been hewn out of the beautiful red stone rocks and the views from the upper seats are just breathtaking. There is also a great little museum at the very top of the seating area that explains the history of the place and also chronicles all of the bands and musicians that have performed there.

June 15th-16th, 2015 - This was an easy two-day trip to the Caribbean Island of St. Maarten. We had a 20-hour layover at a beautiful Westin hotel right on the beach. The rooms were fabulous and the beach bar featured a delicious local drink made with guava and berries. It was a great overnight, but a funny thing happened when we got ready to take off the next day.

In St. Maarten, the end of the airport runway is very close to one of their main beaches. Because of that proximity, a local tradition has developed that encourages beachgoers to try to hang onto the runway fence when a large jet is readying for takeoff. If they are strong enough, they can avoid being blown into the ocean by the jet blasts from the engines. However, I still recall looking out my rear jump seat window just as we were getting ready to take off, and seeing one unfortunate soul lose his grip and get rolled like a sagebrush across the sand. It looked both painful and hilarious at the same time!

June 23rd, 2015 - Today we had NFL Hall of Fame running backs Marcus Allen and Eric Dickerson as well as "The Office" actor Brian Baumgartner on our flight from Los Angeles to Pittsburgh. They were all attending a celebrity golf tournament the next day and were all very pleasant to chat with.

July 7th, 2015 - During our long layover in Salt Lake City, I decided to take the public tour of the Mormon Center. The main temple and the Tabernacle buildings were amazing structures. In fact, we were lucky enough to be in the Tabernacle when their boys' choir was practicing. To hear those amazing voices in a building with perfect acoustics was a wonderful musical experience.

After the tour was over, I then visited their Family History Center which contained hundreds of years of genealogical research. After I spent two hours looking up the Holtzapple family tree, I found out that my paternal grandmother's lineage includes English, French, Irish, and Swedish royalty. It was a great way to spend the day.

August 5th, 2015 - My good friend John McComb and I had been contemplating using my buddy passes to fly into Scotland for a little golf, and a tour of some scotch distilleries. However, since the merger with American, the once cheap passes now cost over $700 each. Therefore, we decided to cancel the trip. I am still so disappointed that this wonderful airline perk has for the most part disappeared.

August 17th-20th, 2015 - Although this was a decent "extra" trip, it was again marred by the reoccurring mistakes of our crew schedulers. On the second day, our Los Angeles-Charlotte flight had a two-hour delay posted that no one on the crew knew about, not even the captain. Again, if we had been informed, we could have stayed at the hotel a little longer. On the last day, there was another long "crew rest" delay out of Providence, Rhode Island, that our schedulers knew about but failed to inform me. I then made a call to our new union representatives, but all they could tell me was that they were "working on it." I tried not to get too upset about this problem because I assumed that the crew schedulers were also working with new company procedures as well. I was sure they were just as frustrated as I was.

September 28th-30th, 2015 - I had another 30-hour layover in Salt Lake City this week, so I decided to return to the Family History Center and do some more genealogical research on my lineage. This time I discovered that my paternal grandmother's family had come to America with the second wave of Pilgrims. Working back from there, I also discovered that my family line eventually married into the English royal family. As was the custom back then, they then proceeded to intermarry into other royal families from other countries. Besides the previously mentioned royal ties, this time I discovered that we are also descended from Danish and Russian royal families.

October 16th, 2015 - This week Karen and I celebrated our 28th wedding anniversary with a trip to Palm Springs. However, a very interesting thing happened while we were passing through the Phoenix Airport on our way back home. It seemed that the final flight of a plane still under the old USAirways colors, was getting ready to push back from the gate for its flight to San Francisco and then to Philadelphia. In honor of its historical past, it was given the flight number of "1939" in reference to the year that Allegheny Airlines (which eventually became USAir) first started flying.

Since their gate was just down the hall from us, Karen and I walked over to check it out. There were lots of historical displays celebrating our long existence, including one lady in her old flight attendant uniform from the 50s! Apparently, I just missed seeing our old CEO Ed Colodny who was a guest passenger on that flight as well. Although it was a little bittersweet to see my airline's history come to a close, what happened next was nothing short of a storybook happy ending.

The weather that day in Phoenix had been rainy and overcast, which was rather unusual for Arizona that time of year. In fact, as the final boarding announcements were being made, there were several claps of thunder that could be heard in the waiting area. (As the reader, please feel free to insert your own conclusions of how those ominous signs might be interpreted.) As Flight 1939 pushed back from the gate, I managed to find a little space near one of the large glass windows and prepared to take a few pictures with Karen's camera. (Yes, this time I did have access to a camera, as opposed to some previously mentioned opportunities when I was unprepared.) I am so very glad that I did!

Now I must admit that I have been incredibly fortunate to have seen or experienced all the amazing coincidences that I have mentioned so far in this book. However, this one just might be the most unbelievable. Because, as if in a magical movie moment, once the plane started both engines and turned to leave, the rain stopped, the sun came out, and a double rainbow appeared... right over the plane! (Although I may have imagined it, I could swear that I also faintly heard heavenly choir voices singing "Hallelujah" as well.)

As I furiously snapped picture after picture, I could hear spectators behind me gasping in disbelief. Karen even squeezed my arm and quietly whispered, "Wow! I hope you got that!" I hoped so too. Fortunately, most of the pictures turned out very well. The very bizarre timing of this event still amazes me to this day.

November 17th, 2015 - Today, I finally received my updated ID badge with my new American Airlines employee number. I am not sure why its delivery was delayed, but I am glad to no longer have to explain to airport security officers why my badge said "USAirways" when the rest of my credentials said, "American Airlines." I am sure that my old ID photograph from the late 80s didn't exactly help the situation either. (That photo showed me with an old hair style and about 30 pounds lighter.)

November 18th, 2015 - Again, I may have spoken too soon. While trying to go through the security line in Pittsburgh, my new ID badge did not register, and I was momentarily detained. After some phone calls to the company verified my status as an employee, I was then allowed to continue. Apparently, someone failed to activate my badge once I signed for it yesterday.

December 1st, 2015 - Today we had actress Mary McDonnell on our flight from Charlotte to Las Vegas. (Although she has been in numerous productions, she might be best known for her role as Kevin Costner's wife in the movie "Dances with Wolves.") She was so very sweet and even brought bags of candy for our crew to enjoy!

December 6th, 2015 - Just when I thought I couldn't possibly have any more strange coincidences happen to me, another one occurred today. I was working the "B" position in the back of an Airbus-321 for our flight to Las Vegas. The passengers had just started to board, and I was attempting to get the rear galley set up before it got too busy. There were just a few passengers already onboard, when I heard a young lady ask me for some help. As I approached her, she seemed confused about her seat assignment.

After looking at her boarding pass, I realized that someone else was already sitting in her assigned seat. After checking the other passenger's ticket, I saw that they both were indeed showing the same seat number. I then pulled out my new H.H.D. and looked up the seat chart for our flight. That chart showed that the young lady was indeed in that seat, but she graciously decided to take the other guy's seat so he wouldn't have to re-pack all of his belongings.

After thanking her for her kindness, I saw that her name was Michelle and somehow, she seemed very familiar to me. She also thought that I looked familiar to her as well, but then admitted that she used to do a lot of flying when she worked in Washington, D.C. Something about that statement jogged my memory, so I then asked her to wait while I proceeded to get up into the overhead bin where my travel bag was stored. After pulling out my address book, I eventually uncovered an old business card. It turned out that it was her card from when she was an assistant to a Senator from Utah...10 years earlier in 2005! If you recall, she had been nice enough to offer to show me around the Senate chambers and White House, so I had retained her information in case I ever had some time off in Washington. Although I never took her up on her offer, we were both amazed that I still had the card.

After chatting with her, I found out that she was now living and working in the Las Vegas area. I then told her about my idea of possibly writing a book about my airline experiences and we both agreed that this highly unusual meeting should definitely be included in my tales. I truly cannot believe my luck with running into people I know!

December 16th-19th, 2015 - This was a very tough four-day trip, mostly because of all the bad weather. It was also my first "Red Flag" assignment, which had been recently created by the company to encourage our flight crews to fly more trips. (The big incentive for us was that we would be paid 50% more than usual for those trip sequences.) Apparently, American's new PBS bidding system wasn't creating enough flying time, so these Red Flag trips were designed to be a short-term solution. The extra pay really came in handy on the third day, when we had a long mechanical delay in Charlotte and didn't arrive in Denver until 6 a.m. I think I ended up making something like an extra four hundred dollars on that day alone!

December 27th-30th, 2015 - My final trip of the year. This week we had a very snowy 34-hour layover in Salt Lake City. Although the approach into the airport between the beautiful snow-capped mountains was breathtaking, once we got on the ground everything was paralyzed by all the snow drifts. After we arrived at the hotel, I bundled up and trudged down the street to the Family History Center and spent some more time researching my family's heritage. This time I discovered that we are related to the famous English historical figure, William the Conqueror. He is best remembered for establishing the very first form of democratic government in the year 1067. Most people wouldn't know that fact, but having been a former history teacher, I was acutely aware of it. Perhaps my connection to old "Uncle Willy" explains why I have always had such a great interest in history.

Chapter Twenty-Eight

2016....J. Peterman, Abbey Road, and a Bad Uniform

January 25th, 2016 - Occasionally, there are times in life where you finally realize that old age is sneaking up on you. Well, today I had one of those moments. After looking at my calendar and my posted flying schedule twice each, I then flew into Charlotte...one day too early for my trip! Once I realized that, I just resigned myself to the fact that since I was already in Charlotte, I might as well stay put. I then decided to contact my old high school friend Terry Bussell who lived nearby, and we ended up having dinner together. I had not seen him since he and his wife had been on one of my flights a few years back out of Las Vegas. It was great to spend some time with him again.

January 26th-29th, 2016 - On the first day of this trip, we had a passenger who apparently had her phone hacked while using our onboard Internet system during the flight. The captain seemed to think that it might be another passenger doing the hacking, so he reset the system and that seemed to take care of the problem.

On the last day, we had New England Patriots defensive back Malcolm Butler on our flight to Charlotte. Sports fans may remember that he was the hero of Super Bowl 49, when he intercepted a pass at the goal line at the end of the game. That play secured the victory and made the Patriots Super Bowl champions once again.

February 3rd-6th, 2016 - Because of very bad weather in Ohio, it took me over three hours to get to the Cincinnati airport for my commuter flight to Charlotte. Once in Charlotte, I discovered that I was going to be the senior flight attendant for the first time in quite a few years. Despite that, it turned out to be a good trip with a great crew. I did, however, have a couple of tense moments up in First Class.

On the second day, I had an already intoxicated First Class passenger board the flight, and then try to order a triple shot of Jack Daniels for his preflight beverage. When I told him that company regulations only permitted him to have one drink, he then called me an "a**hole." He also made the mistake of standing up and challenging me on my decision. After I strongly encouraged him to return to his seat, he finally sat down. I then let the captain know what was happening and he decided to have him removed. Our guideline has always been that if a passenger "appears" to be intoxicated, you can refuse to serve them and/or have them taken off.

On the third day, I had a First-Class passenger spill his drink onto the laptop of the adjoining passenger. Apparently, it shorted out her computer and ruined her earbuds as well. After calming everyone down, I then filled out some reports regarding the incident and even offered her my laptop in case she needed to continue working. She politely declined but did end up writing a nice letter to the company praising my efforts to mitigate the situation.

March 2nd, 2016 - On this date, we had television reporter Steve Hartman on our flight from Charlotte to Albany. Mr. Hartman might be best known for his work on the news program "CBS Sunday Morning." There, he often does heart-warming stories of real people and the challenges that they have overcome. He was just as nice as he seemed to be on television. I even made sure to tell him that I really liked his work; to which he sort of blushed and modestly thanked me for the compliment. (In my humble opinion, if CBS would create a half-hour show featuring just his wonderful stories, I am sure it would be a huge success!)

March 15th, 2016 - Today, we had what would be be our last Recurrent Training in Charlotte. (Starting next year, all of our training sessions will be held at the American Airlines campus near the Dallas-Ft. Worth airport.) During our session on medical emergencies, I was asked again to tell my tale of the night I had three medical situations, including the lady with the leaking butt stitches. Our instructor then used my story to again emphasize the point that I have repeatedly made throughout the book; that anything can happen at any time.

March 17th, 2016 - This is another story of a wonderful passenger interaction that I was privileged to experience. We were working a full flight from Los Angeles to Toronto, and about halfway through our drink service, a very distinguished looking gentleman in an aisle seat wanted to purchase a bottle of wine. After twice running his credit card through my H.H.D. device and not receiving any input, I decided to "comp" his beverage rather than embarrass him by asking for another card. Because of that, the gentleman seemed quite appreciative and then thanked us for our generosity.

In fact, after the meal and drink service was concluded, he made a point to come to the back galley and thank us again for the drink. I even remember him saying that he didn't usually receive such kindness from our airline when he traveled. As we chatted some more, his very distinctive voice and silvery-gray hair seemed more and more familiar.

It turned out that we were talking to actor John O'Hurley. Although his resume' includes soap operas and hosting game shows, he may be best remembered for his stint on the television show "Seinfeld," where he played the ebullient publishing executive J. Peterman. After chatting further, my "trivia brain" kicked in and I also remembered that he was one of the commentators for the annual Westminster Dog Show. That seemed to please him, and we ended up having a nice conversation about different breeds of dogs. Before returning to his seat, he again thanked us for our kindness.

The rest of the flight was uneventful and we had a nice smooth landing in Toronto. After everyone had deplaned, I made my way up to the front of the aircraft. It was then that our senior flight attendant told me that one of our passengers had left something for me in the front galley. There I found that Mr. O'Hurley had left me an autographed photo and a signed copy of his children's book "The Perfect Dog." The book was a sweet story about different types of dogs and was dedicated to his young son. It was one of the nicest gifts I have ever received from a passenger.

March 18th, 2016 - On our last flight of the day from Miami to Charlotte, we had the professional wrestler "Big Show" up in first class. (At almost seven feet tall and probably around 350 pounds, he completely filled his First-Class seat.) He was very personable and even signed a few photos for some fellow passengers.

March 23rd, 2016 - This trip featured a long two-day layover in Seattle. Although I had been there many times, I only found out today about the very unique (and somewhat gross) "Gum Wall," which is located in an alley under the south side of Pike Market. For those who are unaware, both sides of the alley, and everything in the alley, are completely covered with used chewing gum. While the artist in me appreciated the different colors and the creative shapes of the gum wads, the small part of me that is somewhat germophobic, recoiled in horror and reminded my head and hands not to touch anything! I took several photos to show my wife, who was grossed out as well.

April 15th, 2016 - Today was American Airlines' 90th birthday. Although I have only been an employee for a little over two years, I have seen a lot of inefficiencies in their day-to-day operations and experienced their rather casual concern for both passengers and employees. Because of that, I remembered feeling somewhat surprised that they had managed to survive that long.

April 26th, 2016 - According to my logbook notes, we had recently been moved to a different hotel for our long layover in Nashville. However, instead of being close to the downtown area, we were now outside the city limits, near the "Opryland" complex. The hotel was okay, but the only entertainment I could find within walking distance was a store-front business called "Cooter's Place". I soon discovered that it was a museum that featured memorabilia from the television show "Dukes of Hazard."

Apparently, the museum was owned by a gentleman named Ben Jones who had played "Cousin Cooter" on the show. Among his collection of artifacts were Daisy Duke's Jeep, Cooter's tow truck, and one of several orange Dodge Chargers famously known as the "General Lee." Although I had rarely watched the show, I was somewhat impressed by their displays. I even considered getting my picture taken inside the General Lee.

Since we didn't leave the hotel until late the next day, I also managed to squeeze in a late lunch with friends Dave and Sue Rogers, who lived nearby. They are two of my favorite crew members and some of the nicest people I know. I managed to keep them both laughing during our visit by recalling some of my favorite stories. They also both said that I should definitely write a book about my amazing travel experiences.

May 17th, 2016 - During another long layover in Salt Lake City, I returned to the Family History Center and did more research on my family genealogy. Eventually, I was able to trace one side of the family back to 215 AD. According to what I found; I am a distant relative to one of the kings of the Vandals tribe. Those familiar with European history will recall that the Vandals were one of the Germanic tribes that rose to power after the fall of the Roman Empire. Because they were so destructive, their actions eventually gave rise to the term "vandalism" which is associated with mindless destruction of property. (Those genetic traits may also explain why my garage has always been in such disarray!)

June 6th-8th, 2016 - Another three-day trip to London, England. On this layover, I rode the city bus up to Abbey Road Studios and toured the famous studio museum. I also filmed myself walking across Abbey Road like the Beatles did on the famous album cover. Since there are no stop signs in the area, I had to be very careful while crossing that street. (In fact, I saw one couple almost get hit while they were posing for pictures in the middle of the road.) For a music fan like me, seeing that iconic studio was a wonderful experience.

June 10th-17th, 2016 - My wife and I took some vacation time and elected to do a little road trip, rather than try to find open seats on an airplane during the busy summer-travel season. We drove through Pennsylvania, Maryland, and Washington, D.C., and were able to see baseball games at PNC Park in Pittsburgh and the Nationals Park in Washington. We also toured the Gettysburg battlefields and the Arlington National Cemetery. Although these attractions were very educational, because of the emphasis on the heroic loss of life of our soldiers and patriots, it was also very somber. I again came away with a deep appreciation of the sacrifices that so many people have made for our country.

June 27th-29th, 2016 - This was a tough trip. On the second day, we were delayed a little over four hours due to a very large storm system over Dallas, Texas. Eventually we ran low on fuel and had to divert to San Antonio. There, we sat for another three hours before our pilots "timed out" and had to be replaced. We were then sent to a local hotel to wait for the new crew to arrive.

Around 1a.m., we were called back to the airport to ferry the plane to Dallas. Unfortunately for us, we did not get to our hotel rooms until around 4 a.m. We were then informed that our crew would have to work another long day after that very minimal overnight stay. After getting so little sleep, three of us decided to take a "personal day" because of crew-fatigue issues. While I hated to further disrupt the trip, none of us felt alert enough to be able to do our jobs effectively. My supervisor later said that he understood the situation, but in the future we should consider trying to "tough it out." (However, with my background in law, I knew that if something bad had happened during a flight, the company would have used our "fatigue issues" against us, and we could have been fined, or even fired.)

July 15th, 2016 - We have been informed that we will be getting new uniforms this fall and will also be able to order new name tags as well. Apparently, the company will allow us to have just about any variation of our name, a common nickname, or a name that honors your family heritage. Therefore, I am going to attempt to claim Spanish and Asian backgrounds and try to get the moniker "Cervan-Yoo" on my name tag. (Hopefully, no one catches on to the playful twist on "serving you.") I am also considering what I have occasionally been called by some of my passengers... "Mr. Stew," which I have assumed was short for "Mister Stewardess."

July 26th-28th, 2016 - This was a decent trip with a long layover in Toronto. It turned out that our first officer had been a former captain with our commuter fleet. Eventually, I recalled that many years ago, he had gone out of his way to squeeze me onto a nearly-full flight so that I could get home that day. Needless to say, after reminding him of his kindness, I was glad to treat "Captain Josh" to dinner and drinks during our overnight in Toronto.

However, the next day as we were going through the customs line, several other travelers complained very loudly about our crew being allowed to go to the front of the line. Evidently, they were unaware that it is a common procedure to let airline crews go first, in order to speed up the preparation of departing flights. One guy was so obnoxious that the customs officials threatened to kick him out of the airport. We were all glad that none of those folks ended up on our flight that day.

August 1st-4th, 2016 - This was a crazy four-day "extra" trip. On the first night, I stayed in downtown Chicago at the famous Drake Hotel. It was also near the area known as the "Miracle Mile," where I spent the next day exploring. However, later that afternoon, the limousine service that was supposed to take me back to the O'Hare airport, failed to show up, so I had to sweet-talk my way into another crew's van just so I could get to the airport. Once I finally arrived, I discovered that our flight to Phoenix was delayed due to storms in that area.

Eventually we were allowed to take off, but the storms redeveloped, and we had to circle the Phoenix Airport for several hours. Once our fuel ran low, we were then diverted to Tucson. After an incredible 10-hour delay there, they eventually got us to Phoenix, but the rest of my trip was cancelled. I then got to spend 33 hours in downtown Phoenix before dead-heading home on the last day. While in Phoenix, I took in another Arizona Diamondbacks game; highlighted by a very rare home run which landed in their previously mentioned swimming pool in left-centerfield.

August 24th, 2016 - Another good trip to London. This time I made my way over to the Satchii Gallery and took in a wonderful exhibition of my favorite group, the "Rolling Stones." The displays covered all three floors of the museum and encompassed their entire career. The top floor featured an interactive presentation of the Stones in concert, which began when you were personally escorted through the "backstage area." Once on the side stage "VIP" area, you were made to feel that you were watching them perform live. It even gave you the impression that Mick Jagger was waving to you.

If that wasn't enough, I then took the double-decker bus to Hyde Park Corner where I paid another visit to the very first Hard Rock Cafe. This time I took the "Vault Tour" and was allowed to get my picture taken while playing the "Battle Axe" bass guitar made famous by Gene Simmons of "Kiss". Overall, it was a really fun trip!

September 19th-22nd, 2016 - A nice trip with long layovers in Cleveland and the Canadian city of Calgary. While in Cleveland, I walked down the hill to re-visit the Rock and Roll Hall of Fame. I then ended up having a nice conversation with one of their curators about possibly loaning them my guitar pick collection for a limited-time display. I agreed to send them a video presentation of my collection at a later time, to see if we could work something out. As a former history teacher, I know that I would be thrilled to actually have something of mine displayed in a major museum.

On the second day, we were able to wear our new charcoal grey uniforms for the very first time. American Airlines had made a really big push to finally get all employee groups into new clothes, and I must say that our uniforms did look nice. However, I do recall thinking that we would just have to wait to see how comfortable and functional they really were.

September 30th-October 2nd, 2016 - I had to call off sick today from my trip because I had been feeling really nauseous for the last week or so. I remember wondering if perhaps I was getting an early case of the flu or something, because I very rarely seem to get ill. (Spoiler alert: I now wonder if this wasn't some sort of "reaction" to our new uniform pieces. More to come on that topic in a little bit!)

November 8th, 2016 - We didn't get into our hotel rooms in Boston until about 1 a.m. tonight. Once in the room, I turned on the television to watch the results of the presidential elections. Although I personally was not very impressed with either candidate this year, it was amusing to see how shocked all the election commentators were after Donald

Trump was named the winner. It was also a little disconcerting for me because I had always believed that our news channels were supposed to present their stories in an unbiased manner. These guys were all clearly expecting Hillary Clinton to win easily.

November 12th, 2016 - I have always been mildly amused at some of the names of our passengers (and crew members) over the years. Monikers like "Bud" Wiser, Dusty Trale, Rusty Trapp, and Kitty Katz have always made me smile. In fact, I believe it was during my first year of flying that I recall having a passenger named Peter Small onboard. (Although he seemed very nice, I did wonder why his parents didn't more carefully consider the ramifications of such a name.)

I also once had a family of four board my flight and then ask me where their seats were located. Upon checking the manifest, I saw that Ted and Sharon and their two children, were seated in row 14. Their last names were (honest to God) ...the Morons! (Although I did not inquire as to how they pronounced it, I just assumed it wasn't "Marone" or "Moroon.") Despite that negative moniker, they seemed to be very intelligent and polite. However, the next time I overheard other crew members complain by saying, "Geez, I had some real morons on my flight today," I just had to jump in and reply, "Ted and Sharon?? Yeah, they seemed like really nice people!"

Well, believe it or not, today I had a very sweet little Malaysian lady on my flight who wanted to purchase a meal. When I ran her credit card, her name came up as..."Oh Dang!" Once again, I maintained my professional exterior during my interaction with her, but inside I was almost crying with laughter. I really wanted to tell her that I sometimes used her name in vain when things weren't going well. In fact, when our rear galley coffeemaker failed later on that same flight, I'm surprised she didn't come to the back of the plane and inquire as to who it was that kept calling out her name. (As I mentioned earlier, I have a very twisted sense of humor!)

November 28th-December 1st, 2016 - On the third day of this trip, our "extra" flight attendant was my old training classmate Dodi Staggers, who I had not seen in quite a few years. After we started reminiscing about our early days with old USAir, we realized that 33 years later, there were only five of us from our original class of 22 that were still working. We both thought that was rather sad.

December 8th, 2016 - After wearing our new uniforms for only about six weeks, I realized that the pants, and especially the new white shirts, were almost impossible to wear. Although I had no known allergies to anything, the uniform pants continued to make my legs itch, and the new shirts had made my neck and shoulders break out in red welts. Although I had very carefully washed and rinsed all the new pieces, it didn't seem to make them easier to wear. I was also starting to hear rumors of other crew members having similar reactions to the uniform as well.

December 19th-22nd, 2016 - Before this trip started, our union reached an agreement with the company over the multiple crew reactions to the new uniforms. Accordingly, if you still had the old blue uniforms, you would be allowed to continue wearing them, while the company investigated the increasing number of problems with the new clothing. Fortunately, I had not gotten around to disposing of my old uniform, so I decided to go back to the blue apparel, at least for the foreseeable future.

Also, because of the holiday traffic, I had to commute to work via the Columbus airport. Once I finally got to work I ended up swapping trips with another flight attendant. My new trip included a 33-hour layover in Hartford, Connecticut, with the actual overnight at a hotel up in Springfield, Massachusetts. That allowed me to return to the Basketball Hall of Fame (for the first time in over 30 years) and tour the newly renovated facility. Coincidentally, I just happened to be there on the 125th anniversary of the invention of the game of basketball, so there were a lot of basketball dignitaries roaming the halls. Although the Hall of Fame no longer offered my favorite old display where one could shoot baskets at different types of backboards, it was still a really nice museum and a very enjoyable day.

December 26th-27th, 2016 - I finished up the year with an easy two-day trip that had another long layover at the Drake Hotel in Chicago. However, since it was too cold to get out, I just stayed in my room for the most part. I did, however, make sure to call the limo service (twice) to be sure that they wouldn't forget to pick me up this time. (They did in fact show up...but were still 30 minutes late!)

Chapter Twenty-Nine

2017-2018....Tub-thumping, the Constance Conversations, and The Pusher

January 19th, 2017 - This was a good trip that included a Miami-Mexico City turn. It was also my first time going through the Customs area of the Miami International Airport. What a crazy place that was! Thousands of passengers were there and the lines stretched back into boarding areas. During the trip, we also realized that one of my fellow flight attendants was not feeling well. It seemed that his heart rate was erratic, and his blood pressure was high. Since he was usually very fit and health-conscious, we both wondered if it might be a reaction to his new uniform pieces.

February 13th, 2017 - When you chat up your fellow crew members, you never know what stories you may hear. Today I worked with a Philadelphia-based crew, and one of their flight attendants ended up telling me about when he had trained to become a mime. Evidently, he got to spend a week under the tutelage of the great French mime, Marcel Marceau. Because of that, I sort of expected him to break out the old "walking against the wind" routine when he had to open the rear door for the catering truck. (He didn't.)

February 20th-23rd, 2017 - During all my years of flying, I had never experienced what I would call a "life-threatening" situation. However, that changed today after I was involved in a slip-and-fall incident, as I emerged from the shower at our hotel in Nashville. As I recall, I pulled back the shower curtain and tried stepping out over the edge of the tub to reach the bath towel. Suddenly, both feet went out from under me and as I fell, I struck the edge of the tub, right between both shoulder blades. Although it knocked the breath out of me momentarily, I was actually very fortunate. If I had landed on my back just a few inches higher, I could have very easily died from a broken neck. God was truly watching out for me that day!

Eventually I called the hotel manager as well as my supervisor and filled out the appropriate reports. Other than a very large bruise on my back and some pain in my ribcage, I was relatively undamaged. However, as a precaution, I was required to see the company doctors after the trip was over. I then ended up taking a little time off, which included some physical therapy as well. One of my company doctors was a physician's assistant named Ashley. She was very kind and caring, as well as being a great audience. After sharing some of my more hilarious stories with her, she then claimed she didn't want to treat me anymore. Apparently, I made her laugh so hard, that she almost wet herself! (Sorry, Doc!)

March 7th, 2017 - We got to celebrate my mother's 90th birthday today. Although she was still in a memory care unit at a local nursing home, she had continued to do pretty well physically. Despite her increased memory loss, she still seemed to recall her family members. Her sweet nature also continued to shine through as well, which we considered to be a wonderful blessing. She also continued to enjoy hearing stories of my airline adventures and sort of encouraged me by softly saying that "This would be a good book."

March 27th-28th, 2017 - This was my first Recurrent Training at the American Airlines campus near the Dallas-Ft. Worth airport. It was a busy two days that included a stay at the on-campus hotel called "The Lodge," which was an older facility similar to a college dormitory. Those two days also included all the usual drills and testing, as well as some recent security updates. Overall, the training was an interesting mix of incredible stress and occasional boredom. I also recall the wonderful sense of relief that I enjoyed after it was over.

April 20th, 2017- An interesting airline story popped up in the news today. Apparently, the "World's Largest Rabbit" mysteriously died while being transported on a United flight into Chicago. Although that was sad enough, I couldn't help but notice the irony of the fact that the big bunny was flying into...O-"Hare" Airport! (I crack myself up sometimes!)

April 21st, 2017 - We had a long layover in Ft. Worth, Texas, at a new hotel near the downtown area. Since I was unfamiliar with the area, I went out walking and discovered a number of interesting attractions. Among them was a beautiful water park that featured a variety of waterfalls and fountains. There was also a memorial dedicated to President John F. Kennedy, who spent the last day of his life in the Ft. Worth area before his assassination in 1963. I also stumbled upon the annual Ft. Worth Arts Festival which featured lots of crafts, paintings, and metalworks.

April 25th-28th, 2017 - A very tough "extra" trip, mostly due to our schedulers inability to plan far enough ahead for expected crew needs. On the third day, my crew of three "new hires" was pulled off my airplane because another crew had gone over their daily flight-time limits. I was then left to wait for four hours in Phoenix while another group of flight attendants was flown in from Los Angeles.

On the last day, I was told to wait onboard my airplane in Los Angeles until another new crew was flown in from Phoenix. I ended up waiting for over five hours. Since Los Angeles is one of our crew bases, I was surprised that the schedulers couldn't find a local crew instead. It put a terrible burden on our passengers and was a very sad example of the company's inability to cope with what was a relatively simple situation.

July 4th-7th, 2017 - This trip was unusual because my friend Jeannie was working on it, instead of being home with her husband who was dying of cancer. Apparently, her husband had insisted that he was okay and had wanted her to go fly. She had always been a very practical person, so she honored his wishes and stayed on this trip. I tried to make things as easy for her as possible, hoping to ease her mind and lessen her stress. She did well enough, but I heard later that her husband passed away the day after she returned home. It was another example of how flight attendants have to deal with their personal issues while being at work and away from their families.

July 17th, 2017 - This is another tale of our crew scheduler's inefficiencies. Sadly, our flight out of Miami was delayed over four hours because there were no pilots available in the Miami crew base. This was something they should have been aware of ahead of time, but they were still unable to fix the problem. After waiting for pilots to be flown in from Charlotte, we eventually took a very unhappy group of passengers to Las Vegas.

August 21st, 2017 - We had a young, Irish rock band called "The Academics" on our flight to Los Angeles today. Apparently, they were flying to the West Coast because they were scheduled to perform at a record company in hopes of getting signed to a major label. They were also supposedly going to be on a late-night television show as well. After they told me they liked Alice Cooper, I then related to them my story of sitting with him at a baseball game. They were so impressed that one of them wanted my autograph!

September 18th, 2017 - Because hurricane Jose' was churning off the Atlantic coast, we encountered such bad weather that it prevented us from landing in Boston. Instead, the captain decided to turn around and return to Philadelphia. Surprisingly, most of the passengers were okay with that decision; mostly because they had witnessed how bad the weather was in Boston.

September 25th, 2017 - Unfortunately, my mother was becoming less and less responsive and her doctors informed us that it was just a matter of time. We made sure that she was as comfortable as possible, but it was still a sad time for my family.

October 1st, 2017 - My mother passed away late this evening, almost 20 years to the day after my father's death. Although we will miss her, I will always remember her kindness and unwavering support for whatever her three children wanted to accomplish. I was indeed so very fortunate to have had such wonderful parents. It was also very comforting to hear from so many of my airline friends who contacted me afterwards with their condolences.

October 6th-12th, 2017 - After the funeral, my wife and I took some well-deserved time off and celebrated our 30th anniversary in Palm Springs, California. It was just what we both needed to "recharge our batteries" so to speak.

October 18th, 2017 - Today I got to work with one of our most interesting flight attendants. Constance was our "extra" flight attendant and we hit it off immediately. In a nutshell, she grew up in England and still had the most charming British accent. I also discovered that she was good friends with singer Boy George (of the 80s band "Culture Club") and had once vacationed with ex-Beatle Ringo Starr and his family. She was also a Playboy Bunny in the 70s and had even appeared on "The Tonight Show" with Johnny Carson. She was just so entertaining. (In fact, it's possible that she may be one of the few people that I have encountered with better stories than me.)

December 5th-8th, 2017 - This was a good "extra" trip with lots of fun crew members. On the first night, we had a long layover in Portland, Oregon. One of my co-workers was a young lady named Reagan whose father was also a musician. Since she had never seen the downtown area, I offered to show her around. We had a great time exploring their unique urban environment; at least until we witnessed someone's small dog get knocked down by a passing car. After that trauma, we decided to go find a bar and drink a toast to that dog named Carl.

The next day, we had a fairly serious medical emergency on our Phoenix flight. An older lady in row 25 felt very faint and ended up needing three bottles of oxygen. I took charge of the situation and managed to keep her calm until we arrived at our destination. I was just glad she survived and was able to be reunited with her family.

December 10th-15th, 2017 - Although I had some vacation scheduled this week, I ended up staying home in order to close out my mom's estate. Because of all the holiday traffic, I probably couldn't have found an open seat, even if I had wanted to travel.

January 3rd-5th, 2018 - This was a really nice trip with married flight attendants Jeff and Mary. They were both so easy to work with and they even made sure to invite me to have dinner with them once we got to Salt Lake City. After dinner, Jeff and I secured a couple of tickets and attended that night's Utah Jazz basketball game.

January 8th-11th, 2018 - This trip had a 33-hour layover in Austin, Texas, so on my day off, I took the studio tour of the long-running PBS music show "Austin City Limits." For those of you who are unaware, that program has featured hundreds of musical acts over the years on their small, intimate stage. Local celebrity Willie Nelson has been their most frequent guest, but they have also featured other well-established artists, as well as up-and-coming musicians. My tour included visits to the sound room, the backstage "Green Rooms," and the "VIP" lounge. (Fun fact...there is a secret door in Willie Nelson's Green Room that allows him access to a special "smoking balcony" that is reserved just for him.)

February 28th, 2018 - During our layover in Ft. Myers, Florida, I went down to the hotel lobby to await my fellow crewmembers who were going to meet me for dinner. After I started chatting with the nice man sitting across from me, I discovered that he was baseball Hall of Famer Rod Carew. Evidently, he was in town helping out with the Minnesota Twins Spring Training. Mr. Carew was just the coolest guy and even allowed me to take a picture with him. Again, you just never know who you might meet when you start up a conversation with someone.

March 7th-8th, 2018 - While on an "extra" trip, I got hung up in Boston because of some very bad weather. During our delay, however, I entertained my great young crew with a number of my adventures over the years. (Emily, Jacob, and Victoria all said that they can't wait to have similar experiences during their airline careers!) Eventually, our flights that day were cancelled and we returned to the hotel. The next day, I got reassigned to a different crew and ended up finishing up early, which allowed me to commute home out of Philadelphia.

March 22nd, 2018 - Today is my 35th Anniversary with USAir/ American. I cannot believe how fast it seemed to go. It just "flew" by! (Nyuk! nyuk!)

April 10th, 2018 - For the first time in a long time, we had two consecutive missed approaches while trying to land in Miami, Florida. The captain then announced that a small aircraft had been disabled and was blocking the runways. We found out later that it may have been a cartel drug plane that was abandoned by its pilots after it landed.

April 19th, 2018 - I worked with a very nice Philadelphia-based crew today. One of my co-workers was a gentleman named John Damm. It turned out that he was from Celina, Ohio and knew of my paternal grandparents. He also made me chuckle when he told me that his family also owned a local dairy farm and a movie theater there. Those businesses (true story) were known as the "Damm Dairy" and the "Damm Theater."

May 9th, 2018 - While in San Diego on an overnight, I got to see a Padre's baseball game at the new Petco Field. I believe that was the 45th different major league stadium that I have visited over the years.

June 21st, 2018 - We had an interesting flight into Dallas today. Most of our passengers were National Hockey League officials or staff, who were flying in for the upcoming NHL draft. Among them was the league president Gary Bettman and Detroit Red Wings star Steve Yzerman. Just before we opened the front door to allow them to deplane, my co-worker made me laugh when he quietly whispered....

"Should we suggest that they get the puck out of here?"

June 22nd, 2018 - I had my old friend and fellow EKU grad Cindy Newcome on our flight from Denver to Charlotte today. She was still commuting from Montana but let me know that she would be retiring in August. After chatting with her, I realized that this might be the beginning of the next wave of co-workers to start heading out the door. Although things like our uniform issues or those fume events may influence when my peer group decides to leave, it likely will be more of an age-related decision.

July 25th, 2018 - For the first time in my career, I finally got to enjoy a long layover in Spokane, Washington. The best part of the trip was that I also got a chance to visit with my dear friends Bud and Sally Nevers. Bud was still a captain based out of Philadelphia and Sally was one of my original housemates when we were just starting out in Pittsburgh. I got a great tour of the city and also enjoyed a wonderful lunch with the whole family. (And yes, we continued to re-tell the story about "Putting the pumpkin...back!")

August 22nd, 2018 - This was a really nice trip with my old friend Rich Dempsey. We had a long overnight in Los Angeles, so we ended up having drinks and dinner at the Hermosa Beach pier. There, we reminisced about all the fun trips that we had worked together over the last 35 years. He is just the nicest guy and a really fun co-worker.

September 4th-10th, 2018 - My wife and I took some vacation time and spent the week celebrating her birthday at two of her favorite places in Arizona: Sedona and Scottsdale. The weather was terrific and it was surprisingly easy to find seats on our flights in and out of Phoenix.

September 13th-15th, 2018 - Because American Airlines had decided to change their staffing methods, this would end up being the last of my "extra" trips that I had become quite fond of. Although it was sometimes frustrating to not work with the same crew all week, I did enjoy those trips for the long layovers and the chance to meet flight attendants from other crew bases.

October 1st, 2018 - There was an official announcement today that the last of the old USAirways signage and color schemes had been taken down. Again, I understand moving forward as a business, but I must admit that I felt a twinge of sadness that my old airline was "no more."

November 1st, 2018 - An easy one-day trip flying in and out of Minneapolis. It was also my first time on our new Boeing 737-800 aircraft. The passenger seats were much closer together and the rear galley was a little cramped, but the plane had all the new technological features like better television screens and nicer cabin lighting. Additionally, three of the four flight attendants on this crew played guitar, so we had a lot to talk about.

November 7th, 2018 - This was supposed to have been my first layover on the tropical island of Aruba. However, apparently my passport had fallen out of my travel bag at my commuter hotel in Charlotte, and I didn't notice it until they wanted to check our credentials in Miami. Sadly, I then had to get off the trip and find a way home, while my crew enjoyed 18 hours off on the beaches of Aruba.

November 27th-28th, 2018 - This was a good trip with another long overnight in Austin, Texas. However, we had a bit of a problem the next day when our senior flight attendant Diana, was late for our van pickup to go back to the airport. Because of my long-standing rule to "never leave a crew member behind," there was a big argument with the van driver who wanted to leave without her. (When I said no, he threatened to leave all of us there.) She finally arrived some twenty minutes later, and we ended up making our scheduled check-in on time. She eventually made peace with the driver by giving him a nice tip.

December 17th, 2018 - What a crazy way to end the year! On our late-night flight to Los Angeles, we had a lady passenger who sort of flipped out and started hitting another passenger in the row in front of her. When I came up from the back of the plane to see what was happening, she turned her wrath on me and even pushed me in the chest while cursing me out. At that point, I firmly reminded her that it was a federal crime to assault an airline crew member, but that only angered her and caused her to push me for the second time.

When our senior flight attendant Ivy, (who is one of the nicest and most laid-back people I know) arrived to assess the situation, she too was also cursed out by our "problem child." When she started to draw back to push Ivy, I stepped in and got pushed for a third time. It was then that both of us started yelling at her to sit back down immediately or she would be arrested for assault. She finally returned to her seat but continued to swear at everyone around her.

Long story short, Ivy then briefed the captain regarding the situation and he opted to continue on to Los Angeles where he had law enforcement meet our plane. Security then escorted our still-angry passenger off, after taking our statements about what happened during the flight. Despite assurances that she would probably spend the night in jail, we then saw her out in front of the baggage-claim area, a mere 20 minutes later!

Ivy and I were completely stunned and both of us promised to pursue this issue with our supervisors when we got back to Charlotte. Eventually we were informed that no charges were filed against her, but that she would probably be placed on American's "no fly" list. Because of this rather meek response, I really felt like the company failed to support us and definitely did not have our backs in this situation.

Chapter Thirty

2019....The Vampire Woman, Smokey, and the Last of My Firsts

January 14th, 2019 - While trying to make my way to my plane for our first flight of the day, I noticed a fairly large crowd at the next gate. It turned out that my old friend Captain "Sully" Sullenberger was there awaiting the arrival of some passengers who had been on his "Miracle on the Hudson" flight. I then realized that tomorrow was the 10-year anniversary of that fateful flight, so I gradually made my way over to say hello to him. He seemed to remember me and even introduced me to his sweet wife who was there with him. It was so great to re-connect and I came away with the same admiration that I have always had for him.

January 22nd-25th, 2019 - This was a very interesting trip. On the second day, we flew out of Mexico City with literally the most "colorful" passenger I have ever encountered. You see, our female passenger was covered from head to toe with very bright tattoos as well as multiple piercings and under-the-skin implants. The real kicker came when I tried to get her drink order and she revealed her dental "grill," which included two prominent vampire fangs. Despite the outward appearance, she was actually very nice and impressively intelligent. She even shared with us that she was on her way to participate on a talk-show panel for a Miami television station.

Because we ended up staying in Miami that night, I had a chance to enjoy another of my very weird coincidences the next morning. After breakfast, I recall flipping through the television channels, and just happened to pause on a talk show on one of the Spanish-language stations. Suddenly, there was our tattooed friend! The program apparently was all about tattoos and whether they were a lifestyle choice or an addiction. It turned out that our lady friend was a bit of a celebrity and was famously known as the "Vampire Woman of Mexico." Although my Spanish was a little rusty, I generally understood most of the conversations, and she again came off as very well-spoken. Also, since we are not allowed to photograph our passengers without their permission, I was able to take a few photos of her off the television to show my wife. (She was not as impressed.)

February 5th-8th, 2019 - My co-workers on this trip were the very sweet Patricia and Catalina, who I nicknamed "Patty and Catty." On the second day, we got to fly into Camaguey, Cuba, for the first time. Before we left, our crew was informed that the terminal there was a bit antiquated and had very few amenities. We were also firmly instructed that we were to stay onboard after the passengers deplaned in Cuba. (In fact, we were told that if any of us tried to leave the aircraft for any reason, we could be arrested!) The only exception was that we would be allowed to step out onto the set of boarding stairs that they would bring up to the front door of our plane.

After landing there, we discovered that Camaguey was located in the middle part of the island and, like much of Cuba, had not seen much technological innovation since Castro took over in the mid-1950s. The airport was surrounded by sugarcane fields, and the few vehicles that were on the airport grounds were all at least 70 years old.

I also clearly remember stepping out onto the top of the boarding stairs when the plane started getting warm. Seeing no one around, I decided to walk to the bottom of the stairs and sat down on the next-to-last step. After thinking that I just wanted to touch the ground (in order to accurately claim that I was in fact IN Cuba), I then pretended to stretch my legs and lightly brushed the tarmac with my feet. Even though there was no one in sight, I could swear that I heard the metallic clicking sounds of gun safeties being turned off. (I then chickened out and wisely retreated back up the stairs!)

On the third day we went in and out of Tegucigalpa, Honduras, which was another city and country that I had never experienced before. On that third night we got to enjoy a long layover in Miami. In fact, our hotel there was close to an area known as the Lincoln Road Shops, which afforded us the chance to go exploring. We then discovered lots of interesting attractions and some really good Cuban restaurants. The girls also found a couple of fun nightclubs where they danced the night away.

February 14th, 2019 - We had another entertaining flight full of celebrities out of New York LaGuardia today. Up in First Class were Cheryl "Salt" James (of the female rap group "Salt-N-Pepa") and veteran actor Michael Rappaport, who coincidentally played the bartender in the movie "Sully" about my captain friend, Sully Sullenberger. In the main cabin we encountered former Obama aide Reggie Love who had also played college and pro basketball. Once we finished up in Charlotte, I also once again ran into my old high school wrestling teammate Mike Carpenter, who was mentioned earlier. Since we were both heading into Cincinnati, we rearranged our seats so that we could get caught up during the flight home.

March 12th-15th, 2019 - On this trip, I ran into old flight attendant friends Art Hartz and Dean Kroh while passing through the Phoenix Airport. (They were both around my seniority and I had not seen either of them since we had flown together many years earlier.) In addition, I also worked on flights in and out of Vail, Colorado, for the first time. The mountain views there were spectacular, but the weather suddenly worsened, and we almost got stuck at their airport.

April 16th, 2019 - After missing two possible commuter flights out of Cincinnati, I then drove up to Dayton to try for a flight out of there. Although the first flight was full, while waiting for the second flight, I did get a chance to meet Republican State Representative Jim Jordan, who had been a terrific high school wrestler back when I was a teacher and wrestling coach. (Sports trivia note: Mr. Jordan was only the second student in Ohio wrestling history to be a four-time state champion. A few years later, his brother Jeff also became a four-time champion; as did two nephews after that!)

April 29th-30th, 2019 - A very easy two-day trip with my old friend Billy Walton. On the flight to San Diego, we had a gentleman named John Walsh, who had been the host of the television crime show "America's Most Wanted." Mr. Walsh was very nice to chat with, but unfortunately, he had suffered a broken leg recently and had to be taken on and off the flight in a wheelchair. On the last day, we had a very drunk frequent flyer on our flight to Charlotte who loved our crew and promised to write a "glowing" letter about us to American Airlines. (Somehow, that letter never arrived.)

May 14th-17th, 2019 - A very good trip with my friends Mike Parrish and Jeannie Boyce. On the third day, our crew was invited to a very high-end VIP soiree' at our hotel in Orlando. Unlike my experience many years earlier at Terrible's Casino, this gathering was actually very impressive, and featured lots of great food and excellent drinks. (And... no one at this party was wearing bib overalls or their pajamas!)

May 28th, 2019 - This was a rather unusual day. On my morning drive to the Dayton Airport, I encountered a little bit of bad weather which fortunately dissipated before I reached the airport parking lot. Although I had noticed some debris along the highway, I was unaware that there had just been a tornado that touched down near the northern part of the city. It had apparently also knocked out all power at the airport, which of course meant all flights were cancelled. After quickly checking my I-pad for available options, I found that the only open flight to Charlotte was out of Louisville, some three hours later. Despite the estimated three-hour drive time, I made that frantic dash in 2.5 hours and got the last seat to work. However, after my trip was over, it took me a full day just to get back to my car in Louisville, let alone to then make the three-hour drive home in the dark. This was one of several times where I really hated commuting.

June 18th-21st, 2019 - On this trip, I achieved another career "first" when I flew with my first all-female crew. Captain Caron, First Officer Allison, and fellow flight attendants Marianne and Deborah were all a joy to fly with. (I also had fun teasing them by occasionally reminding them that, "Hey...my eyes are up here!")

On the third day we experienced a huge Southern California traffic jam while trying to get to our hotel in downtown Los Angeles. After that two-hour ride, I was still able to get out and explore the area a little bit. I ended up taking the tour of the Grammy Music Museum and then later checked out the Staples Center where the L.A. Lakers play basketball.

July 19th, 2019 - As I have said before, you just never know what you might discover when you start a conversation with someone. On our San Diego-Charlotte flight, I chatted up one of our passengers who had some interesting stories about being a photographer during an oil spill near Boston. At some point, he created a liquid emulsifier that helped break up the oil spill, and that product eventually became a shaving cream called Edge Gel.

July 23rd-26th, 2019 - A really fun trip with three Texas layovers (Dallas, Austin, and San Antonio) and a really good crew of Stan Ashmore, Mike McCloskey, and my new friend Deanna. The highlight of the trip was a fun overnight on the San Antonio Riverwalk with the whole crew. At dinner, Deanna joined the growing list of friends and family who really urged me to start sorting through all my logbooks and to begin writing this book. (Thanks Deanna!)

July 30th, 2019 - On our second flight of the day, we had an older female passenger whose dialysis punctures opened up while in flight. My co-worker Jeff and I spent some time bandaging her wounds and monitoring the situation. Once we landed in Charlotte, the paramedics came onboard and afterwards said that we did a great job taking care of her.

August 8th, 2019 - Today ended up being the last time I would ever work on one of our Boeing 757s. I had not been on one of those airplanes in quite a while, and the old air- conditioning system made the flight to Las Vegas a little bit "toasty." However, that little bit of airplane nostalgia warmed my heart as well.

August 13th-16th, 2019 - This was a really good trip with my new friends Max, Vili, and Karen. On the second day, we experienced a rather long delay in Dallas. After the captain decided to not waste any more time waiting for our catering supplies to be delivered, Vili and I then closed and locked the galley doors in preparation for our pushback. However, the caterers surprised us with a very late arrival and consequently tried to open the rear door. Vili then resembled Superman for a second as he dove across the galley to unlock that door and prevent the slide from accidentally deploying. It was as close as I would ever come to seeing my first "blown slide." (Whew!)

On the third day, the whole cabin crew experienced a wonderful afternoon exploring the French Quarter in New Orleans. My young friends also seemed to enjoy several of my impromptu "history lessons" regarding various landmarks around the downtown area. Afterwards, I treated them to some of the local cuisine. That also brought to mind how warmly I had been treated by veteran crew members when I was just starting out. (Hopefully they will all have long, rewarding careers, and then share their experiences with the next generation of flight attendants as well.)

August 19th-20th, 2019 - During my commuter flight to start my trip, some storms developed over Charlotte which forced us to divert to the Tri-Cities Airport in Tennessee. After a two-hour delay, we finally arrived in Charlotte just in time for my check-in. That made for a rather long day.

On the second day, we had to wait around in Chicago for three hours while crew scheduling tried to find us some pilots. Because of that delay, we didn't finish up in Charlotte until 2 a.m., which kept me from finding an available hotel room. Therefore, I tried to doze off in the sleeping area of our crew room, but I was unable to get any rest because of very noisy construction work going on right above me in the Charlotte terminal. I then walked over and tried instead to sleep on the floor of our international crew room. However, after an hour or so, I just gave up and then flew back home for some sack time in my own bed.

August 31st-September 6th, 2019 - My wife and I attempted to take some vacation time in the Myrtle Beach area this week but only got as far as Charlotte. That was because hurricane Dorian was threatening the entire southern coastline. Instead, we rented a car in Charlotte and "road-tripped" home through Virginia, West Virginia, and Kentucky. (Again, in the airline business, you always have to be flexible with your travel plans!)

September 12th, 2019 - Another first for me. This time our flight was delayed in Phoenix for two hours for of all reasons; a clogged sink. None of us could believe that they couldn't just close off that lavatory and let us leave on time.

September 23rd-25th, 2019 - An easy redeye trip to Portland, Oregon. On the second day, I had a chance to explore some old bookstores downtown where I purchased several books written by flight attendants. It was the beginning of my research on the airline genre and the motivation for actually starting to organize and record my lifetime of stories. Strangely, as if to encourage me in that effort, the universe presented me with another unique passenger interaction, which I feel I must include here.

After we got back from Portland, I hurried over to our commuter gates to try to catch an early flight home. There I was informed that although there were indeed seats open, I would still have to wait until the end of boarding to see what seats were left. Sure enough, at about 10 minutes before departure, the gate agent told me there was an open seat in the back of the plane and let me down the jetway.

My plane home that day was a small 50-seater, so there was still a line of passengers waiting to enter the plane. Since I was at the end of the line, I had time to talk with the flight attendant at the front door while waiting to get to my seat. However, apparently there was some sort of double-seat assignment, so the crew asked me not to go any further until they could get things worked out. At that point, I was standing in the middle of First Class, so I ended up chatting with the nice man seated in row two. After a few minutes, I realized that I was conversing with long-time singer/songwriter Smokey Robinson, who had been in the classic Motown group "Smokey Robinson and the Miracles."

Once I knew who he was, I introduced myself and told him how much I had enjoyed his music over the years. I also recalled that his current wife was the mother of one of my flight attendant friends (Lynnette M.) who I had flown with early in my career, but had not seen in a few years. Mr. Robinson then said that she was doing great and was currently out in Los Angeles. He also thought that I looked familiar and that I might have worked on one of his flights a few years back. After a few minutes, I was finally cleared to proceed, so I wished him good luck with his upcoming show in Dayton that night and took my seat in the back of the plane.

Now, over the course of my airline career, I have been fairly proficient at remembering enough random details to be able to carry on a decent conversation with most of our passengers. In fact, as I got squared away for the flight home, I was mentally congratulating myself for recalling that Mr. Robinson was Lynnette's stepfather. However, what happened next might be a sign that either I was getting old and forgetful, or perhaps I was just fatigued from my redeye flight.

Anyway, as I curled into the fetal position in my tiny little seat for a quick nap, I had a nagging feeling that there was something else that I should have known about Mr. Robinson. However, I dozed off pretty quickly and only stirred when I heard the captain make his approach announcement about an hour later. As I was trying to wake up, I suddenly remembered this great story from one of my favorite old captains from early in my career.

If I remember correctly, my captain friend had grown up in rural Pennsylvania in the late 50s and early 60s. Apparently, he had decided at age 17 that he wanted to become an aviator, so he started working several jobs in order to secure enough money for flying lessons. One of those jobs was working the late-night shift at a gas station up in the Pocono Mountains. I also recalled him saying that the work was fairly easy because it was out in the middle of nowhere and generally there was very little business during those late-night hours.

According to his story, it was about 2 a.m. on a Saturday night, when he looked up and saw a big Cadillac pull into his gas station. He then saw four guys, all dressed in the same fancy tuxedos, get out of the car and come into his store. Apparently, they had just suffered a blown tire on their car, and had no spare. Needless to say, they were quite relieved to have come across the only service station around. They then inquired if my friend had replacement tires, and if so, what it would cost them.

According to his tale, my friend let them know that the cost of a new tire (back then) was around eight dollars and there was also a charge of one dollar to put the tire on. At that point, the four gentlemen sighed heavily and explained that their manager had left ahead of them in another car, and that he had all of their money. When my friend inquired as to why they had a manager, one of them explained that they were a singing group and that they had just performed at one of the resorts up in the Pocono Mountains.

Apparently, my captain friend then asked how much money they did have, so they fished through their pockets and came up with about four dollars in change. Realizing that it was the middle of the night, and the guys were in a tough position, my friend grudgingly agreed to sell them the tire for the four dollars and even said he would put the new tire on for no charge. However, in a stroke of genius, he then reasoned that since they were a singing group, (and to make up the difference of the cost of the tire) they had to agree to sing to him while he worked on their car.

Based on his story, the four gentleman looked at each other and happily agreed to his request. My friend then claimed that during the time that it took to change out the tire, they sang five or six songs and that they were really talented. When he finally took their car down off the lift, he then thanked them for the entertainment and inquired as to who they were. The lead singer then introduced himself as Smokey Robinson and his friends as "The Miracles." Evidently, they were just starting out on their long and successful career.

Now that I had this great story in my brain, I could only hope that Mr. Robinson was still up in First Class, so that I could share it with him. Unfortunately, by the time I could work my way up from the rear of the aircraft, he had already deplaned. When I didn't see him in the baggage claim area or out in front of the airport, I could only assume that he had already been whisked away for his upcoming show. That seemed like a real shame, because I really think that he would have enjoyed that story. I also believe he would have remembered that particular situation, because although Smokey Robinson has been in the music business for over 50 years, I just couldn't imagine that he had sung to that many people while they changed his flat tire.

October 21st, 2019 - We had a rather unique opportunity presented to us before our flight from Charlotte to Tampa. Before boarding the passengers, we were asked to place advertisements on the seats promoting a new display of Medal of Honor recipients at the Tampa Airport. To my surprise, one of the honorees was a gentleman from my hometown named Gordon Roberts. (Sgt. Roberts had received the Medal of Honor for his heroism during the Vietnam War in 1969.) After we arrived in Tampa, we all took a few extra minutes to check out the wonderful display which honored some our most heroic military veterans.

October 29th-November 1st, 2019 - This turned out to be a fairly good trip. On the third day, one of our passengers was guitarist "Captain Ray" Earls who plays in the band "Green Jelly." Eventually I discovered that he also worked as part of our ground crew at the Orange County Airport and was a huge aviation fan as well. After a short conversation about his music, he was also nice enough to show me his guitar and even let me play it a little. Once I showed him a video of my guitar pick collection, he also gifted me with one of his custom picks as well. He was such a terrific guy!

November 14th, 2019 - During our long layover in Los Angeles, I enjoyed watching some beach volleyball near Hermosa Pier. That was followed by a good meal, a few frosty beverages, and then a pause to take in the sunset over the Pacific Ocean. Looking back, it also ended up being a little symbolic of where I was on my career path as well. I could not have known it at the time, but I was enjoying my final sunset...so to speak.

December 2nd-5th, 2019 - This was an interesting trip. On the first day, our flight to Boston was delayed over three hours due to heavy snow over much of New England. Because we arrived so late, our trip got rescheduled and we later ended up instead with a 33-hour layover in downtown Philadelphia. Fortunately for us, our Philadelphia hotel was located across from their main square and that allowed us to take in the annual tree-lighting ceremony the next night. That celebration included lots of free "swag" and plenty of great holiday food and drink. I even got to shake hands with Mr. and Mrs. Santa Claus during their guest appearance.

December 9th-16th, 2019 - Because our vacation in September had been foiled by a hurricane, Karen and I had to shift that time off to mid-December in Orlando, Florida instead. However, trying to "non-rev" during a holiday month was usually pretty tricky, so we eventually settled for flying into Tampa and then renting a car to Orlando. Although that took considerably longer, it worked out just fine.

My sister Sherri and her husband Tim, even flew in and spent a few days with us as well. That also allowed us to enjoy a small family reunion with my other sister, Cindy, and some cousins over in nearby Plant City. It was a very relaxing week. Unfortunately for us, after it was over, it was nearly impossible to find a seat home. We eventually had to fly through Dallas-Ft. Worth and into Columbus, Ohio, instead. Because of how long it took for us to get home, I decided to push back my next trip by an extra day, so I could get some Christmas decorations up for the holidays. It turned out to be one of the most pivotal decisions I have ever made.

Chapter Thirty-One

2020....The Five "Miracles" and the Final Months

December 17th, 2019 - This date will be etched into my memory for all time, because our lives were changed forever today. We had just finished dinner and because we had not been able to hang any Christmas decorations before we left for Florida, we decided to finally put up the tree. Karen had just enjoyed her after-dinner cigarette and as she returned to the kitchen she suddenly stopped talking and her eyes sort of glazed over. When she didn't answer my query of "Are you okay?" I immediately sensed that something was wrong. That is apparently when her stroke occurred. I then yelled to my son who was downstairs in the basement, to call 9-1-1!

Looking back at that moment, I am thankful for two things. First, I had decided to stay home instead of working a trip that day. (In fact, I consider that to be the first of what would be a series of "miracles" that would shape the rest of our lives!) Second, I had been trained every year since 1983 to spot the possible signs of a stroke. Once I sensed what was happening, I then went through the checklist of stroke symptoms, which I will list for you readers. Please consider committing them to memory, as they could save the life of someone you love.

1. Have the person raise both arms out in front of them. If a stroke is happening, one arm will generally be higher than the other one.

2. Have the person stick out their tongue. In a stroke situation, the tongue will not be in the middle of their mouth but will tend to drift to either the left or right side of the lips. (You may also consider asking

them to smile for you. If one side of the mouth is drooping or crooked, it may be another indication of a stroke.)

3. Have the person repeat a simple phrase or sentence. If a stroke is happening, they may be unable (or only partially able) to repeat what you say.

Long story short, the paramedics arrived within a few minutes and agreed that she was most likely having a stroke. They then transported Karen to a local hospital in Dayton, where she received tremendous care. However, we were informed that her condition was very serious, and that it would be "touch-and-go" for the next few days. We were even advised to be ready to make some "end-of-life" decisions if her recovery did not go well.

At that point, I will just say that she was in bad shape. Karen was unable to speak or move her right arm and only had limited motion in her right leg. Fortunately, we had the love and support of our families and a wonderful circle of friends. The medical staff couldn't have been nicer and the hospital clergy continued to offer up prayers for Karen's recovery.

It was somewhere around the third day that I eventually recalled a conversation that Karen and I had while on vacation in Florida. Apparently, after going through her father's effects, my wife had been unable to find any records of her baptism as a child. Since she had recently been taking bible classes and consequently exploring her spiritual faith, it seemed to bother her that she didn't know for sure. Therefore, the next time the hospital chaplain stopped in to check on Karen, I floated the idea of possibly having her baptized.

The chaplain then explained that a baptism was indeed possible and in fact she could perform anything from a simple service to a more detailed ceremony with complete water immersion. Since Karen was still in and out of consciousness, we settled on a more moderate service. Within a couple of hours, everything was organized and as we began the ceremony, I was also pleasantly surprised to see about 20 members of our medical staff join us in our hospital room.

In a very sweet and moving ritual, Karen was then blessed and anointed by our chaplain, followed by a joyous round of applause from many of her caregivers. It was a very heartwarming day indeed.

However, the very next morning we were all witnesses to another "miracle" (number two for those keeping track) when Karen eventually woke up and discovered that she could now use her right arm and right leg!

Although her doctors were amazed at her recovery, I knew that her inner toughness was also probably playing a part in this scenario. However, as a long-time believer, I was also not discounting the interesting timing of her sudden improvement. I knew in my heart that God had heard our prayers and had decided to bless us. In fact, when the chaplain stopped by later that day to visit, she was nearly moved to tears by what she saw. We all then offered up sincere prayers of thanksgiving, followed by many, many hugs.

Karen continued to improve so much that after 11 days in their I.C.U. unit, she was discharged to a local rehab facility. There she was nurtured and cared for while undergoing extensive physical therapy. Fortunately, I was again allowed to stay with her each night, just like at the hospital. Thanks to a great team effort, Karen continued her amazing recovery and after thirty days, we were finally allowed to bring her back home.

However, during that period, I had used up much of my accumulated "sick time" and was starting to get some pressure from American Airlines about my extended absence. According to them, I was supposed to have already filed for an F.M.L.A. (Family Medical Leave Act) leave. Although we managed to eventually work through all the red tape, my company still chose to "write me up" and I received disciplinary points on my work record. Although that didn't sit well with me, I figured Karen's health was more important. So once I knew she was healthy enough, I made plans to return to flying at the beginning of March.

March 3rd-6th, 2020 - This was my first trip in over two months. It was also my first time wearing our new uniforms designed by Land's End. (The new apparel was the company's eventual response to three years of rashes and other negative reactions to the previous uniform.) I was also fortunate to have a good crew, which included old friends Mary Hardy and Sherri Fogleman. That was comforting because after being away for so long, I felt a little rusty.

Despite the easy trip, there was still a lot of concern about the newly prevalent Corona virus that was going around. According to some medical officials, that particular virus could be extremely dangerous and therefore our company was recommending that we wear surgical masks and gloves while on the airplane.

March 11th-13th, 2020 - While on a layover in Dallas, I had a chance to drop by the Dallas crew room and visit with my old Pittsburgh pal Tom Kilheeney, who had recently been promoted to base supervisor. Despite his new corporate position, Tom was still the coolest guy. He even reminded me that "us old dudes" were starting to slowly disappear from the workforce. He also expressed great concern about my wife's health and made sure that I had his contact information in case I needed any help dealing with American Airlines in the future.

March 19th-20th, 2020 - I was supposed to fly into Dallas-Ft. Worth for two days of our annual CQT training. However, with the increasing concern over the Corona virus, the company wisely relented and temporarily suspended all training. It was anybody's guess as to when things would get back to normal.

March 22nd, 2020 - Today marked my 37th anniversary as a flight attendant. Although I still loved my job, my wife's recent health problems and the company's occasionally callous treatment of it's workforce, had skewed my enthusiasm a bit. However, I just refused to ever let it show to my passengers.

March 25th-27th, 2020 - This was originally a three-day trip that was repeatedly altered due to an increasing amount of flight cancellations. (Apparently, many of our passengers had decided to curtail their flying after the government had recommended more isolation and less social interaction.) On the plus side, we got an extra day off at our hotel which was right on the beach in Ft. Lauderdale, Florida. However, that day seemed almost eerie, because there was no one on the beach or in the water during what should have been a very busy Spring Break week. In fact, the term "ghost town" actually seems appropriate when I recall that situation.

April 6th, 2020 - Due to the increasing severity of the Covid-19 pandemic, I was starting to get more worried about its effects on our health and whether or not I might accidentally bring it home to my family. Today, I woke up with a scratchy throat and a little bit of congestion. To be safe, I then used one of my "personal days" and called off my four-day trip.

I felt better after a couple of days, but while I was home, American Airlines announced that they would soon be offering a number of leaves of absence to their flight crews. Apparently, they were estimating around a 70% reduction of passengers during the summer, and possibly more for the rest of the year. I eventually signed up for a three-month leave.

April 15th-16th, 2020 - This was originally a redeye trip that was changed to an easy two-day with a long layover in Las Vegas. On what would have normally been completely full flights, we only had 20 passengers going into Vegas and just 11 on our return flight the next day. Everyone wore masks and our passengers were evenly spread throughout the cabin. We were instructed to provide only the basic service and to limit our interactions with the customers as much as possible. I remember thinking how weird that felt.

Well, that was only the beginning of the weirdness. Once we arrived at our hotel in Las Vegas, we were informed that we were just about the only guests staying there. Because of that, there would be very limited food and drink options available to us, as most of the restaurants and casinos in town had closed down in response to the outbreak. In what would resemble a scene from some bizarre, post-apocalyptic movie, there was literally no traffic on or around the famous Las Vegas Strip, and all the normally bustling casinos were empty.

Because very little food was available at the hotel, I opted to head out for an afternoon stroll in hopes of finding something more substantial to eat. After heading north toward the Stratosphere hotel, I soon discovered that our hotel manager's assessment was absolutely accurate: everything was closed! I did eventually find one McDonald's that was only providing service through their drive-up window. Despite the fact that there was a very long line of cars, none of the drivers wanted to engage with this hungry flight attendant, or even roll down their windows. (In fact, I remember feeling like an underage minor with cash, trying to convince someone to go into the liquor store and buy me some beer.) One conversation actually went something like this:

Me: (tapping on a random car window) "Please sir, could you get me a cheeseburger and some fries? I have money."

Them: (from behind the glass) "Go away, weirdo. We are not risking getting sick."

The good news was that eventually I did discover an open Subway store that agreed to make me a couple of sandwiches, as long as I wore a mask and stood about 15 feet away from the counter. I was so appreciative of their kindness that I even left them an extra twenty-dollar bill as a tip! In fact, after all that effort to find food, I couldn't recall any recent meal that I actually enjoyed more.

April 20th-22nd, 2020 - This was an easy three-day trip that featured a long overnight in Austin, Texas. My crew was a rather rare "all-guy" grouping consisting of longtime friends Tony Diaz, Keith Whatley and Willie Whitmore. (To say that we were "veterans" might be understating it a bit. Someone figured out that we had over 150 years of flying experience between the four of us!) Tony and Keith were also fellow musicians who both played in a great local band called "Groove 8." That gave us lots to chat about during our trip, which was good because we hardly had any passengers this week, again due to the Covid-19 pandemic.

In fact, the airports and restaurants were also deserted, as well as our hotels. (Again, I can't stress enough how bizarre it was to see these normally bustling venues so completely silent.) Once we arrived in Austin, we were re-assigned to a different hotel that was away from the downtown area and had no access to any nearby restaurants. After the food fiasco the previous week in Las Vegas, I had finally learned to bring more food in my travel bag. However, I had already eaten most of it by the time we got to Austin, so we really had to be creative in order to get something to eat.

Fortunately, Tony was able to arrange an Uber ride for the four of us to the only open grocery store within 10 miles. Again, in a very bizarre scenario, we had to wait outside the store (spaced evenly apart in our full mask-and-gloves regalia) and were only allowed to enter the store in very small groups. We then managed to purchase enough groceries for our next few meals. However, when our return Uber driver showed up with a much smaller car, we also had to figure out a way to get it all back to the hotel. (Imagine a very tiny circus "clown car" completely packed with various arms and legs protruding from the windows!) It was quite the adventure.

On the third day, right before our last flight from Dallas to Charlotte, I received a text from the company that they were re-starting our CQT Trainings and I was being assigned a slot for the May 6th -7th class. Even though my leave started on May 1st, I figured I would go ahead and get it out of the way, so I wouldn't have to worry about it during my three months off. Reviewing all the test material also gave me something to occupy my time during our last leg, because we only had five passengers to care for on the way to Charlotte.

It has been said that you never know when the last time for something might occur. Although I was aware that I would not be doing any flying for the next few months, (and I was a little suspicious as to when our normal flight schedules would return) I decided to be sure to thank my crew for a great trip and wished them all good luck with what appeared to be a rather uncertain future. The rest of my crew must have felt the same way, because Tony then encouraged us to pose for a group picture after we landed in Charlotte. I was so glad that we did, because that photo ended up being a nice souvenir of my final crew and my final trip. Again, I just didn't know it at the time.

Even as I made my way down to the crew room, I remember thinking that I had better get everything out of my crew mailbox, since I wasn't going to be back for a while. I also grabbed a few extra masks and a box of gloves for the commute home to Cincinnati. Additionally, I saw a few flight attendant friends who I would have normally greeted with a big hug, but for health reasons elected to go with a gloved "fist bump" instead. Since I may never see them again in person, I will regret not hugging them for a long time.

May 6th, 2020 - In short, I spent the next two weeks at home, preparing for the always- stressful two days of CQT training. My wife's health had improved quite a bit during the last few months, and she was even able to quiz me on some of the test material. On the morning of May 6th, I got up early and quietly prepared to head to the Dayton Airport for my flight into Dallas-Ft.Worth. I remember kissing my wife on the forehead as she mumbled, "Good luck with your training" from under her covers. I also recalled thinking that she still looked cute in the morning, even with rumpled "bed-head" hair. I would end up holding on dearly to that image for the next few years.

During the three-hour flight to the DFW airport, I alternately slept or studied my test material in preparation for what always felt like the longest two days of the year. I arrived early at the training center, and then used that time to practice opening and closing all the different doors and windows of each aircraft that I was certified on. I managed to get re-qualified on all but one plane, which was normally the most difficult part of our training. Once class started, we were told to turn off our cell phones so that we could not be interrupted during our training.

The next few hours were a bit of a blur. I remember thinking that the "what if" scenarios offered this year (used to test your knowledge and reactions to possible threatening situations) seemed pretty tame. Eventually, I was selected to be the flight attendant who had to calm down an overly agitated passenger. The fact that I not only calmly answered all his nervous questions, but also managed to get him laughing, earned me high praise from our instructors. During our dinner break, I did turn on my phone to see if there were any messages. Since nothing popped up, I then turned my phone off for the rest of the evening.

Somewhere around 10 p.m., we finished up with the first day and were then bussed back to our hotel. It was only after I checked into my room, that I bothered to turn on my phone again. When about 15 frantic messages from my son appeared on my screen, I then called home. It turned out to be the most upsetting phone call I ever made.

Apparently, Karen had suffered another, much more serious stroke soon after she had finished dinner that night. In what I would describe as our third "miracle," Brian fortunately, was with her when it occurred and immediately called for an ambulance after she failed to respond to him. (Had he been in his room or away from the house at the time, she could very well have died on the kitchen floor.)

According to my son, she was then transported back to the same hospital in Dayton that had treated her during her first stroke. However, this time the newly initiated Covid-19 restrictions would keep her isolated from Brian and the rest of her family while they treated her. She was considered to be in critical condition and our only updates would come from a hospital spokesperson via Brian's cell phone.

After furiously writing down all the pertinent information regarding Karen's condition and then calming my son, I then made multiple calls to her family members to alert them. I also tried to contact anyone at the American Airlines training center, but everyone had already left. I also sadly discovered that the first available flight to Dayton was not until 2 p.m. the next day. Therefore, I offered up numerous prayers for my wife's well-being, and then futilely tried to get some sleep.

The next day, I got up very early and made my way back to the training center, where I eventually found a supervisor and carefully explained what had happened. He was most supportive and not only secured a guaranteed seat on that first flight to Dayton but also managed to get me placed in an earlier class, so that I could finish my training and then leave quickly for the airport to fly home.

The rest of that day was also a bit of a blur. I vaguely recall sitting inside a life raft during the final class, which was our "ditching" seminar. I also remember a review of what happened during the "Miracle on the Hudson," but I was too distracted to really care. Once that class was over, I bolted for the airport and was given a seat in the first row of coach class. Fortunately, my seatmate was a nice young man who sensed my distress, and after kindly listening to my situation, then offered up prayers for my wife and family as well.

As soon as we landed, I hurried to my car and then drove to Karen's hospital to check on her condition. Unfortunately, because of the Covid-19 protocols in place, I was not allowed to see my wife, or even have a seat inside the building. Instead, I was forced to sit in my car in the parking lot and just stare up at where I imagined her room was located. Two hours later, I received a phone update from one of her doctors that she was still sedated, and that more testing was needed. After verifying her medical records and history of strokes, I was again informed that there was no way that I could get in to see her. I then reluctantly left to drive home and be with my son.

Over the next few days, I tried to stay busy and not let my mind wander. I usually received Karen's medical updates in the morning, and then again around dinnertime. On the second day, I even drove back to the hospital and sat in the parking lot near her window, just to feel closer to her. It was during that time that I fervently prayed to God to allow her to heal. I also recall asking for any opportunity to be allowed to see her, because I felt that was truly what would be best for her... and for myself as well. I then ended my prayer with the option that if I couldn't get in to see her, that God might possibly send me a sign that things were indeed going to be okay.

Well, be careful what you ask for. Out of the blue, the very next morning, (and what I consider to be our fourth "miracle") I received an unexpected phone call from one of Karen's doctors. He then informed me that if I could make it up to the hospital within the next hour, he would then arrange a "consultation" with me regarding Karen's medical treatment. I would also be allowed a two-hour visit with her while we discussed her care. I not only agreed, I then drove up to that hospital like I was shot out of a cannon!

Once at the hospital, I was required to wear a mask and gloves. I was also warned that Karen was still very groggy and may or may not be able to respond to me. She was indeed sleeping when I first got there, so her physician and I took that time to review her brain scans and medical information. Apparently, this stroke was much worse than the first one and there was extensive damage to several areas of her brain. The doctor cautioned that although Karen would most probably survive, she would require extensive physical and occupational therapy. While all the options for her care were discussed, I remember taking lots of notes and trying to just keep my emotions in check.

The really good news was that at the end of our meeting, my wife started stirring and even opened her eyes for a short time. As I held her hand, I gently explained what had happened to her and where she was. I also reassured her that her family was fine and that we were all praying for her. Although she couldn't speak, she was able to nod her head and to follow me around the room with her eyes. Overall, our visit was exactly what we both needed and before I left, I offered another sincere prayer of thanks for this unexpected opportunity to see and hold her again.

I dimly recall the 30-minute drive home after that visit. Once I pulled into the driveway however, our son met me and wanted to know how his mother was doing. After patiently explaining what the doctor had related to me, I also told him about how my prayer to see her had been answered. He and I were both amazed at the incredible timing of the doctor's phone call, and we were both encouraged somewhat by her prognosis. Afterwards, I recall telling Brian that I needed some fresh air and elected to head out for a nice afternoon walk around the neighborhood. It was a walk that I wouldn't soon forget.

As I left the house, I was faced with a number of options. I could turn left out of the driveway and either head into town or go up the hill into a residential neighborhood. If I turned right, I could end up walking on the nature trail in the woods behind our house, or take the stroll around the big city block which took me near the downtown area. For whatever reason, I elected to turn right and do the big-city-block walk.

As I started out, I vaguely recall going over all the details in my mind regarding my wife's expected care and recovery. I remember thinking that I was so fortunate to have taken advantage of the extended Covid-19 leave, so that I could concentrate on Karen's health and not have to worry about missing more work. I was also doing a little bit of accounting as well; trying to estimate how much our insurance would cover and how much money we might have to spend for additional expenses. I am sure there were also a thousand other nagging concerns bouncing around in my head, but that all came to a screeching halt as I turned left at the second corner of the block.

There, sitting right next to the sidewalk, was a triangular message board that often advertised services for the little Baptist church on the corner. (Strangely enough, it was the same church that I had occasionally attended as a young man.) For whatever reason, that day's message was a Bible passage from the book of Psalms. As if it had been written just for me, it stated in big block letters...”The Lord is my Rock and my Deliverer.”

Now if you recall, I had prayed not only to be able to see my wife in the hospital, but also for a sign that things were going to be okay. In what I consider the most amazing and coincidental timing yet, (and my fifth and final "miracle") I had asked for a "sign," and I literally got...a sign! I remember stopping dead in my tracks, taking a few seconds to try to comprehend what I was seeing, and then looking up into the beautiful blue sky. I then felt what I can only explain as a warm feeling of calm and peace that washed over me. All my concerns went away, and I just knew that we were indeed going to be okay.

At this point, I can only guess what you, the reader, must be imagining. As I look back at what I have written so far for this chapter, I myself have a hard time rationalizing it. Throughout my life, I have always been an optimistic, "glass half full" kind of guy, and have felt that most things have a reasonable explanation. However, this chapter does not seem to fall in that direction. My mother (the math teacher) had instilled in me early on, that the "law of averages" will balance out all things eventually. However, based on everything that happened to us over the last six months, that law of averages had been severely skewed. Based on the absolutely incredible timing of those five amazing "miracles," I can now only surmise that we had been extremely blessed by God. It is the only answer that works.

Chapter Thirty-Two

Epilogue

Following her second stroke, Karen was eventually transferred to a nearby facility for rest and rehab. This time, the second stroke had once again affected her right side and she again was unable to use her right arm or leg. She also could only speak a few words. Unfortunately, because of the severity of the Covid-19 pandemic, she was also isolated by herself in that rehab facility for about nine weeks. During that period, I was only able to communicate with her over the phone or through her bedroom window.

Once again, I felt so very fortunate to have taken advantage of that three-month leave, because I ended up using that time to remodel our house into a more wheelchair-friendly abode. I also spent every evening of those nine weeks sitting outside her room window, trying to either entertain her or inform her of current events. Our most memorable night came during week six, when her nurse forgot to lock her window, and I managed to lift it up high enough to actually reach in and hold her hand for about 15 minutes!

Although my original leave of absence ran from May through July of 2020, American Airlines then allowed me to extend that twice; to include the months of August and September. That turned out to be extremely beneficial because Karen had a rough time in August. She not only fell and fractured her hip, but she also had some kidney and lung complications as well. That caused her to spend the entire month of August back in the hospital. Because she was unable to speak, her doctors arranged a special exemption, which allowed me to stay with her in her room and essentially act as her "interpreter."

As I mentioned in the Introduction chapter, because I needed something to occupy my time, it was then that I began to compose this book. Each day, I would bring a different logbook with me to the hospital; then re-read each one and start cherry-picking the really good stories. Most of the time, Karen was usually either sleeping or undergoing physical therapy, so my research permitted me to at least feel somewhat productive. It also allowed me to entertain the severely overworked staff with some amazing tales. I think it was good for their spirits, and most importantly it gave me some great feedback about the entertainment level of my stories

Eventually, Karen was able to come home for good by the end of August. To celebrate, we then organized a "drive-by parade" for her on her birthday in early September. This gathering allowed all of her family and local friends to safely "isolate" in their cars, but still honk and wave at her as they drove by with balloons and hand-made posters encouraging her to continue to heal! She absolutely loved every minute of it, and it was a great boost to her morale as well.

By mid-September, American Airlines announced that because so few people were flying, they would be offering more extended leaves to their workforce. Since Karen was still recovering, I elected to take a 15-month leave which would run through December of 2021. I reasoned that if my wife was healthy by that point, I could then return to my amazing career. If not, I would then be old enough to retire with full benefits.

As it turned out, we spent the rest of 2020 and most of 2021 in "Covid isolation." That allowed my son and I plenty of time to acclimate to our new roles as full-time caregivers and to assist Karen in getting used to her physical limitations as well. Although we sort of missed our normal social routines during that period, it really did give us a chance to bond as a family.

In March of 2021, I remember thinking that I would have been celebrating my 38th anniversary as a flight attendant. Since my father had worked as a farm manager for nearly 40 years and my mother had been a teacher and school librarian for 30 years, I was also apparently upholding the family tradition of finding one job that you really liked and staying with it. I clearly recall that they had both emphasized to me over the years, that it was so much better having work that you enjoyed doing.

In early July of 2021, I received several texts from fellow flight attendants, warning me that American Airlines was seeing an increase in passenger loads and that they were considering recalling some of their workforce. Sure enough, in mid-July I was sent an official notice that all crew member leaves were being rescinded. Our only options were to return to work in either November or December of 2021, or officially resign from the company. We would also have to let them know our decision by July 29th.

For most of my airline career, I never actually considered retiring. In fact, I can say that at one point I loved my job so much that I would have found a way to continue flying, even if I was so old and feeble that they would have had to strap me to the end of the drink cart with bungee cords. However, during the last few years, there had been a number of irritating changes to our airline culture. Despite that, I had always found a way to make the most of every trip and I still enjoyed the job. Although I may not have liked or completely understood some of the corporate changes made by our management, I still appreciated what I did for a living.

This time was different. First and foremost, this was no longer just about me. I had to consider what was best for Karen and her health. My usual pattern of being away for several days in a row would no longer work well with her needs. If I had to bring in professional caregivers to watch her while I was away, that would essentially cost as much as any pay I brought home. Other factors, including the difficulty in commuting to and from work and the risk of bringing home the Covid-19 virus, also complicated the situation.

Perhaps the most frustrating problem was the very real possibility that I might have to go back on "reserve" again under American's "rotating reserve" program. (This shameful policy was originally supposed to have been limited to the bottom 15% of our block holders, but had been continually expanded to include long-time veterans like me.) That uncertainty alone made my options pretty clear. Therefore, after careful consideration, I notified the company that I would be retiring in October.

The next few months were rather hectic as I prepared to become a retiree. There was exhaustive research on applying for Medicare and an extensive compilation of paperwork related to our retirement accounts. I even had to push back my original retirement date of October 1st to October 21st, just so I could complete all the forms in time. Because I was so busy, I hadn't even considered a retirement party, until my son asked if the company was going to have any sort of ceremony for me. Unfortunately, the answer was, no.

One of the sad truths of the airline industry is that trying to gather a large number of crew members together in one place at one time, is a lot like herding cats; it is nearly impossible. That was generally because at any given time, your airline friends might be scattered across the far corners of the globe. The ones who might be off-duty that day, may or may not be able to find an open seat in order to fly to your location. Consequently, with those logistics to consider, I knew there would not be any fanfare regarding my retirement.

With that in mind, I did decide to stage my own "going-away party" on Facebook. Beginning about two weeks out, I elected to post one personal photograph each day from some point in my career. That allowed many of my friends to reminisce and comment about my flying adventures on each day that I posted. Under the circumstances, it was the best way to share some sweet sentiments with some wonderful people before I left.

October 21st arrived before I could blink twice. On that day, I made a call to my long-time supervisor Sammie Reid, to make sure that he had received all the necessary paperwork and to thank him for all his support and kindness. Other than that conversation, the day itself was a little anticlimactic. Because of some Covid-19 restrictions still in place, I didn't even have to fly into Charlotte to return my ID badge. Instead, I just mailed it in.

Looking back over my career, I am utterly amazed at the number of wonderful experiences I had the chance to enjoy. Although there had been a few "cringe-worthy" moments here and there, generally I can say that I was just very blessed! When I realize that God somehow allowed this farm boy from Ohio to lay down his pitchfork and put on his airline wings, I just feel so grateful. In fact, I also believe that my farming background contributed to my ability to keep a good perspective about my work life. No matter how frantic or stressed I may have felt some days, remembering all the cow manure I shoveled during my youth, always made me think that my flight attendant life was so much easier. (It usually smelled better too!)

Additionally, it warms my heart to recall how many wonderful crew members I got to work with over the years. Back when I was starting out, the flight attendant position was a highly coveted job. Only those folks with outstanding personalities and great "people skills" could even make the cut. Consequently, those types of people were also so much fun to fly with that they made it a joy to come to work each week. I hope they all know how much I treasured flying with them!

Also, after looking back at my airline career and writing about how many times we drank, I just didn't realize how often I was imbibing. As I mentioned in Chapter Two, there had always been opportunities to enjoy a frosty beverage or two while on our layovers. Because I rarely went over what I considered my "limit" or encountered other problematic behaviors with drinking, I just didn't consider it to be more than a fun social activity. However, as I got older and more health-conscious, I eventually realized that it was just not the smart thing to do. Also, because of my wife's medical condition and the demands of constant caregiving, I finally decided to put it all aside. As of this writing, I have not had a drink since June of 2020.

I also feel like I should address the issue of the sheer number of bizarre coincidences that I encountered during my airline career. For whatever reason, my family has always seemed to have unusual things happen around us. Because my parents constantly reminded us to "pay attention," we were usually alert to what was going on. Also, throughout my career, we were constantly reminded to exercise "situational awareness" whether on the airplane or at our layovers. When you combine that awareness with my mental capacity for remembering trivial details, it would appear that I became a bit of a lightning rod for those ironic situations. However, I believe that most people probably have similar types of coincidences happening around them as well. It's just that I seem to pay more attention to them.

To emphasize that point, I recently received the final bit of data that I needed to finish up my last chapter, titled "The Hall of Records." After my friend Jayme sent me some measurements on the volume of our airplane coffee pots, I then worked on some formulas that would help me try to estimate the amount of coffee I made during my airline career. However, I had to put that research aside while I tended to my wife and didn't get back to it until the next day. After finally completing that work, I realized that I was essentially finished composing this book. It was only then that I noticed the date: March 22nd, 2023. Ironically, I had completed writing about my airline adventures on the 40th anniversary of me becoming a flight attendant! As I have stated several times previously..."What are the odds of that??"

Finally, I also want to mention that I was raised with God in my life, and I have always been so very glad to be able to call on Him during moments of doubt or weakness. Perhaps because of all the medical problems that my wife has had to endure, He now seems to have instilled in me an unexplainable sense of peace and calm that maybe wasn't so prevalent before. In fact, despite all the calamity, God has allowed us to not only carry on, but to actually prosper as well. Again, although my life has been far from perfect, it has at least been...entertaining! I hope you think so as well.

Chapter Thirty-Three

Hall of Records

As I mentioned several times throughout the book, I have always enjoyed interesting mathematic categories and fun trivia facts. After researching my logbooks, here are a few personal statistics that I thought were entertaining.

AIRLINE CEO'S THAT I WORKED FOR....Ed Colodny (1983-1991), Seth Schofield (1991-1995), Stephen Wolf (1996-1998), Rakeesh Gangwal (1998-2001), Stephen Wolf (2001-2002), David Siegel (2002-2004), Bruce Lakefield (2004-2005), Doug Parker (2005-2021)

CITIES THAT I HAVE FLOWN TO/FROM....According to my logbooks, there were 167 different U.S. airports and 37 international airports in 24 other countries, for a total of 204 individual airports.

TOTAL NUMBER OF FLIGHTS THAT I WORKED....A grand total of 16,135 flights, with 734 of those being either deadhead or ferry flights, where I rode as a passenger.

TIME SPENT WAITING FOR DIET COKE FIZZ TO SUBSIDE....Since most flight attendants hate having to pour the fizziest of all sodas, I wanted to know how much of my life I spent waiting for those accursed bubbles to die down. Therefore, I estimated that I probably averaged 6 Diet Cokes per flight x 15,401 working flights. If I waited 10 seconds per drink for the carbonation to subside, that equals....10.6 days!

TYPES OF AIRPLANES I HAVE WORKED ON....A total of 17 different types of aircraft. BAC-111, McDonnell-Douglass DC-9 and MD-80, Boeing 727-100, 727-200, 737-200, 737-300, 737-400, 737-800, 757-200, 767-200, Fokker-100, Airbus-319, A-320, A-321, A-330, and Embraer E-190.

AMOUNT OF TIME SPENT COMMUTING TO/FROM WORK....Although too mind-boggling to even contemplate, I will give it a try. I started commuting in February of 1986. With a minimum of at least 4 hours per trip and at the worst maybe 12 hours per trip, I am going to assume an 8-hour average for every trip. At about 40 trips per year, that equals somewhere around 11,300 hours or 470 days' worth of added travel time. (However, being home with your family and getting to sleep in your own bed, always seemed worth it to me.)

VOLUME OF COFFEE THAT I MADE FOR OUR PASSENGERS....I estimated about 5 pots of coffee per flight. (More on longer flights and morning flights, less on shorter flights.) Assuming 48 ounces per pot, that would be 240 ounces made per flight. Since there are 128 ounces in a gallon, and I worked 15,401 flights, that would be 3,696,240 ounces or about 28,877 gallons of coffee made in my career. (That also equals about 525, 55-gallon drums, and about 616,040 6-ounce cups of caffeination!) The really weird thing is, I never learned to drink coffee, so I have never even had one cup of airline java. However, it always smelled wonderful, especially early in the morning!

DIFFERENT WAYS TO TELL PASSENGERS "GOODBYE"....Some flight attendants simply repeated the same things during our deplanings. However, I liked to mix it up a little bit. Here are some of my favorites: "bye," "so long," "see ya," "see ya later," "bye now," the infamous "SNL" version of "buh-bye," "take care," "take care now," "ta-ta," and occasionally..."farewell," "later dude," or "till we meet again." For certain international flights I might go with the French "Au revoir" or Spanish "Adios." However, I could never quite get the right pronunciation for the German "Auf Wiedersehen," so I occasionally uttered "Our feet are stained" instead. (No one ever acted like they caught that one). Of course, there was that mash-up mentioned in Chapter 3 of "good...bye-bye," but it was only used that one time!

THINGS THAT I ALWAYS HAD IN MY TRAVEL BAG.... comb, Chapstick, my passport, some handy-wipe packets, enough coins to make a few pay phone calls (I didn't own a cell phone until after 9/11), a photo of my "Pride and Joy," ink pens from the hotels, a "trip sheet" of each day's scheduled flying, my address book, some sort of stain/spot remover, a few surgical masks for fumes and/or flu (or Covid-19), our big heavy "safety manual" (at least until we got the HHD's), and some American Express travelers checks. (To quote the old ads, "I didn't leave home without them!")

TOTAL NUMBER OF CELEBRITIES I ENCOUNTERED DURING MY TRAVELS....I went back through my logbooks and compiled a list which consisted of sports figures, actors/actresses, politicians, television personalities, comedians, newsmakers, authors, and musicians...and a few others. (I counted entire teams and/or musical groups as one entity, unless there were a number of significant members with outstanding individual accomplishments.) Total: 478

SIGNIFICANT PUBLIC HEALTH SCARES DURING MY CAREER .... AIDS 1983-1984, MRSA (superbug) 1990-1991, Hantavirus 1993, H1N1(bird flu) 1997, Mad Cow disease 2000, SARS 2002-2003, Swine flu 2009-2010, Anthrax 2009-2010, Mersa 2012, Ebola virus 2014-2016, Zika virus 2015-2016, Covid-19 virus 2020-2021. (Despite all this, I rarely got sick!)

SAGE ADVICE THAT REALLY HELPED ME DURING MY AIRLINE CAREER....Although I may be an old retired guy, I don't want to appear like those elderly folks who reminisce about their lives, then offer anyone who is listening unsolicited advice. However, these bits of wisdom actually came in handy during the course of my career. Some came from my very wise parents. A few were the results of the old "trial-and-error" method. I hope they can help you as well.

1. Appreciate the kindness of those around you. A simple, heartfelt "Thank you" can go a long way toward creating good will.

2. Master the art of the sincere complement. Being noticed and appreciated makes others feel good about themselves.

3. Having a sense of humor can deflect a lot of stress and/or pressure. Having a twisted sense of humor will make you memorable.

4. Be honest with yourself about what you can (and cannot) do well. Be patient and attempt to improve your weaknesses. The more you work at something, the easier it becomes.

5. "Seize the day" is still good advice. Your opportunities may only be present once, or for a limited time. Some of the world's most miserable people are those with regrets.

6. Ask intelligent questions. Then listen...and remember the answers.

7. Surround yourself with good people who will love and support you. Your friends and family can be a valuable asset during stressful situations.

9. Give love. Be happy. Appreciate the blessings you experience on your journey.

FAVORITE LINE TO USE ON A PASSENGER....When/if someone asked for just a half of a cup of coffee, I would pour a smaller amount, then squint at the cup and say, "That's about 9/16ths...is that close enough?" Most people just stared at me, but a few "math whizzes" got it! A close second might be the few times that a passenger asked for orange juice, and I pretended to crush the juice box before pouring their drink. I then presented their beverage with the announcement that their juice was...."fresh squeezed!"

WEIRDEST THING THAT I DID NOT WRITE ABOUT.... During a flight I once dropped an unopened, plastic 16-ounce bottle of water from about about waist-high, and somehow it hit the floor... and then bounced right back up to me! After I caught it, I got curious and wanted to know how and why that happened. After considering the structural design of the bottle and/or the angle at which it hit the ground, I uncovered the secret: It contained "Spring" water!! (nyuk! nyuk!)

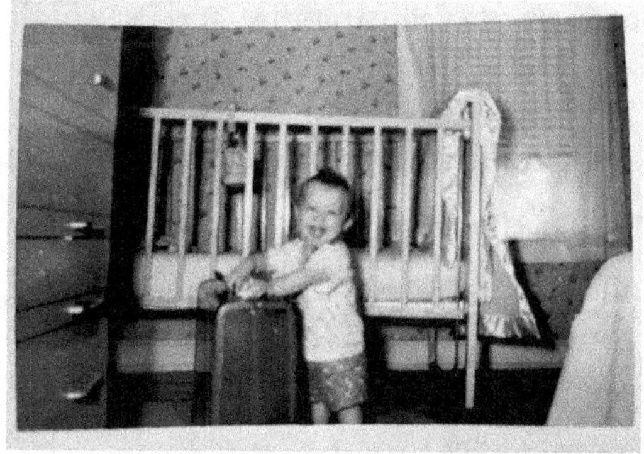

Even at a very young age, Larry
already knew he would be going places!

Special Thanks

This book was a labor of love. However, I had a lot of help along the way. My sincere thanks go out to the following individuals who encouraged me with this project.

My wife Karen and son Brian for your unending support.

My parents, Jack and Mary, who helped me to try new things.

My sisters Sherri and Cindy and their families, mostly for putting up with "Uncle Lar!"

Steve Moore for the illustrations and a wonderful life long friendship.

Gail Snyder for editorial suggestions and for tolerating my weird sense of humor.

David Braughler for publishing suggestions and support.

Wendee Wilson for suggesting that I try the flying business.

A wonderful circle of airline friends who I was fortunate enough to work with over my career.

Those friends and family members (and sometimes complete strangers) who tolerated my many stories, and especially the ones who encouraged me to start writing them down.

The folks at USAir, who in 1983 took a chance and hired a young farm boy/teacher with no airline experience.

God, who during a time of crisis and doubt, gave me great peace and the reassurance that things would eventually be good again.